RUSSIAN CYBER
OPERATIONS

Other Titles of Interest from Georgetown University Press

Conflict and Cooperation in the Global Commons:
A Comprehensive Approach for International Security
edited by Scott Jasper

Cyber Blockades
by Alison Lawlor Russell

Cyberspace and National Security: Threats, Opportunities, and
Power in a Virtual World
edited by Derek S. Reveron

Hacking the Bomb: Cyber Threats and Nuclear Weapons
by Andrew Futter

Optimizing Cyberdeterrence: A Comprehensive Strategy for
Preventing Foreign Cyberattacks
by Robert Mandel

The Russian Understanding of War: Blurring the Lines between
War and Peace
by Oscar Jonsson

Strategy, Evolution, and War: From Apes to Artificial Intelligence
by Kenneth Payne

Understanding Cyber Conflict: Fourteen Analogies
edited by George Perkovich and Ariel E. Levite

RUSSIAN CYBER OPERATIONS

CODING THE BOUNDARIES OF CONFLICT

SCOTT JASPER

Foreword by Gen. Keith Alexander, USA (Ret.)

GEORGETOWN UNIVERSITY PRESS
WASHINGTON, DC

Library of Congress Cataloging-in-Publication Data

Names: Jasper, Scott, author.
Title: Russian Cyber Operations : Coding the Boundaries of Conflict / Scott Jasper.
Description: Washington, DC : Georgetown University Press, 2020. | Includes bibliographical references and index.
Identifiers: LCCN 2019038780 (print) | LCCN 2019038781 (ebook) | ISBN 9781626167971 (hardcover) | ISBN   9781626167995 (ebook)
Subjects: LCSH: Cyberspace operations (Military science)—Russia (Federation) | Information warfare—Russia (Federation) | Hybrid warfare—Russia (Federation) | Asymmetric warfare—Russia (Federation) | Cyber intelligence (Computer security)—United States. | Computer security—United States.
Classification: LCC U167.5.C92 J375 2020 (print) | LCC U167.5.C92 (ebook) | DDC 355.4/1—dc23

LC record available at https://lccn.loc.gov/2019038780
LC ebook record available at https://lccn.loc.gov/2019038781

21 20   9 8 7 6 5 4 3 2 First printing

Printed in the United States of America.
Jacket design by Martyn Schmoll.

Contents

Illustrations

Maps

Figures

Foreword

Since World War II, we have faced Russia in the Cold War and now, after the "fall of the Wall," in a new era of both conflict and competition. Scott Jasper, on the faculty at the Naval Postgraduate School, does an excellent job of laying out the facts and the issues that Russia poses to the United States and other nations. We are at a critical juncture, and it is not clear how Russia will evolve. Scott helps us frame key issues in the cyber domain from both a technical and legal perspective.

On November 9, 1989, East German spokesman Günter Schabowski said that the people of East Germany would be free to travel to West Germany, which led to the fall of the Berlin Wall and the unification of Germany. These actions led not only to the dissolution of the Soviet Union on December 26, 1991, but also to the end of Russia's position as a superpower rival of the United States. These facts continue to impact Russian politics today.

Much has changed since 1991. Amazon, iPhones, "the cloud," Twitter, Facebook, and the underlying financial strength of Internet-based businesses have been huge for the US economy. But not for Russia. Its economy has been weak, and sanctions have had a significant and detrimental impact on the country.

But Russia has not been quiet during this time.

In 2007, we predicted that cyber power would be used as an element of national power and that cyber operations would evolve from disruptive to destructive attacks. This in part was based on the fact that international networks were moving from analog to digital—a process that the invention and development of the iPhone helped to accelerate. As the networks became more digital, it was logical to see that they could also be avenues for exploitation and attack. And Russia has led the way in the offensive use of cyber power across a number of operations.

In April and May of 2007, Russian hackers attacked Estonia over a disagreement on the relocation of the Bronze Soldier of Tallinn, an elaborate grave marker for Soviet soldiers. Cyber power was now being used as an element of national power. Russia used cyberattacks in its physical attack on Georgia in August of 2008. It attacked the Georgian government and financial companies at the same time that its military units crossed into Georgia.

In October 2008, the United States detected malware in classified networks. It is ironic that the intrusion into Department of Defense networks would lead to the formation of US Cyber Command. On November 11, 2008, Secretary Bob Gates delegated the operational control of DOD defensive units under me, placing both offense and defense under one commander and paving the way for the creation of US Cyber Command.

In the first posture statement to the House Armed Services Committee on September 23, 2010, we noted that "competition and even conflict in cyberspace are a current reality." Since then, by closely watching the Russians, we have observed them increasing the intensity of overt and covert confrontation in every domain. In large part, this is in order to achieve their goal of restoring Russia to the status of a great power and fulfill their objective of reasserting influence on the global stage.

Russia has incorporated cyber operations into new models and forms of warfare, as we witnessed in their annexation of Crimea, followed by the havoc and disruption they are creating in Ukraine over the Donbass region. In Ukraine, the Russians have undermined the international norms of responsible behavior they originally helped establish. These attacks are testing legal criteria for qualification of their cyber operations as a wrongful act or an armed attack.

In 2016, Russia used cyber-enabled information operations to subvert and interfere in elections here in the United States, in our allies' European Union elections, and in the 2017 French presidential election. In using new tools of influence, Russia has simply adapted tried and tested techniques and measures from the Cold War to the Internet age.

Russia has also conducted disruptive and destructive attacks (named Bad Rabbit and NotPetya, respectively). On June 27, 2017, Russia used NotPetya to attack key Ukrainian organizations. While the majority of the attacked companies were in Ukraine, companies that did business with the country were also affected, including Maersk, Merck, FedEx subsidiaries, and a number of other global companies. Tom Bossert, former Homeland Security adviser to the White House, claimed the total damage from this one attack was over $10 billion, as noted by Andy Greenberg in *Wired* magazine on August 23, 2018.

US diplomacy, sanctions, indictments, and other government responses have not altered Russian behavior in cyberspace. Russian cyber activities are prompting a new US cyber strategy of persistent engagement in day-to-day competition to defend US interests. At the same time, Russian state and proxy actors have increased the speed, scale, and sophistication of their cyber operations. They are using innovative techniques and tools, some stolen and released, including fileless malware and legitimate applications.

Scott highlights that commercial security capabilities have evolved in automated cyber defenses to defeat cyber offensive operations. Commercial entities are integrating endpoint detection and response capabilities into security operating platforms with cloud-based threat intelligence. The implementation of these defenses in a technical offset strategy that embraces data-correlation technologies holds promise to diminish Russian advantages.

In reply to Russian cyber operations that act as aspects of conflict or components of competition, Scott examines actual cyber campaigns and incidents to understand how Russia exploits technical means and legal regimes to evade attribution and retribution. The most concerning example of this strategy was when Russia penetrated the control rooms of American electric energy utilities in 2018. To counter these operations that routinely and adeptly fall below the threshold of an armed attack, Scott evaluates methods for cost imposition and argues for robust solutions for resilience to withstand attacks.

This book is a must-read as the possibility for future cyber engagements with Russia grows. Scott Jasper provides a great foundation and analysis that all of us would benefit from knowing.

Gen. Keith Alexander, USA (Ret.)
former commander of US Cyber Command and former director of the National Security Agency

Acknowledgments

Knowing his expertise and time are in extreme demand, I especially want to thank Gen. Keith Alexander, the first commander of US Cyber Command and former director of the National Security Agency, for graciously writing the foreword. At the Naval Postgraduate School, I also owe much to Clay Moltz and Mohammed Hafez, the present and past chairmen of the National Security Affairs Department; to Dan Boger, chairman of the Cyber Academic Group; and to Steve Peterson, director of the Institute for Security Governance for the opportunity to design and teach courses in residence, online, and overseas related to the content of this book. I also want to thank John Arquilla, Clark Robertson, and Sharon Runde for their confidence in my ability to lead and teach a school-wide initiative in cyber education. I sincerely appreciate the vision and support of Joe LoPiccolo, Chris Gaucher, Robert Sweeney, Chris Angelopoulos, and Justin Brown in installing, testing, and measuring on campus the robust solutions for cyber resilience described in this book.

In addition, I would like to thank numerous industry experts for discussing and demonstrating their cybersecurity products. I want also to recognize the pertinent guidance from Don Jacobs and Hanna Greco in the organization and construction of this book. Finally, I want to thank my wife, Annie, who provided the inspiration to take on this field of study.

Abbreviations

A2/AD	antiaccess/area-denial
APT	advanced persistent threat
CIA	Central Intelligence Agency
CIS	Center for Internet Security
CNSSP	Committee on National Security Systems Policy
DDoS	distributed denial of service
DHS	Department of Homeland Security
DLL	dynamic link library
DNC	Democratic National Committee
DCCC	Democratic Congressional Campaign Committee
DOD	Department of Defense
EDR	endpoint detection and response
EU	European Union
FBI	Federal Bureau of Investigation
FSB	Federal Security Service
GDP	gross domestic product
GGE	Government Group of Experts on Information Security
GRU	Main Intelligence Directorate
G7	Group of Seven
G20	Group of Twenty
HTTP	Hypertext Transfer Protocol
ICS	industrial control system
ICS-CERT	Industrial Control System–Computer Emergency Response Team
ICT	information and communication technology
IHL	international humanitarian law
IO	information operations
IoT	Internet of Things
IP	internet protocol
IRA	Internet Research Agency
IT	information technology
IW	information warfare
MMS	multimedia messaging service
NATO	North Atlantic Treaty Organization
NIST	National Institute of Standards and Technology

NSA	National Security Agency
PDF	Portable Document Format
PPD	presidential policy directive
RMF	Risk Management Framework
RT	Russia Today
SAP	State Armament Program
SCADA	supervisory control and data acquisition
SIEM	security information and event management
SMB	Server Message Block
SMS	short message service
SOAR	security orchestration, automation, and response
SOC	security operations center
SSH	Secure Shell
UK	United Kingdom
UN	United Nations
URL	Uniform Resource Locator
US-CERT	United States Computer Emergency Response Team
VPN	virtual private network
WMI	Windows Management Instrumentation

Introduction
Below the Threshold

Cyber operations possess the means to achieve really mischievous, subversive, and potentially destructive effects, but how is an injured state supposed to respond? The United States, its allies, and its partners face this dilemma in responding to Russian cyber operations. In March 2017, US senator John McCain said on Ukrainian television that the alleged Russian-sponsored breach of the computer systems of the Democratic National Committee (DNC) was "an act of war."[1] Michael Schmitt, a professor of international law applicable to cyber operations, cringed at the comment and argued that while Russian interference in the 2016 US presidential election was alarming, it did not amount to an act of war. Schmitt said the hacking and dumping of emails by Moscow to WikiLeaks was not "an initiation of armed conflict."[2] A few months earlier at a congressional hearing, Senator McCain had taken issue with a similar assessment reached by Adm. Michael Rogers, director of the National Security Agency (NSA). Admiral Rogers stated that "Russian cyber-attacks on the electoral system would have to have produced more significant impact or physical destruction to constitute an armed attack."[3] The challenge today, as succinctly outlined by Schmitt, is that "the Kremlin is adept at carrying out operations that fall short of breaching undisputed legal red lines that would invite robust responses."[4] Russian cyber operations sow discord in societies and threaten critical infrastructure in the United States and across Europe. The United States in particular is now engaged in day-to-day competition with Russia in cyberspace below the level of armed conflict.

In reply to Russian cyber operations that adeptly avoid crossing perceived thresholds for war, this book will examine methods to counter them through cost imposition or defensive solutions. It will provide an analytical framework to evaluate how and whether past, ongoing, and future Russian cyber operations rise to the level of armed conflict or function as a component of strategic competition.[5] This book will examine actual cyber campaigns and incidents to understand how the Kremlin exploits technical means and legal regimes to evade attribution and retribution. More specifically, it will explain how Russia uses advanced tactics and techniques for intrusion and evasion to prevent detection and verification of its cyber operations. It will also explore how Russia uses deception through proxies and other means to sustain plausible deniability and avoid responsibility for its cyber operations. The book will explain how Russia tests legal criteria for qualification of its cyber operations as neither a wrongful act nor an unlawful attack. The Russians abuse uncertainty in technical attribution and ambiguity in legal classification to elude repercussions inflicted by injured states through lawful use of countermeasures—for example, by cyber means or by a variety of other methods, such as economic sanctions or legal indictments.

In a speech in Poland in 2019, Secretary of State Mike Pompeo proclaimed that "Russia has grand designs of dominating Europe and reasserting its influence on the world stage. Vladimir Putin seeks to splinter the NATO [North Atlantic Treaty Organization] alliance, weaken the United States and disrupt Western democracies."[6] The 2017 US National Defense Strategy asserts that the Russians are using "areas of competition short of open warfare to achieve their ends (e.g., information warfare [IW], ambiguous or denied proxy operations, and subversion)."[7] Cyber operations are merely a means for Russia to obtain political goals and objectives. An examination of their use in asymmetric tools, in hybrid warfare, and through IW is warranted to understand their role and results. Russia continues to modernize its armed forces with an emphasis on asymmetric weapons, in particular subsonic cruise and hypersonic aeroballistic missiles, the latter part of a potentially invincible arsenal designed to penetrate and evade limited US antimissile defenses.[8] Cyber operations serve in another asymmetric arsenal of nonmilitary methods but achieve the same aim of penetration and evasion of cyber defenses. Russia has employed new models of warfare, the most debatable called "hybrid." Since the Russian incursion into Ukraine in 2014, the Western strategic community has been "trying to come to grips with the concept of hybridity,"[9] although NATO does define hybrid threats as a "type of threat that combines conventional, irregular and asymmetric activities in time and space," which invariably includes cyber operations.[10] Finally, in the arena of competition of IW, Russia prevails primarily by social media exploitation and cyber-enabled information operations (IO) that influence populations and challenge democratic processes.

The first evidence of Russian foreign policy turning to confrontation with the West was Putin's blunt Munich speech in 2007. In it, the Russian president accused the United States of imposing an unacceptable unipolar world model, characterized by an "almost uncontained hyper use of force" and a "greater disdain for the basic principles of international law."[11] Putin openly demanded that Russia, with "the privilege to carry out an independent foreign policy," be given a leadership position in making international policy. The following year, Russia exerted this privilege by invading Georgia, using cyber operations as a new component of warfare. Russian hybrid aggression expanded into Ukraine in 2014 and has continued with cyber campaigns that intend to desovereignize the nation.[12] Russia has also attempted to influence the public policy of NATO allies, in particular Estonia in 2007 and the United States during the 2016 election. Through use of cyber operations in these and other cases, Russia seeks to advance its national interests, even if it undermines or circumvents established norms for responsible state behavior. US and international responses to counter harmful or wrongful acts by Russia in the cyber domain through methods for cost imposition have not altered Moscow's behavior. Therefore, in reply to Russian usage of legal ambiguity and technical complexity, this book argues to leverage emerging solutions for resilience to withstand attacks and continue operations. It will examine the adequacy of cybersecurity measures and describe proven capabilities for automated cyber defense. Given continued legal uncertainty that hampers meaningful responses, the book will explore conditions for a technical offset strategy. Specifically, the use of data-correlation technologies in an integrated security operating platform has the potential to diminish Russian advantages through cyber operations, whether they rise to the level of armed conflict or function as a component of strategic competition.

Conceptual Foundations

Russia seeks to restore its status as an independent great power. The long-term ambition of President Vladimir Putin and that of his inner circle is for Russia to resume on its own terms what they decree to be a rightful geopolitical position.[13] That position is as one of the two or three most important nations in the world.[14] To achieve this obsessive ambition, Russia competes against the United States and its allies and partners.[15] Russia competes across "political, economic, and military arenas" using "technology and information to accelerate these contests in order to shift regional balances of power in their favor."[16] The reemergence of long-term, strategic competition challenges the prosperity and security of the United States and its allies and partners. In the decades after World War II, these nations "constructed a free and open international order to better safeguard their liberty and people from aggression and coercion."[17] The Western concept of international order is generally defined by its alliances, institutions, and rules.[18] However, today, according to Gen. Curtis M. Scaparrotti, the commander of US European Command, Russia is "engaged in strategic competition" while "pursuing a strategy that undermines the international order."[19] Russia does this "within the system by exploiting its benefits while simultaneously undercutting its principles and rules."[20] Russia perceives itself to already be in conflict with the West, led by the United States.[21] This perception drives actions by Russia in a wide range of domains, including cyberspace, and also in disinformation campaigns and military interventions in third countries. The debate is perpetual over whether Russia believes "it is defending itself against an actual and genuine threat from the West or is simply expressing its nature as an unreconstructed expansionist power."[22]

Cyber operations have become a central aspect of Russian forms of conflict or competition. Cyber operations are defined as "the employment of cyberspace capabilities where the primary purpose is to achieve objectives in or through cyberspace."[23] The domain of cyberspace consists of "the interdependent network of information technology infrastructure and resident data,"[24] whereas a cyberspace capability is a "device or computer program, including any combination of software, firmware, or hardware, designed to create an effect in or through cyberspace."[25] Examples of cyber operations include those operations that "use computers to disrupt, deny, degrade, or destroy information resident in computers and computer networks, or the computers and networks themselves."[26] In regard to what is meant by an effect "in cyberspace," an example would be the deletion of resident data, while an effect "through cyberspace" would be the destruction of connected equipment. A cyber incident is the result of a single cyber operation, whereas a cyber campaign is a planned series of cyber operations, over time, designed to accomplish objectives.[27] Russia has expanded long-term strategic competition with the United States and its allies and partners with persistent campaigns "in and through" cyberspace.[28]

The United States intends to "work with like-minded partners to attribute and deter malicious cyber activities with integrated strategies that impose swift, costly, and transparent consequences."[29] Although the extent of that response is limited by attribution to the responsible state under international law, US military doctrine clearly delineates that "to initiate an appropriate defensive response, attribution of threats [actors] in cyberspace is crucial for any actions external to the defended cyberspace."[30] Furthermore, the doctrine states that "the most challenging aspect of attributing actions in cyberspace is connecting a particular cyber-persona or action to a named individual, group, or nation-state, with sufficient confidence and verifiability to hold them accountable."[31] Russia uses uncertainty in technical attribution and ambiguity in legal classification to evade repercussions for covert actions that routinely fall below the threshold of armed conflict. A thorough examination of the role and use of Russian cyber operations in their methods of conflict and competition is imperative for formulating and deciding on cost-imposition options or defensive-solution choices to counter them.

Book Overview

This introduction has provided the context and basis for an evaluation of Russian cyber operations as a facet of conflict or a component of competition. Chapter 1 will describe the technical (means used for intrusion, evasion, and deception) and legal (regimes for classification as an armed attack, a use of force, or an internationally wrongful act) framework to analyze and evaluate Russian cyber operations, known henceforth as the analytical framework. It will then depict the application of the analytical framework in a case study of Russian cyber operations against critical infrastructure in Ukraine. Each chapter will then present one or two case studies of the full range of Russian cyber operations (for theft, espionage, denial, and destruction) for analysis and evaluation by the analytical framework. Each case study will examine Russian exploitation of evolving technical means and disparate legal regimes. The book is organized into three parts to describe the role of Russian cyber operations, their rationality to use them, and cost-imposition options or defensive-solution choices to counter them.

Part I, "Cyber Operations," explains the use of Russian cyber operations in the setting of strategic competition. Chapter 2 begins with a theoretical review of asymmetry and how cyber operations fit into the Russian asymmetric arsenal. It then applies the technical and legal framework to analyze the 2007 cyber assault by Russian "patriotic hackers" (ordinary citizens expressing nationalistic/political views through cyberspace) on Estonia. It compares similar usage in the 2008 conflict with Georgia but introduces the role of cyber operations as a component of warfare. Chapter 3 discusses the Western theory of hybrid warfare in comparison to Russian doctrine. Next, the chapter applies the analytical framework to Russian cyber operations during the 2014 annexation of Crimea. After a review of the Russian model for new-generation warfare, it analyzes Russian cyber operations in the ongoing Eastern Ukraine separatist conflict. Chapter 4 explains the Russian concept of IW, arguing that the current Russian practice is a reinvigorated aspect of the subversion campaigns seen in the Cold War but adapted to the Internet age. Next, the chapter uses the technical and legal framework to analyze Russian cyber-enabled interference in the 2016 US presidential election.

Part II, "Security Dynamics," frames the difficulties and deficiencies in the use of cost-imposition options to counter Russian cyber operations. Chapter 5 begins with a review of the theory of rationality and why the use of cyber operations by Russia is considered to be rational. It then uses the analytical framework to demonstrate how Russia circumvented norms of responsible state behavior in the 2017 NotPetya mock ransomware attack. Chapter 6 commences with a review of deterrence theories and methods to impose cost. The chapter explains why US responses to wrongful acts in the cyber domain have failed to alter the undesired behavior of Russia, as seen in subsequent hacks of the 2017 French presidential election.

Part III, "Defensive Solutions," offers and reviews a range of defensive choices to counter Russian cyber operations. Chapter 7 examines cybersecurity risk management and by what degree current strategies improve the security of networks and systems. It then analyzes how Russian cyber operations defeated defenses to penetrate critical infrastructure in the US energy sector. It concludes by examining security measures suggested by the United States

Computer Emergency Response Team (US-CERT) to prevent similar attacks and deny the Russians any benefit from irresponsible behavior in cyberspace. Chapter 8 starts with a theoretical review of resilience and how automation in cyber defense reduces the time needed to detect, analyze, and remediate cyber threats. Next, the chapter analyzes the 2017 Bad Rabbit ransomware attack, demonstrating the utility of automated cyber defenses that operate at network scale and attack tempo against sophisticated techniques. Chapter 9 explores the employment of technical offsets to counter Russian cyber operations. It illuminates how continued manipulation of international norms, for instance in the Kerch Strait confrontation, hampers forceful responses. It argues that similar to Russian pursuit of technical offsets in military innovations, the West must respond in cyberspace with data-correlation advances.

The conclusion reiterates how the Kremlin uses legal ambiguity and technical complexity to maintain anonymity and uncertainty in its cyber operations. It examines the application of a more aggressive approach to defend forward through the strategy of persistent engagement. It concludes that risk in deterrence through this aggressive cost-imposition method mandates the use of resilience solutions to withstand attacks and continue operations.

Notes

1. Raphael Satter, "What Makes a Cyberattack? Experts Lobby to Restrict the Term," Associated Press, March 28, 2017.
2. Ellen Nakashima, "Russia's Apparent Meddling in U.S. Election Is Not an Act of War, Cyber Expert Says," *Washington Post*, February 7, 2018.
3. Michael J. Adams and Megan Reiss, "How Should International Law Treat Cyberattacks like WannaCry?," Lawfare Institute, December 22, 2017.
4. Nakashima, "Russia's Apparent Meddling."
5. Strategic competition is for influence and advantage in political, economic, and military arenas.
6. Lorne Cook and Robert Burns, "NATO Chief Says Allies Keen to Avoid Arms Race with Russia," *Stars and Stripes*, February 13, 2019.
7. Jim Mattis, "Summary of the National Defense Strategy of the United States of America," Department of Defense (hereafter DOD), January 2018, 3.
8. Julian Cooper, "Russia's Invincible Weapons: Today, Tomorrow, Sometime, Never," Changing Character of War Centre, University of Oxford, May 2018, 2.
9. Michael Ruhle, *Deterring Hybrid Threats: The Need for a More Rational Debate*, NDC Policy Brief no. 15 (Rome: NATO Defense College, July 2019), 1.
10. NATO, *NATO Glossary of Terms and Definitions*, AAP-6 (Brussels: NATO Standardization Office, 2018), 62.
11. President of Russia, "Speech and Following Discussion at the Munich Conference on Security Policy," Kremlin Event Transcripts, Moscow, February 10, 2007.
12. Volodymyr Horbulin, *The World Hybrid War: Ukrainian Forefront* (Kiev: Ukrainian Institute for the Future, 2017), 25.
13. Keir Giles et al., *The Russia Challenge* (London: Chatham House, June 2015), 51.

14. Keir Giles, *Moscow Rules: What Drives Russia to Confront the West* (Washington, DC: Brookings Institution Press, 2019), 13.
15. Donald Trump, *National Security Strategy of the United States of America* (Washington, DC: White House, December 2017), 25.
16. Trump, 25.
17. Mattis, "Summary of the National Defense Strategy," 2.
18. Thomas Wright, "The Return to Great-Power Rivalry Was Inevitable," *The Atlantic*, September 12, 2018.
19. Gen. Curtis M. Scaparrotti, USA, "Statement before the United States Senate Committee on Armed Services," March 8, 2018, 19–20.
20. Mattis, "Summary of the National Defense Strategy," 2.
21. Giles, *Moscow Rules*, xix.
22. Giles, xix.
23. Joint Chiefs of Staff, *Cyberspace Operations*, Joint Publication 3-12 (Washington, DC: Chairman of the Joint Chiefs of Staff, June 8, 2018), vii.
24. DOD, *DOD Dictionary of Military and Associated Terms* (Washington, DC: Secretary of Defense, April 2018), 59.
25. Joint Chiefs of Staff, *Cyberspace Operations*, GL-4.
26. DOD, Office of General Counsel, *Law of War Manual* (Washington, DC: Secretary of Defense, June 2015; updated December 13, 2016), 1012.
27. Gregory Conti and David Raymond, *On Cyber: Towards an Operational Art for Cyber Conflict* (San Bernardino, CA: Kopidion Press, 2017), 7.
28. DOD, "Summary: Department of Defense Cyber Strategy," 2018, 1.
29. Donald Trump, *National Cyber Strategy of the United States of America* (Washington, DC: White House, September 2018), 21.
30. Joint Chiefs of Staff, *Cyberspace Operations*, i-x.
31. Joint Chiefs of Staff, I-12.

CHAPTER 1

Analytical Framework

Joel Brenner, a former counterintelligence leader for the US director of national intelligence, has noted that "cyber is one of the ways adversaries can attack us and retaliate in effective and nasty ways that are well below the threshold of an armed attack or laws of war."[1] The term *cyberattack* is used in a colloquial sense in discussing cyber operations that refer to various types of "hostile or malicious cyber activities, such as the defacement of websites, network intrusions, the theft of private information, or the disruption of the provision of internet services."[2] Therefore, cyber operations described as a "cyberattack" are not necessarily an "armed attack" or an "act of war." They might qualify under thresholds and conditions for less severe classifications such as a "use of force" or an "internationally wrongful act." The classification matters, for it determines under international law to what extent injured states can respond to a cyberattack—either with force in self-defense or by lesser means, known as countermeasures. Even though various legal conditions must be met, in any case, attribution to the responsible state under international law is a required condition for appropriate action.

Russian cyber operations exploit legal regimes to avoid thresholds and classifications that prompt or justify meaningful responses. They also use technical means to avoid attribution that is necessary for injured-state responses to an internationally wrongful act or any other type of unlawful attack under international law. The term *attribution* is defined simply as "determining the identity or location of an attacker."[3] Technical attribution is associated with indicators, such as tradecraft, code styles, domain registration, Internet Protocol (IP) ownership, resource language, and time zone information. Political attribution is more declaratory, usually based on cumulative or circumstantial evidence. For malicious actors, the goal is not only to avoid attribution but also to maintain anonymity for as long as possible during a cyber operation. Thus, in the cyber realm, *anonymity* infers not only the inability to identify an individual, group, or state actor but also the "inability to recognize an attack is occurring, and the inability to isolate the target or objective of the attack."[4] In order to thoroughly analyze and evaluate Russian cyber operations, this chapter will provide a technical (means used for intrusion, evasion, and deception) and legal (regimes for classification as an armed attack, a use of force, or an internationally wrongful act) framework. It will then demonstrate an application of the analytical framework to a case study of destructive Russian cyber operations against the energy sector in Ukraine.

Act of War

No clear legal definition exists for when exactly a cyberattack would constitute an act of war.[5] US Code defines the term *act of war* to mean "any act occurring in the course of (A) declared war; (B) armed conflict, whether or not war has been declared, between two or more nations; or (C) armed conflict between military forces of any origin."[6] The term *armed conflict* infers an armed exchange. A more informal interpretation for an act of war is "a hostile interaction between two or more states."[7] The challenge is defining what cyber operations could prompt an initiation of armed conflict or a political declaration of war. In the physical domains, the answer might be more obvious. Take, for instance, the devastating attack on the American fleet at Pearl Harbor in 1941 that resulted in the US declaration of war against Japan.[8] While metrics exist for what counts as a physical act of war, they do not exist for a cyber act of war.[9]

In May 2016, Sen. Mike Rounds introduced the Cyber Act of War Act of 2016, which is a bill "to require the President to develop a policy for determining when an action carried out in cyberspace constitutes an act of war against the United States." [10] A few months later, in September 2016, Marcel Lettre, undersecretary of defense for intelligence, declared at a Senate hearing that cyberattacks which "proximately result in a significant loss of life, injury, destruction of critical infrastructure, or serious economic impact should be closely assessed as to whether or not they would be considered an unlawful attack or an act of war."[11] His statement affirms the reality that an assessment of what amounts to an act of war is "more a political judgement than a military or legal one."[12] Professor Michael Schmitt and Liis Vihul, the chief executive officer of Cyber Law International, state that war is a "historical term that no longer enjoys the normative meaning associated with it for centuries, when the fact that states were 'at war' or had engaged in 'an act of war' meant that certain bodies of law, such as the law of war and neutrality law, applied."[13] Instead, "the traditional understanding of war has fallen into desuetude, replaced by a complex admixture of legal concepts."[14]

After World War II, a normative scheme in the form of the Charter of the United Nations (UN) was crafted by the international community. The charter, combined with customary international law norms, dictates how and when states may employ force.[15] The rules applicable during warfare were also reexamined by the international community, which abandoned the need for a declaration of war as the threshold for the application of the law of war.[16]

Instead, this body of law was relabeled the "law of armed conflict," commonly referred to as "international humanitarian law," which applies whenever armed conflict occurs. The United States has interpreted "armed conflict" according to Common Article 2 of the 1949 Geneva Convention to include "any situation in which there is hostile action between the armed forces of two parties, regardless of the duration, intensity or scope of the fighting."[17] Therefore, by these standards, "the concept of armed conflict implies forceful acts at whatever level."[18] For cyber operations to satisfy the armed criteria of armed conflict, they would have to result in injury or death of persons or damage or destruction of property. A host of legal regimes provide the basis for the further interpretation of how international law is applicable to cyber operations.

Legal Regimes

Article 2(4) of the UN Charter prohibits the use of force "against the territorial integrity or political independence of any state."[19] Unlike the charter, no similar international convention exists today for cyber operations. The closest consensus treatise is the *Tallinn Manual 2.0 on the International Law Applicable to Cyber Operations* (hereafter *Tallinn Manual 2.0*), written by lawyers, practitioners, and researchers, albeit primarily through Western perceptions, who called themselves the International Group of Experts. The aim of the *Tallinn Manual 2.0* is to place existing international law, known as *lex lata* (the law as it exists), pertinent to cyber operations into statutory form.[20] Rule 68 of the *Tallinn Manual 2.0* decrees that "a cyber operation that constitutes a threat or the use of force . . . is unlawful."[21] The Cyber Act of War Act of 2016 introduced to Congress mirrors the US administration's evaluation of a cyber operation "in terms of the use of force rather than acts of war."[22] It specifically asks the president to determine when an action in cyberspace constitutes an act of war by considering which effects may be equivalent to "an attack using conventional weapons, including with respect to physical destruction or casualties."[23] Harold Koh, a legal adviser at the Department of State, made this same correlation in 2012 by stating, "In analyzing whether a cyber operation would constitute a use of force, most commentators focus on whether the direct physical injury and property damage resulting from the cyber event looks like that which would be considered a use of force if produced by kinetic weapons."[24]

Koh explained that if a cyberattack created the same physical consequences caused by dropping a bomb or firing a missile, that cyberattack should equally be considered a use of force.[25] Likewise, the US Department of Defense (DOD) *Law of War Manual* delineates that cyber operations may constitute a use of force within the meaning of Article 2(4) if they "cause effects that, if caused by traditional physical means, would be regarded as a use of force under *jus ad bellum*," the law of war governing the resort to force.[26] Such cyber operations include those that "(1) trigger a nuclear plant meltdown; (2) open a dam above a populated area, causing destruction; or (3) disable air traffic control services, resulting in airplane crashes."[27] In addition, cyber operations that "cripple a military's logistics systems" would qualify as a use of force,[28] although "not every use of force rises to the level of an armed attack" according to the International Court of Justice.[29]

Michael Schmitt, who served as the general editor of the *Tallinn Manual 2.0*, says that while "it is clear that every an armed attack must at least amount to a use of force," consistent with the approach of the International Court of Justice, "only the gravest uses of force are armed attacks."[30] Therefore, the qualification of a cyber operation as an armed attack "requires the resulting harm, or the harm that is intended to result, to reach a certain threshold of severity."[31] That threshold is measured in the scale and effects of the cyber operation. The International Group of Experts agreed that "a cyber operation that seriously injures or kills a number of persons or that causes significant damage to, or destruction of, property would satisfy the scale and effects requirement."[32] In contrast, they also concluded that cyber operations for intelligence gathering or theft, as well as cyber operations that "involve brief or periodic interruption of non-essential cyber services, do not qualify as armed attacks,"[33] although Schmitt argues that states will treat cyber operations "with very severe consequences, such as the targeting of the state's economic well-being or its critical infrastructure as armed attacks to which they are entitled to respond in self-defense."[34]

Article 51 of the UN Charter demarcates "the inherent right of individual or collective self-defense if an armed attack occurs against a Member of the United Nations."[35] The charter also recognizes the inherent right of states to use force in self-defense—which is a just cause for military action,[36] though many constraints on self-defense exist. Rule 72 of the *Tallinn Manual 2.0* declares, "A use of force involving cyber operations undertaken by a State in exercise of its right of self-defense must be necessary and proportionate."[37] *Necessary* implies that a use of force is needed to repel an imminent or ongoing attack. *Proportionate* limits the "scale, scope, duration and intensity" of the response.[38] Once an armed attack is over, the right of self-defense ceases. However, if the victim state concludes that "its attacker intends to conduct further cyber operations at the armed attack level," it may treat the operations as "an ongoing campaign against which it may take defensive action at any point."[39]

Cyber operations that qualify as an armed attack certainly constitute an "internationally wrongful act." However, numerous cyber operations that fall below the threshold of armed attack in this category of acts are unlawful. Rule 14 of the *Tallinn Manual 2.0* defines an internationally wrongful act as "an action or omission that both (1) constitutes a breach of an international legal obligation applicable to that State; and (2) is attributable to the State under international law."[40] The first condition for a breach of an international legal obligation "may consist of a violation of a State's treaty obligations, customary international law, or general principles of law."[41] Prominent examples of relevant customary norms that constitute internationally wrongful acts "are respect for sovereignty (Rule 4), the prohibition of intervention (Rule 66), and the prohibition of the use of force (Rule 68)."[42] Rule 4 delineates that whether sovereignty has been violated by remote cyber operations depends on "two different bases: (1) the degree of infringement upon the target State's territorial integrity; and (2) whether there has been an interference with or usurpation of inherently governmental functions."[43] Rule 4 explains that the first is based "on the premise that a State controls access to its sovereign territory . . . and the second on the sovereign right of a State to exercise within its territory 'to the exclusion of any other State, the functions of a State.'"[44]

In regard to what degree of infringement qualifies as a violation of sovereignty, the majority of the International Group of Experts agreed on "damaging operations, including those that interfere in a relatively permanent way with the functionality of the targeted cyber infrastructure."[45] For cyber operations that do not result in physical damage or the loss of functionality, some experts were willing to characterize violations of sovereignty from cyber operations "causing infrastructure or programs to operate differently; altering or deleting data stored in cyber infrastructure . . . and causing a temporary, but significant, loss of functionality, as in the case of a major DDoS [distributed denial of service] operation."[46] The International Group of Experts could not definitively define the second basis on which a violation of sovereignty occurs "when one State's cyber operation interferes with or usurps the inherently governmental functions of another State."[47] While some functions are obviously inherently governmental, such as the conduct of elections, diplomacy, and national defense activities, the range of other functions is less clear.[48]

The second condition required to establish the existence of an internationally wrongful act is equally problematic to determine—namely, that the conduct in question must be "attributable to the State under international law."[49] The element of breach has sometimes been described as "objective" and the element of attribution as "subjective."[50] The standard for breach is irrelevant of state organs or agents, whereas attribution necessitates intention or knowledge of state organs or agents.[51] In the clearest case, attribution is "when State organs, such as the military or intelligence agencies, commit the wrongful acts."[52] Cyber operations conducted by a person or group of persons are attributable to a state when "acting on the instructions of, or under the direction or control of, that State in carrying out the conduct."[53]

In response to "a breach of an international legal obligation that it is owed by another State," Rule 20 of the *Tallinn Manual 2.0* says, "A State may be entitled to take countermeasures, whether cyber in nature or not." Countermeasures are "measures which would otherwise be contrary to the international obligations of [an] injured state . . . if they were not taken . . . in order to procure cessation and reparation."[54] In the cyber context, countermeasures "often represent an effective means of self-help by allowing the injured state to take urgent action that would otherwise be unavailable to it, such as 'hacking back,' to compel the responsible state to cease its internationally wrongful cyber operations."[55] Examples could include "taking control of remote computers to stop attacks" or "launching denial of service attacks against attacking machines."[56] Countermeasures must not themselves "affect the obligation to refrain from the threat or use of force."[57]

Despite these well-established legal regimes, Rep. Dan Donovan framed the political dilemma in his statement that "we currently do not know when a cyber attack is an act of war."[58] The closest criteria offered by Secretary Lettre are actions in the cyber realm that "threaten our ability to respond as a military, threaten national security, or threaten national economic collapse."[59] However, Lettre pointed out each action would be discussed based on type and consequences. Likewise, the European Union (EU) declares that cyberattacks from hostile actors "can be considered an act of war that under the most serious of circumstances justifies a response with conventional weapons."[60] This obscurity shows that America, and its European partners, continue to lack a clearly defined threshold at which cyber operations are perceived as an act of war. It might not matter since the term *war* has been replaced by the term *armed conflict* for most international legal purposes.[61] Accordingly, a solid international legal framework exists to govern how the United States and other countries should respond to cyber operations. Therefore, this book will draw on expert interpretations of the UN Charter, together with related customary international law, to classify Russian cyber operations and the methods allowed to counter them, with appropriate legal terms and references.

Technical Means

To retain anonymity and avoid attribution, malicious actors employ technical means for intrusion, evasion, and deception to prevent detection and verification, association of responsibility, and determination of intent. Attack vectors are methods for intrusion into an information asset. Examples of common attack vectors are phishing individuals and use of stolen credentials.[62] Malicious actors are constantly refining social-engineering methods to trick users to click malicious links or attachments that contain malware or to provide their username and password for a protected website.[63] Common tactics to make bogus emails appear authentic are using domains named to look valid yet with an intentional minor error (often only a single wrong letter or number) so as to deceive the target, adding subdomains under a valid domain, or disguising a website URL with a shortener.[64] Credentials can also be stolen by keyloggers (used to monitor and log keystrokes) and password dumpers (used to obtain a hash or a clear-text password from the operating system).[65] Attackers also compromise legitimate websites for what is known as a watering hole attack. Victims who routinely visit the site are tricked into activating pop-up alerts or are infected by embedded exploit kits that automatically scan their machines for vulnerabilities in an operating system or application. The exploit code in the kit takes advantage of the vulnerability, such as a coding flaw, to gain access to a system.[66]

Malicious actors also infect software-update processes with malware in what are termed software-supply-chain attacks. These attacks have recently been observed in destructive campaigns, in addition to nation-state espionage.[67] Malware is malicious code intended to perform an unauthorized process and is inserted into a system to compromise the victim's data, applications, or operating system.[68] Attackers use polymorphic malware that changes its signature to evade detection. By making simple changes to the code, an entirely new binary signature is generated for the file.[69] Polymorphic malware also changes its characteristics, such as file names or encryption keys, to become unrecognizable by common detection tools.[70] Other techniques used by malware for evasion include encryption during execution, compression of the file, binding with a legitimate file, and increasing the size of the file.[71] Obfuscation of the malware code, by encoding plain-text strings or adding junk functions, makes analysis difficult. Malware can also avoid detection in a sandbox, which is a virtual analytical environment, by detecting related registry keys, files, or processes.

The latest trend for the category of evasion is the use of fileless malware, which infects a system by inserting itself into memory instead of writing a file on the disk drive, making detection difficult because antimalware products search for static files that attempt to run on a machine's local storage.[72] Fileless malware attacks are estimated to account for 35 percent of all attacks in 2018 and are ten times more likely to succeed than file-based attacks.[73] Threat actors can use scripting language such as Microsoft PowerShell to infect a system with fileless malware—for example, to retrieve and execute a ransomware payload into memory. PowerShell is normally used to automate administration tasks such as running background commands, checking services installed on the system, terminating processes, and managing configurations of systems and servers. Adversaries can use PowerShell to run an executable using the Start-Process cmdlet or to run a command locally or on a remote computer using the Invoke-Command cmdlet. Since PowerShell has resided in every Windows operating system since 2009, it is unlikely to be blocked outright by system policy.[74] Hence, scripting languages such as PowerShell, JavaScript, VBScript, and PHP aid attackers in operations and perform tasks that otherwise would be manual. Scripts have replaced traditional code and corresponding traditional delivery mechanisms.[75] They are also easy to obfuscate and thus difficult to detect. For instance, PowerShell can be obfuscated by command shortcuts, escape characters, or encoding functions.[76] Its efficiency to run directly from memory makes it even stealthier. Attackers have also made malware more potent by adding self-propagating, worm-like functionality to cause widespread damage.[77] Worms leverage software vulnerabilities to spread across networks in an automated fashion.[78] In addition, attackers use legitimate administrative tools such as PsExec to move laterally across networks and either infect other systems or find valuable data.

The use of the category of deception can mislead others "while they are actively involved in competition with you, your interests, or your forces."[79] Deception causes ambiguity, confusion, or misunderstanding in adversary perceptions.[80] Cyber deception effects for the attacker include "fail to observe (prevent the defender from detecting the attack), misdirect (focus the defender on a different attacker), and misattribute (induce the defender into thinking that the attacker is someone else)."[81] An example of technical means for the classification of "fail to observe" are DDoS attacks that serve as a diversion. For the second classification of "misdirect," attackers use false flag operations, where false claims or implanted evidence imply that a third party was responsible.[82] For instance, Russian hackers belonging to APT28 cyber-espionage group took control of the television channel TV5Monde in France in April 2015 and posted jihadist messages supposedly by the Cyber Caliphate (linked to the terrorist group ISIS), most likely to cover its destructive tracks.[83] Likewise, an implanted language string, time zone, or build environment used does not mean the attack originated from a certain actor. For example, Russian hackers from the Main Intelligence Directorate, the GRU, used North Korean IP addresses to make an attack on South Korea during the 2018 Winter Olympic Games look like the work of North Korean hackers.[84] Finally, for the classification of "misattribute," states employ proxies to divert or take the blame. Proxies are generally defined as "non-state actors with comparatively loose ties to governments."[85] Proxies in cyber space are normally found in patriotic hackers, criminal organizations, hacker groups, or advanced persistent threat (APT) groups. Adm. Michael Rogers, the former commander of US Cyber Command, testified that foreign governments' use of criminals and other hackers gives them the "ability to say, it's not us, its criminal groups."[86]

Framework Application

James Clapper, former director of national intelligence, testified that "Russia is assuming a more assertive cyber posture based on its willingness to target critical infrastructure systems."[87] An examination of Russian cyber operations employed in a 2015 cyber incident targeting critical infrastructure in the energy sector in Ukraine demonstrates an application of the technical and legal framework for classification of the attack and any allowable response. The Russians were able to breach isolated power systems by the theft of field workers' credentials and eventually cause damage to systems and disrupt services. Their use of a proxy group hampered a definitive determination of attribution necessary to lay blame for a violation of sovereignty, which is an internationally wrongful act.

Ukraine Power Grid

On December 23, 2015, three different distribution *oblenergos* (energy companies) in Ukraine experienced unscheduled power outages starting at 3:35 p.m. local time. External hackers had remotely accessed their control centers to take over their supervisory control and data acquisition (SCADA) distribution-management system. The hackers opened breakers at thirty distribution substations, causing more than 225,000 customers to lose power.[88] The cyberattacks appeared to have been synchronized and coordinated following extensive reconnaissance. Company personnel reported they occurred at the three locations within thirty minutes of each other.[89] At the conclusion of the onslaught, hackers wiped some systems with KillDisk malware, most likely in an attempt to interfere with expected restoration efforts.[90] The oblenergos were forced to move to manual operations and fortunately were able to restore service in several hours. In addition to the intrusions, the attackers conducted a remote telephonic denial of service during the period of the outage. Thousands of bogus calls flooded the energy companies' call centers to prevent impacted customers from reporting the outages. The intent seemed to be to frustrate the customers since they could not find out when the lights and heaters were expected to come back on in their homes.[91]

At the onset of the attack, an operator at the Prykarpattya region oblenergo witnessed the cursor on his computer move purposely toward buttons controlling the circuit breakers at a regional substation. The cursor then clicked on a box to open the breakers, taking the substation off-line. The operator stared helplessly as one breaker after another was clicked open.[92] However, the assault had begun long before this mysterious remote control occurred, when the perpetrators conducted reconnaissance of the company networks and stole operators' credentials. The attacks began in the spring with a spear-phishing campaign that targeted both information technology (IT) staff and system administrators at multiple electrical distribution companies throughout Ukraine.[93] The phishing emails, which appeared to come from a trusted source, contained Microsoft Word documents that were weaponized with embedded BlackEnergy 3 malware.[94] When workers clicked on the attachment, a pop-up alert asked them to enable macros. If they complied, Black-Energy infected their machines and opened a backdoor avenue for further infections. This method for intrusion exploited an intentional feature in the Microsoft Word program, instead of a vulnerability in an operating system or application.[95]

After being downloaded, BlackEnergy 3 connected to a command-and-control channel for the hackers to communicate with the malware.[96] The hackers mapped networks and moved laterally throughout the environment, blending into the target's systems to evade detection.[97] Eventually they gained access to the Windows domain controllers and harvested workers' credentials. Even though the companies had segmented the corporate network from the SCADA networks that controlled the grid, the hackers now had a way to access the latter through virtual private networks (VPNs) the grid workers used to remotely log in.[98] Once inside the SCADA networks, they reconfigured the uninterruptible power supply for two of the control centers so operators would lose and not regain power during the assault.[99] They also wrote and uploaded malicious firmware for the serial-to-Ethernet converters at more than a dozen of the substations. Replacing legitimate firmware meant the attackers could prevent operators from sending remote commands to reopen breakers during the blackout. Now that they were "armed with the malicious firmware, the attackers were ready for their assault."[100]

Shortly after the outage, the Security Service of Ukraine claimed that Russian security services were responsible for the cyber incident.[101] Robert Lee, cofounder of Dragos Security, shied away from quick attribution but suggested different types of actors worked on different phases of the operation in saying, "It could have started out with cybercriminals getting initial access to the network, then handing it off to nation-state attackers who did the rest."[102] Eventually the cyber-threat intelligence firm iSight Partners blamed the Russian hacking group known as Sandworm for the power outage.[103] Its conclusion was based on detailed analysis of the Black Energy 3 and KillDisk malware used in the operation. Although iSight said it was not clear whether Sandworm was directly working for Moscow, its director of espionage analysis, John Hultquist, stated that it was "a Russian actor operating with alignment to the interest of the state."[104] A profile of politically oriented operations by the Sandworm team suggests "some affiliation to the Russian government."[105] However, alignment with Russian state interests "does not prove state support."[106] No proof has been presented that Sandworm operated on the instructions of, or under the direction or control of, the Russian government.

Regardless of lack of clear attribution to the state, the fact remains that the pro-Russian group Sandworm conducted the first-ever cyberattack on another country's electric grid.[107] The hackers had the ability to cause more damage to the circuit breakers, permanently taking the stations off-line, but chose not to. This restraint may have been "meant to signal Russia's capability to attack Ukraine's physical infrastructure, but without doing irreparable damage."[108] The signal could have been more of a warning, for the Ukrainian parliament was considering at the time a bill to nationalize privately owned power companies in Ukraine, some owned by Russian oligarchs.[109] Either way, the widespread impact, during winter, was mainly psychological. Power was restored in one to six hours, and even though the malicious firmware operationally impaired the breakers for months, workers could still control them manually.

Without injury or death and without significant damage, the cyber incident at the regional electrical distribution companies in Ukraine in December 2015 would not be viewed by most analysts as a use of force. Furthermore, the scale (number of customers) and effects (duration to restoration) of the cyber operation would probably not reach the threshold of severity to qualify as an armed attack. At most, the cyber incident was a violation of sovereignty in accordance with the two different bases for remote cyber operations delineated in Rule 4 of the *Tallinn Manual 2.0*. As for the first base, the degree of infringement on the state's territorial integrity was met by the enduring loss of functionality of critical infrastructure. For the second base, the experts who wrote the *Tallinn Manual 2.0* agreed that "a cyber operation that interferes with data or services that are necessary for the exercise of inherently governmental functions is prohibited as a violation of sovereignty."[110] This determination amounts to a violation of international law under the principle of sovereign equality of states, explained in Rule 4 of the *Tallinn Manual 2.0* and enshrined in Article 2(1) of the UN Charter. However, since the violation of sovereignty was not clearly attributable to a state under international law, the incident does not necessarily meet both of the conditions (breach of an international legal obligation and attributable to the state) to qualify as an internationally wrongful act, and therefore countermeasures by the injured state are not justified or allowed.

Conclusion

The 2017 US National Security Strategy clearly recognizes that "the U.S. is now engaged in a strategic competition with Russia every bit as broad and dangerous as that which existed during the Cold War and which is, in some ways, much more complex."[111] Cyberspace, according to David Luber, the civilian executive director of US Cyber Command, has become "the center of strategic rivalry in this era of renewed great power competition."[112] President Donald Trump has described Russia's leader, Vladimir Putin, as a competitor rather than an enemy.[113] The term *competitor* fits well in the economic arena, such as for natural gas exports, where the United States has surpassed Russia as the world's top natural gas producer, although competition in the market could spill into the political arena by reducing the ability of Russia to leverage natural gas as a means to exert political pressure in Europe.[114] In addition to economic and political competition, new means of influence and coercion are found in the spread of technology and communications.[115] In this manner, US Cyber Command contends that competitors, some considered to be adversaries, constantly operate below the threshold of armed conflict.[116] Russia is a competitor that uses cyber operations to influence events and gain advantage and, in some cases, test the thresholds of conflict, without fear of legal or military consequences.

The cyber operations against the energy distribution companies in Ukraine in 2015 demonstrated Russia's willingness and capability to target critical infrastructure. The intrusion sent a message or a warning to influence and coerce the Ukrainian parliament. Ciaran Martin, the head of the National Cyber Security Centre, part of the Government Communications Headquarters in the United Kingdom, warned the UK parliament that in addition to "traditional" targets such as energy infrastructure, Moscow is deploying cyber technology "against the west as a whole" with a view to undermine "democratic institutions, media institutions and . . . free speech."[117] The next month, Deputy Attorney General Rod Rosenstein warned the Aspen Security Forum of the growing threat from Russian influence operations. He said Russian actions "are persistent, they're pervasive, they are meant to undermine democracy on a daily basis."[118] However, these persistent actions appear designed to avoid designation as an armed attack. In the United States, cyber incidents are assessed on a "case-by-case basis."[119] US officials are hesitant to articulate red lines within cyberspace, since they provide "adversaries a defined line they can walk right up to without fear of reprisal," which Russian cyber actors would certainly do.[120] Instead, this book offers an analytical framework to analyze and evaluate Russian cyber operations, whether they rise to the level of armed conflict or function as a component of strategic competition.

Notes

1. Nicole Perlroth, "Chinese and Iranian Hackers Renew Their Attacks on U.S. Companies," *New York Times*, February 18, 2019.
2. DOD, Office of General Counsel, *Law of War Manual* (Washington, DC: Secretary of Defense, December 2016), 1013.
3. David A. Wheeler and Gregory N. Larsen, "Techniques for Cyber Attack Attribution," Institute for Defense Analysis, November 11, 2013.
4. Aaron Franklin Brantly, *The Decision to Attack* (Athens: University of Georgia Press, 2016), 80.
5. Bryant Jordan, "US Still Has No Definition for Cyber Act of War," Military.com, June 22, 2016.
6. Legal Information Institute, 18 US Code §2331: Definitions, Cornell Law School.

7. Saundra McDavid, "When Does a Cyber Attack Become an Act of War?," InCyber-Defense, American Public University, July 31, 2017.

8. Ronald H. Spector, *Eagle against the Sun: The American War with Japan* (New York: Free Press, 1985), 1–8.

9. Blair Hanley Frank, "When Is a Cyber Attack an Act of War? We Don't Know, Warns Ex-Obama Adviser," VentureBeat, September 14, 2017.

10. Mike Rounds, "Cyber Act of War Act of 2016," S. 2905, 114th Congress, 2nd Session, May 9, 2016.

11. Marcell Lettre, "Cybersecurity, Encryption and United States National Security Matters," Hearing before the Committee on Armed Services, S. 114-671, 114th Congress, 2nd Session, September 12, 2016, 85.

12. Ellen Nakashima, "When Is a Cyberattack an Act of War?," *Washington Post*, October 26, 2012.

13. Michael N. Schmitt and Liis Vihul, "The Nature of International Law Cyber Norms," *The Tallinn Papers*, no. 5, special expanded issue (2014): 7.

14. Michael N. Schmitt, "Cyber Operations in International Law: The Use of Force, Collective Security, Self-Defense, and Armed Conflicts," in *Proceedings of a Workshop on Deterring Cyberattacks: Informing Strategies and Developing Options for U.S. Policy* (Washington, DC: National Academies Press, 2010), 152.

15. Schmitt, 152.

16. Schmitt, 152.

17. DOD, *Law of War Manual*, 82.

18. Michael N. Schmitt, "Classification of Cyber Conflict," *International Law Studies* 89, no. 233 (2013): 240.

19. UN, Charter of the United Nations, Chapter I, Article 2(4), October 24, 1945.

20. Michael Schmitt, "Tallinn Manual 2.0 on the International Law Applicable to Cyber Operations: What It Is and Isn't," Just Security, February 9, 2017, https://www.justsecurity.org/37559/tallinn-manual-2-0-international-law-cyber-operations/.

21. Michael Schmitt, ed., *Tallinn Manual 2.0 on the International Law Applicable to Cyber Operations*, 2nd ed. (Cambridge: Cambridge University Press, 2017), 329.

22. Net Politics Program, "The Cyber Act of War Act: A Proposal for a Problem the Law Can't Fix," Council on Foreign Relations, May 12, 2016.

23. Rounds, "Cyber Act of War Act of 2016."

24. Harold Hongju Koh, "International Law in Cyberspace: Remarks as Prepared for Delivery to the USCYBERCOM Inter-Agency Legal Conference," September 18, 2012, reprinted in *Harvard International Law Journal Online* 54, nos. 3–4 (December 2012).

25. Koh.

26. DOD, *Law of War Manual*, 1015.

27. DOD, 1015.

28. DOD, 1016.

29. Schmitt, *Tallinn Manual 2.0*, 341.

30. Michael N. Schmitt, "Peacetime Cyber Responses and Wartime Cyber Operations: An Analytical *Vade Mecum*," *Harvard National Security Journal* 8, no. 2 (2017): 245.

31. Schmitt, 245.

32. Schmitt, *Tallinn Manual 2.0*, 341.

33. Schmitt, 341.

34. Schmitt, "Peacetime Cyber Responses," 246.

35. UN, Charter of the United Nations, Chapter VII, Article 51, October 24, 1945.

36. DOD, *Law of War Manual*, 40.

37. Schmitt, *Tallinn Manual 2.0*, 348.

38. Schmitt, 349.
39. Schmitt, "Peacetime Cyber Responses," 248.
40. Schmitt, *Tallinn Manual 2.0*, 84.
41. Schmitt, 84.
42. Schmitt, 85.
43. Schmitt, 20.
44. Schmitt, 20.
45. Michael Schmitt, "In Defense of Sovereignty in Cyberspace," Just Security, May 8, 2018.
46. Schmitt.
47. Schmitt, *Tallinn Manual 2.0*, 21.
48. Schmitt, 22.
49. Schmitt, *Tallinn Manual 2.0*, 84.
50. International Law Commission, "Draft Articles on Responsibility of States for Internationally Wrongful Acts, with Commentaries," Article 2, 2001, 34.
51. International Law Commission, 34.
52. Schmitt, *Tallinn Manual 2.0*, 87.
53. International Law Commission, "Draft Articles on Responsibility of States," Article 8.
54. International Law Commission, chap. II, commentary, para. 1.
55. Michael N. Schmitt and Liis Vihul, "Proxy Wars in Cyberspace: The Evolving International Law of Attribution," *Fletcher Security Review* 1, no. 2 (Spring 2014): 59.
56. Matthew Monte, *Network Attacks and Exploitation: A Framework* (New York: John Wiley, 2015).
57. International Law Commission, "Draft Articles on Responsibility," Article 50, 1a.
58. Scott Maucione, "Lawmakers Still Looking for Definitive Answer on What Constitutes Cyber War," Federal News Radio, April 16, 2018.
59. Lettre, "Cybersecurity, Encryption," 85.
60. Bradley Barth, "New EU Framework Allows Members to Consider Cyber-Attacks Acts of War," *SC Magazine*, October 31, 2017.
61. Schmitt, *Tallinn Manual 2.0*, 375.
62. Verizon, "2018 Data Breach Investigations Report," 11th ed., April 2018, 8.
63. Tao Yan, Bo Qu, and Zhanglin He, "Phishing in a Nutshell: January–March 2018," Palo Alto Networks, Unit 42 Blog, June 18, 2018.
64. Cisco, "2018 Annual Cybersecurity Report," May 2018, 21.
65. Sandra, "Top 10 Free Keylogger Software in 2019," Elite Keylogger (blog), January 17, 2019.
66. National Institute of Standards and Technology (hereafter NIST), *Glossary of Key Information Security Terms*, draft NISTIR 7298, revision 3, September 2018.
67. Elise Thomas, "As the West Warns of Chinese Cyber Spies, Poorer Nations Welcome Gifts with Open Arms," *Wired*, June 11, 2018.
68. NIST, *Glossary of Key Information Security Terms*.
69. Radware, "Five Ways Modern Malware Defeats Your Defenses . . . and What You Can Do about It," 2018.
70. Julia Sowells, "Polymorphic: Refers to a Malware's Ability to Change," Hacker Combat, August 20, 2018.
71. McAfee Labs, "Quarterly Threats Report," June 2017, 8–10.
72. CrowdStrike, "Who Needs Malware?," white paper, 2017, 2.
73. Kevin Jones, "Fileless Ransomware: The Next Big Threat for the US in the Waiting," Hacker Combat, December 30, 2018.
74. Red Canary, "Threat Detection Report," 1st ed., 2019, 6.
75. Red Canary, 8.

76. McAfee Labs, "Quarterly Threats Report," September 2017, 38, 53.

77. Cisco, "2018 Annual Cybersecurity Report," 6.

78. FireEye, "Advanced Malware Exposed," white paper, 2011, 16.

79. Joseph Caddel, "Deception 101: Primer on Deception," Strategic Studies Institute, US Army War College, December 2004.

80. Joint Chiefs of Staff, *Military Deception*, Joint Publication 3-13.4 (Washington, DC: Joint Chiefs of Staff, January 26, 2012), I-6.

81. Gregory Conti and David Raymond, *On Cyber: Towards an Operational Art for Cyber Conflict* (San Bernardino, CA: Kopidion Press, 2017), 246.

82. James Scott, "Information Warfare," Institute for Critical Infrastructure Technology, 2018, 85–86.

83. Gordon Corera, "How France's TV5 Was Almost Destroyed by Russian Hackers," BBC News, October 10, 2016.

84. Ellen Nakashima, "Russian Spies Hacked the Olympics and Tried to Make It Look like North Korea, U.S. Officials Say," *Washington Post*, February 24, 2018.

85. Tim Maurer, *Cyber Mercenaries* (Cambridge: Cambridge University Press, 2018), 5.

86. Ian Duncan, "Cyber Command Chief: Foreign Governments Use Criminals to Hack U.S. Systems," *Baltimore Sun*, March 16, 2016.

87. James R. Clapper, "Worldwide Threat Assessment of the US Intelligence Community," statement for the record, Senate Armed Services Committee, February 9, 2016.

88. Electricity Information Sharing and Analysis Center, "Analysis of the Cyber Attack on the Ukrainian Power Grid," defense use case, March 18, 2006, v.

89. ICS-CERT, "Cyber-Attack against Ukrainian Infrastructure," alert (IR-Alert-H-16-056-01), February 25, 2006.

90. Michael J. Assante, "Confirmation of a Coordinated Attack on the Ukrainian Power Grid," SANS (blog), January 9, 2016.

91. Electricity Information Sharing and Analysis Center, "Ukrainian Power Grid," 9.

92. Kim Zetter, "Inside the Cunning, Unprecedented Hack of Ukraine's Power Grid," *Wired*, March 3, 2016.

93. Zetter.

94. GReAT, "BlackEnergy APT Attacks in Ukraine Employ Spearphishing with Word Documents," Securelist, Kaspersky (blog), January 28, 2016.

95. Zetter, "Inside the Cunning."

96. JASmius, "Russian Hackers Take Down Power Grid in Ukraine," Political Pistachio, January 5, 2016.

97. Electricity Information Sharing and Analysis Center, "Ukrainian Power Grid," 6.

98. Zetter, "Inside the Cunning."

99. Zetter.

100. Zetter.

101. SBU Press Center, "Russian Hackers Plan Energy Subversion in Ukraine," Ukrinform, December 28, 2018.

102. Zetter, "Inside the Cunning."

103. Ellen Nakashima, "Russian Hackers Suspected in Attack That Blacked Out Parts of Ukraine," *Washington Post*, January 5, 2016.

104. Jim Kinkle, "U.S. Firm Blames Russian 'Sandworm' Hackers for Ukraine Outage," Reuters, January 7, 2016.

105. Donghui Park, Julia Summers, and Michael Walstrom, "Cyberattack on Critical Infrastructure: Russia and the Ukrainian Power Grid Attacks," Henry M. Jackson School of International Studies, University of Washington, October 11, 2017, https://jsis.washington.edu/news/cyberattack-critical-infrastructure-russia-ukrainian-power-grid-attacks/.

106. Park, Summers, and Walstrom.
107. Dan Goodin, "First Known Hacker-Caused Power Outage Signals Troubling Escala-tion," Ars Technica, January 4, 2016.
108. Michael Connell and Sarah Vogler, "Russia's Approach to Cyber Warfare," CNA, March 2017, 20.
109. Connell and Vogler, 21.
110. Schmitt, *Tallinn Manual 2.0*, 22.
111. Daniel Gouré, "A Competitive Strategy to Counter Russian Aggression against NATO," Lexington Institute, May 2018, 5.
112. Julian E. Barnes, "U.S. Cyber Command Bolsters Allied Defenses to Impose Cost on Moscow," *New York Times*, May 7, 2019.
113. Alissa de Carbonnel, "Trump Says Putin 'Competitor,' Not Enemy," Reuters, July 12, 2018.
114. Anna Mikulska, "When Trump Calls Russia a 'Competitor' for the US, He Might Be Talking about Natural Gas Exports," The Conversation, July 13, 2018.
115. Michael Rogers, "Achieve and Maintain Cyberspace Superiority: Command Vision for U.S. Cyber Command," US Cyber Command, March 2018, 3.
116. Rogers, 3.
117. "Threat of Cyber Attack from Russia Has Intensified, British MPs Told," *The National*, June 25, 2018.
118. Morgan Chalfant, "Rosenstein Warns of Growing Threat from Russia, Other Actors," *The Hill*, July 19, 2018.
119. Aaron Hughes, deputy assistant secretary of defense for cyber policy, Statement before the House of Representatives Committee on Oversight and Government Reform, In-formation Technology and National Security Subcommittee, July 13, 2016, 1.
120. Mark Pomerleau, "Why DoD Leaders Are Increasingly Worried about the 'Gray Zone,'" C4ISR Networks, February 5, 2018.

PART I
Cyber Operations

CHAPTER 2

Asymmetric Arsenal Tool

Asymmetric approaches can generate significant advantage over a stronger power by leveraging vulnerabilities that are either overlooked or tolerated.[1] A 2018 report for the United States Senate noted that cyber operations are a prominent tool in the Kremlin's asymmetric arsenal, which includes military invasions and other nonmilitary methods, such as organized crime, disinformation, corruption, and energy coercion.[2] The Kremlin has refined the role and use of asymmetric tools over time while increasing the production and deployment of formidable conventional and nuclear forces. In December 2015, President Putin approved a new National Security Strategy for his country. It declares that "one of the country's fundamental long-term interests" is consolidating "Russia's status as one of the world's great powers."[3] The notion of great power status is a key component of Russian national identity and one that it appears impossible to relinquish.[4] Therefore, the regime appears intent on using all means and measures, military and nonmilitary, at its disposal to achieve this status. In an energy-dependent economy constrained by Western sanctions and volatile oil prices, cyber operations are not a burden in macroeconomic terms.[5] They are also not manpower intensive—ideal for Russia, which faces a shrinking population.[6]

In military operations, the term *asymmetric* infers "the application of dissimilar strategies, tactics, capabilities, and methods to circumvent or negate an opponent's strengths while exploiting his weaknesses."[7] For Russia, that opponent is the United States and the North Atlantic Treaty Organization. The latest Russian National Security Strategy asserts that "the U.S. and its allies are seeking to contain Russia in order to maintain their dominance of world affairs, which Russia's independent foreign policy challenges."[8] In response, an asymmetric approach permeates Russian military doctrine and the state armament program to execute it. To support great power ambitions, Moscow has prioritized the building of a robust military to project power and add credibility to Russian diplomacy.[9] The result is visible posturing of the Russian military near NATO borders that alarms force commanders and foreign ministers.[10] While Russia uses its military to overawe and misdirect the West, the country is in no position to wage a real conflict.[11] Instead, Russia prefers to test the thresholds of armed conflict, using cyber operations and other ambiguous means in its asymmetric arsenal in continual "day-to-day" competition with the United States and its allies.[12]

Two significant early incidents signaled Russian preference for cyber operations. The first occurred in Estonia in 2007, where they were used in an independent manner in a political dispute. The second happened in Georgia in 2008, where they were integrated "into a kinetic battle, not as a standalone effect, but rather as a force multiplier."[13] Russian cyber operations for denial of service in Georgia were familiar in tactics and methods to their application the year prior in Estonia. The only difference was that in Estonia they served as a form of coercion, while in Georgia they acted as a component of warfare. This chapter will describe how cyber operations fit into Russian national strategy and military doctrine. It will then evaluate the role and use of Russian cyber operations in the virtual protests in Estonia and in the state conflict in Georgia. The chapter will conclude with trends in Russian investments in asymmetric weapons, which indicate that cyber operations will remain prominent in Russian strategy and doctrine.

Asymmetric Approach

The term *asymmetry* in warfare denotes the use of "some sort of difference to gain an advantage over an adversary."[14] One acts, organizes, and thinks differently from opponents to maximize one's strengths and exploit their weakness. Critical components of asymmetry are cost, means, time, will, and behavior. Asymmetric approaches are well suited for the cyber domain as cyber operations can be low cost, technically superior, and persistent over time. They are often employed by an antagonist with the will to defend its survival or vital interests. Usually the actor operates under different views on ethics or laws while demonstrating irresponsible behavior. Asymmetry in the cyber domain is often presented by scholars in the context of the offense over the defense.[15] A prevailing view is that "offensive operations are low cost and have a high payoff for the offense, whereas defensive operations are expensive and ineffective."[16] Part of this assessment is based on the seemingly endless ways to exploit human and machine vulnerabilities. The attacker has to succeed only once to penetrate a system, while the defender has to install layers of security to prevent every attack vector. Gen. Joseph Votel, the commander of US Central Command, further elaborates that "the cyberspace domain provides our adversaries an asymmetric advantage where they can operate at the speed of war without bureaucratic obstacles or concern for collateral damage, and at relatively low cost."[17]

Strategic theorist Everett Dolman argues that "strategy, in its simplest form, is a plan for attaining continuing advantage."[18] Advantage may take the form of material, will, and ways to employ forces to achieve aims. Professor Lukas

Milevski, at the University of Leiden, asserts that strategy may be "interpreted as the generation and exploitation of asymmetry for the purposes of war."[19] His conclusion is in line with an observation by Capt. Roger W. Barnett, from the Naval War College, that "asymmetries arise if opponents enjoy greater freedom of action, or if they have weapons or techniques available to them that one does not. Perpetrators seek to void the strengths of their adversaries and to be unpredictable. They endeavor to take advantage of an ability to follow certain courses of action or to employ methods that can be neither anticipated nor countered effectively."[20] Milevski argues this statement could be conceived as the "very essence of strategy."[21] He points out that famed military theorist Sir Basil Henry Liddell Hart focused his strategic theories "on the indirect approach to create situations in which the enemy would be utterly helpless."[22] Russia continues to employ strategies designed to render the enemy hopeless and gain its surrender without undue bloodshed.

The Russian General Staff has "systematically explored the role of asymmetry in modern warfare, learned lessons from historical evidence worldwide, followed Western discourse on the subject, and generated insights from the benefits of the military theory and practice."[23] The result of this exploration is evident in the observation by Andreas Jacobs and Guillaume Lasconjarias, at the NATO Defense College, that "Russia has developed the ability to employ non-linear and asymmetric tactics, in place of—or alongside—conventional means of warfare."[24] Diego A. Ruiz Palmer, of the NATO International Staff, argues that what makes Russia's use of asymmetric tactics and techniques different than other weaker opponents "is its scale."[25] He claims that Russia has the "strategic capacity to use a mix of hard and soft power instruments to isolate and coerce weaker neighbors, while intimidating and deterring more distant, but also more capable, opponents." Furthermore, Palmer states that Russia will apply hard and soft power "in ways that maximize asymmetric advantages for Russia, as well as minimize risks and costs."[26] In an asymmetric approach, advanced technologies for military functions offer decisive advantage in the context of hostilities, while other advances in technologies for computer hacking aim to attain political advantage short of conflict.

Strategy and Doctrine

The 2015 Russian National Security Strategy defines national interests and priorities in the sphere of domestic and foreign policy. The strategic planning document focuses on national defense, state security, economic growth, education, health care, culture, ecology, and strategic stability.[27] While the 2009 version had the same basic concerns, the new document "contains fiercer and more explicit criticism of the West."[28] It directly accuses the United States and NATO of "pursuing actions that cause instability and threaten Russian national security."[29] The 2015 National Security Strategy claims Western powers are "flouting international law" and intervening in "countries to change their regimes, consequently spawning terrorism" and "destabilizing the international security environment."[30] The buildup of NATO is singled out as a threat that could spark conflict "because the alliance is expanding its military infrastructure towards Russian borders."[31] Primarily in reaction to Western practices, the 2015 National Security Strategy makes it clear that the "Kremlin considers Russia to be a major power within the global system."[32] It consequently recognizes that there has been an increase in Russia's role "in resolving the most important international problems, settling military conflicts, and ensuring strategic stability and the supremacy of international law in interstate relations."[33]

The recognition of an increased role in the global system confirms Moscow's intentions to assert influence with all the tools at its disposal.[34] The 2015 National Security Strategy states with flagrant transparency that "interrelated political, military, military-technical, diplomatic, economic, informational, and other measures are being developed and implemented in order to ensure strategic deterrence and the prevention of armed conflicts."[35] While the strategy appears to prioritize the use of nonmilitary methods and means based on the "principles of rational sufficiency and effectiveness," it does note that the capacity of the armed forces is essential for the achievement of both precepts of deterrence and prevention. Thus, plans to improve the state's military organization are outlined in the new strategy, including "equipping the Armed Forces of the Russian Federation, other troops, military formations and agencies with modern weapons and military and specialist hardware."[36]

The 2015 National Security Strategy also identifies a number of domestic challenges that could undermine the ability to play a leading role on the world's stage. In the sphere of the economy, the main threats to national security are a stagnant export / raw materials model, lagging introduction of future technologies, a progressive shortage of labor, and the persistence of a shadow economy and conditions for corruption. In addition, restrictive economic measures imposed against Russia are seen as a negative impact on economic security. Although Russia has survived four years of sanctions,[37] gross domestic product (GDP) growth in 2017 was far lower than neighboring countries such as Poland and Turkey.[38] In regard to demographics, the 2015 National Security Strategy seeks to create the conditions for stimulating the total fertility rate, which at 1.3 births per woman is well below the replacement rate of 2.1 to maintain a stable population, and reducing mortality, where the death rate is far higher than the world's average, reflected in a life expectancy of Russian men at 59 years.[39] For Russia, a country with a GDP ($1.28 trillion) smaller than that of the state of Texas ($1.70 trillion), the need to modernize the economy and overcome demographic pressures hampers the fielding of a military worthy of a great power.[40]

The 2015 Russian National Security Strategy states that the "fundamental principles of military policy" are set out in the Military Doctrine of the Russian Federation. The latest such document was approved by President Putin on December 25, 2014. This edition contains little that is new, other than an emphasis on information warfare and concerns over the establishment of regimes in bordering states whose policy threatens Russian interests.[41] The Military Doctrine opens with an assessment of world development as "characterized by the strengthening of global competition."[42] It identifies main external military risks, including the expansion of the NATO alliance, deployment of military contingents and exercises in territories contiguous with the Russian Federation, and deployment of strategic missile defense systems. It also describes the features of current military conflicts, including the integrated employment of military force and political, economic, informational, or other nonmilitary measures, and the use of indirect and asymmetric methods of operations. It recognizes that information and communication technologies (for cyber operations) are being used for military-political purposes counter to international law and are being "aimed against sovereignty, political independence, [and] territorial integrity of states."[43] Although the use and aim of these technologies is stated as a danger to the Russian Federation, the case studies in Estonia and Georgia demonstrate the contrary—of a "mirror image" imposed by Russia on other nations on its periphery.

Cyber Coercion

Scholar Dmitry Adamsky claims that the current Russian art of strategy is one of "cross-domain coercion."[44] The strategy of coercion, according to Thomas Schelling, "includes 'deterrent' as well as 'compellent' intentions."[45] The deterrent component prevents undesirable actions by instilling a fear of consequences into a targeted actor if the act in question is taken, whereas the compellent component offers the actor positive reinforcement for taking actions he otherwise would not. Compellence usually "involves initiating an action . . . that can cease . . . only if the opponent responds."[46] The 2014 Military Doctrine codified the ideas inherent in nonnuclear deterrence (and possibly compellence).[47] By employing asymmetric means, the weak player can impose its political will on a stronger one, without a traditional decisive battlefield victory. The asymmetric approach prevents military confrontation or mitigates its consequences. Cyber operations are an element of cross-domain coercion, but their ability to produce strategic effects was tested in the crisis in Estonia, against a member of the NATO alliance (see map 2.1). The Russians sought to achieve coercive concessions by "demonstrating their power to hurt digitally and by imposing costs."[48] Although the cyber operation "achieved a dramatic effect," Professors Brandon Valeriano, Benjamin Jensen, and Ryan Maness conclude in their seminal work on cyber strategy that there "was no concession."[49] The Russians were able to shut down governmental and civilian websites in Estonia with DDoS attacks generated by individuals and botnets (swarms of computers hijacked by malicious code). Their use of patriotic hackers and refusal to allow investigations on their territory prevented attribution for what could have qualified as a use of force.

2007 Estonia Assault

During the months of April and May 2017, Estonia suffered through a blistering cyber onslaught. The incident began with rioting and looting in the streets over the relocation of a Soviet war memorial, and the remains of Soviet soldiers buried beneath it, from the center of Tallinn to a war cemetery on the outskirts of the capital. The six-foot-tall bronze statue of a soldier wearing a uniform of the Red Army signified the supreme sacrifice of eleven million comrades made during the "Great Patriotic War," the Russian term for World War II.[50] Yet for a country no longer under Soviet occupation, the monument, located at a busy intersection, had become to many Estonians a symbol of suppression of independence. A beleaguered Russian minority begged to differ and protested as the date for dismantling the monument approached. The initially calm protests escalated into violence with looting. Estonian police arrested hundreds, and one fatality occurred. The Kremlin vocally expressed displeasure at this perceived violation of Russian rights, although instead of military action, Russia imposed retaliatory economic measures and severed passenger services between Tallinn and Saint Petersburg.

Estonian leaders were fully aware of the potential for an ensuing "cyber-riot," a catchy term coined by *The Economist* magazine.[51] The Estonian director of computer emergency response said, "If there are fights on the streets, there are going to be fights on the Internet."[52] The danger was clear, for Estonia had evolved since the mid-1990s into an e-state with Internet-based service solutions. Hence, the Internet in Estonia had become a daily feature of life for many citizens. For instance, some 40 percent read a newspaper online daily, and 97 percent of banking transactions took place electronically over the Internet. Estonians used Internet connections to pay for street parking and bus tickets, to vote, and to pay taxes.[53] By 2007, 98 percent of the territory in Estonia had Internet access, either fixed line or mobile wireless.[54] Despite nearly ubiquitous Internet access and usage, Estonia was not ready for a cyber onslaught of the scale, intensity, and duration that it experienced in 2007.

The rioting in cyberspace started on the evening of April 27 against po-

Map 2.1. Estonia

Source: Central Intelligence Agency, "Europe: Estonia," *The World Factbook,* https://www.cia.gov/library/publications/resources/the-world -factbook/geos/en.html.

litical institutions and news portals. Over roughly four weeks, waves of DDoS attacks swamped the websites of banks, ministries, newspapers, and broad-casters. Botnets deluged sites with bogus requests for information. At its peak more than one million computers created data-request traffic equivalent to five thousand clicks per second on targets.[55] Jaak Aaviksoo, the Estonian defense minister, remarked, "The attacks were aimed at the essential infrastructure of the Republic of Estonia. . . . This was the first time that a botnet threatened the national security of an entire nation."[56] Internet traffic that exceeded average-day peak loads by a factor of ten shut down the Estonian governmental website and those of numerous ministries, some for hours and others for days. Many sites were also defaced. The Estonian prime minister and other politicians were spammed, and the Estonian parliament's email system was taken off-line. In addition, the Estonian news outlet *Postimees Online* closed foreign access to its networks after attacks on its servers.[57]

The second phase commenced on April 30 with four waves against mostly governmental websites and financial services. It delegated attack coordination to the command-and-control servers of botnets while the short first phase depended on forum communication and synchronized human actions.[58] Initially, Russian-language Internet forums posted calls and instructions for patriotic hackers to launch ping commands, which check the availability of targeted computers. The instructions did not require advanced technical knowledge to follow—just a computer with an Internet connection. Later, executable files were made available to copy onto computers and launch automated ping requests. When coordinated across many users, the pings were effective but easily mitigated.[59] The main attack in the second phase continued use of forum calls to schedule attacks at specific times to generate simultaneous large volumes against targets. However, the first wave on May 4 showed intensification and precision, which indicated the use of botnets.[60]

The DDoS attacks increased on May 8 (in conjunction with Victory Day in Russia, commemorating the defeat of Germany in World War II).[61] On May 9, up to fifty-eight sites were shut down at once.[62] The attackers used a giant network of enslaved computers, as far away as North America and the Far East, to amplify the impact.[63] Banks were hit hard, especially Hansabank, the largest in Estonia, which suffered customer outages for hours. The third wave, on May 15, saw strong DDoS attacks via a botnet of eighty-five thousand hijacked computers.[64] The Web portal of SEB Eesti Ühispank, the second-largest bank, went off-line for an hour and a half.[65] In addition, hackers infiltrated and defaced individual websites while posting their own messages.[66] The final wave struck on May 18, with diminished interruptions afterward.[67] Over the course of the assault, at least three major Internet-service providers, three of the six largest news organizations or portals, and three mobile network operators in Estonia were disrupted to some extent.[68] While the DDoS attacks definitely achieved effects on public and private targets, they did not achieve their larger goal, for after all the disruptions finally ended, the bronze statue remained in the tranquility of the cemetery.

The origin of the attacks was mainly, although not exclusively, from sources outside of Estonia. Furthermore, the source was worldwide, by compromised computers from 178 countries, indicative of a global botnet. A substantial number of the attackers were "crowds affected by nationalistic/political emotions" that carried out the attacks according to Russian hacker sites and Internet forums that appeared on April 28.[69] Some were identifiable by their Internet Protocol (IP) addresses, and many were Russian, including some Russian state institutions and the presidential administration. However, Russian authorities denied any involvement.[70] The first time anyone claimed responsibility was in March 2009, when Konstantin Goloskokov, a commissar of the Kremlin-backed Russian youth group Nashi, said that "he and some associates had launched the attack."[71] The Nashi claim added to assumptions concerning involvement by the Russian government. Besides the IP locations, there is also evidence that the Russian government rented time on botnets from transnational criminal syndicates at the peak of the assault. The editor of *Postimees*, Merit Kopli, said bluntly, "The cyber-attacks are from Russia. There is no question. It is political."[72] The timing and effects of the cyber assault did fit nicely into Russia's overall foreign policy strategy of preserving its influence and safeguarding Russian minority populations in its neighboring countries.[73]

Madis Mikko, a spokesman for the Estonian defense ministry, said, "If a bank or an airport is hit by a missile, it is easy to say that is an act of war" and then asked, "But if the same result is caused by a cyber attack, what do you call that?"[74] The "same result" charge of lasting physical damage is debatable, especially since the 2007 cyber operations against Estonia, which were widely referred to as "cyber war," were not publicly characterized by "the international community as an armed attack."[75] The International Group of Experts, the author of the original *Tallinn Manual*, "agreed with this assessment on the basis that the scale and effects threshold was not reached."[76] Although the cyber operations caused no deaths, injuries, or physical damage, they did fundamentally affect the operation of the entire Estonian society. The effects were immediate and direct upon governmental services, the economy, and daily life. The consequences were more than mere inconvenience or irritation, albeit difficult to quantify since most involved denial of service rather than destruction or damage.[77]

Overall the cyber operations intentionally frustrated governmental and economic functions. Thus, Michael Schmitt concludes that "taken together as a single 'cyber operation,' the incidents arguably reached the use of force threshold. Had Russia been responsible for them under international law, it is likely that the international community would (or should) have treated them as a use of force in violation of the UN Charter and customary international law."[78] The attribution to Russia is lacking due to "no definitive evidence that the hacktivists involved in the cyber operations against Estonia in 2007 operated pursuant to instructions from any State, nor did any State endorse and adopt the conduct."[79] The most likely employment of proxies in the form of patriotic hackers confounds the second condition of "attributable to the State under international law" that is required to firmly establish the existence of an internationally wrongful act. Indisputable facts of this relationship do not exist, only indications that Russia was involved, although arguments are bolstered because the Russian Federation refused to cooperate with the Estonian Public Prosecutor's Office in identifying the hacktivists behind the attacks.[80] According to the prosecutor's office, earlier similarly phrased requests under the Agreement on Mutual Legal Assistance had been met, but in the cyber operations case, the Russian Prosecutor's Office conveniently took a different interpretation.[81]

Cyber Warfare

Paul Cornish, at Chatham House, argues that cyber warfare could be "the archetypal illustration of 'asymmetric warfare'—a struggle in which one opponent might be weak in conventional terms but is clever and agile, while the other is strong but complacent and inflexible."[82] His definition for cyber warfare encompasses "a conflict between states, but it could also involve non-state actors in various ways. . . . The target could be military, industrial or civilian."[83] The Russian definition for cyber warfare is translated as "cyber attacks carried out by states, groups of states, or organized political groups, against cyber infrastructure, which are part of a military campaign,"[84] whereas the US government's definition is "an armed conflict conducted in whole or part by cyber means. Military operations conducted to deny an opposing force the effective use of cyberspace systems and weapons in a conflict."[85]

Two distinctions exist between the Russian and US versions. The first is the originator, which for the Russians extends beyond the state apparatus to organized political groups, whereas the US definition infers the use of only the armed forces in military operations. The second is the target, which for the Russians is cyber infrastructure and for the United States is opposing force systems and weapons. This implies Russia intends to attack civilian cyber infrastructure in armed conflict, although in Russia the term *cyber warfare* is used primarily to signify US and allied activity.[86] Yet both pretenses, the originator and the targets, of the Russian version were seen in the interstate war with Georgia in 2008 (see map 2.2). During the Russian incursion into Georgia, organized political groups took down civilian infrastructure and defaced websites in conjunction with kinetic military operations. Therefore, the disruptions and manipulations could have qualified as part of armed conflict.

2008 Georgian Invasion

In August 2008, Russian military forces mounted a large-scale land, air, and sea invasion of Georgia, ostensibly in response to Georgian artillery shelling of the South Ossetia capital of Tskhinvali. The Kremlin argued its actions were driven by an imperative need to defend the Russian peacekeeping contingent there and protect Russian citizens abroad.[87] The real objectives were strategic and geopolitical, specifically to terminate Georgian sovereignty in South Ossetia and Abkhazia, bring down pro-American president Mikheil Saakashvili, and prevent Georgia from joining NATO.[88] Russia had enacted a creeping annexation of the two separatist republics by granting the majority of their populations Russian citizenship and forging close economic and bureaucratic ties. They also had abused their mandate as peacekeepers—for instance, by staging additional troops, shipping containers of weapons, and repairing a key railroad

Map 2.2. Georgia

Source: Central Intelligence Agency, "Middle East: Georgia," *The World Factbook,* https://www.cia
.gov/library/publications/resources/the-world-factbook/geos/gg.html.

line in Abkhazia.[89] Russia also infiltrated advance elements of motorized rifle
regiments into South Ossetia prior to hostilities. In addition, on July 19, hackers conducted a dress rehearsal "for an all-out cyberwar."[90] Unknown parties
used a computer "located at a U.S. '.com' IP address to command and control
a multi-pronged DDoS attack" against Saakashvili's website.[91] The command-
and-control server instructed its botnet to attack the website with a variety
of flooding methods, exploiting the TCP-, ICMP-, and HTTP-type protocols
(Transmission Control Protocol, Internet Control Message Protocol, and Hypertext Transfer Protocol, respectively).[92] The website became unavailable for
more than twenty-four hours. Although experts were unable to trace the attack, they identified the server as "a MachBot DDoS controller written in Russian and frequently attributed to Russian hackers."[93] Yet, in effect, the attack
seemed to be from a civilian computer of a presumed ally of Georgia.

The first Russian interstate post-Soviet war lasted only five days, from August 7 to August 12, 2008. After initial skirmishes of forces already in Georgia near the city of Tskhinvali, large columns of Russian soldiers and tanks
advanced into South Ossetia on the second day through the Roki Tunnel.[94]
On the third day, Russia opened a second front in Abkhazia, with military elements landing from the Black Sea and arriving by the repaired railroad line.[95]
Cyber operations against Georgian targets commenced at the onset of physical
hostiles. Russian hacktivist websites posted lists of Georgian sites for patriotic
hackers to attack, along with instructions and downloadable malware.[96] The
main phase of the cyber operations began on August 8, when multiple command-and-control servers hit Georgian websites. Among those targeted were

the Georgian president, the central government, the Ministry of Foreign Affairs, the Ministry of Defense, and popular news outlets, such as the television station R2. TBC, the largest commercial bank of Georgia, came under attack the next day. On August 11, the website of the Georgian parliament was struck, and a defacement of the president's website occurred, where a slideshow depicted doctored images comparing Mikheil Saakashvili and Adolf Hitler. A similar defacement and replacement happened at the National Bank of Georgia website, with President Saakashvili included within a gallery of twentieth-century dictators. Although military operations ended on August 12 by a cease-fire agreement, the DDoS attacks continued until the end of the month.[97]

The methods used to deface websites and launch DDoS attacks against numerous public and private targets in Georgia were similar to those used in Estonia the previous year. Lists of Georgian sites vulnerable to remote injections of Structured Query Language, or SQL (an attack technique that takes advantage of poorly secured application coding for databases), which would facilitate automatic defacements, were distributed on Russian-language websites and message boards, in addition to a Microsoft Windows batch script, with instructions to flood sites. The Russian blogs and forums were located in Estonia, the Russian Federation, and elsewhere.[98] The websites StopGeorgia.ru and Xakep.ru appeared to coordinate targeting and attacking of Georgian websites.[99] They provided DDoS attack tools and identified thirty-six major websites as primary targets. Also, botnets associated with criminals were used in both Estonia and Georgia. The largest DDoS attack against Estonia came from a botnet linked to a Russian cybercrime group operating out of Saint Petersburg, with connections to the Russian Business Network. In the Georgian conflict, the six command-and-control servers that launched the largest DDoS attacks were managed by a cybercrime group. The servers themselves were registered through www.naunet.ru, a known "bulletproof hosting" provider in Russia, and the domains used to launch the attacks were hosted by www.steadyhost.ru, a known front for cybercrime activities.[100]

The concerted and sophisticated DDoS campaign constrained the ability of the Georgian government to convey its narrative in the early stages of the conflict to the international community. Therefore, the significance of the disruptions and manipulations should not be understated, for although the domestic impact upon society was not as great as in Estonia, the state's loss of control of the narrative in Georgia may have led to a delayed international response.[101] Overall, the attacks were not particularly complicated since they were facilitated by prefabricated tools and techniques disseminated to willing participants. In addition, the attacks had limited operational or tactical benefit from a conventional military perspective. Yet the use of cyber operations set the conflict apart as the first of its kind in modern warfare. Additionally, the reliance on local proxies of dubious loyalties to carry out both conventional and unconventional tasks signaled a new way of warfare.[102] These actors, in the form of peacekeepers, militiamen, and hackers, gave Russia a way to feign plausible deniability and avoid deploying more of its armed forces, including organic cyber assets.

A report by the US Cyber Consequences Unit, an independent, nonprofit research institute, concluded that "the cyber attacks against Georgian targets were carried out by civilians with little or no direct involvement on the part of the Russian government or military."[103] The forensic evidence fell upon patriotic hackers recruited by social networking forums and on criminal organizations, who contributed Web servers and botnets. However, the timing of the attacks indicates that the organizers had advance notice of Russian military intentions. For instance, the quick start of packet assaults meant the writing of attack scripts, registering of new domains, and hosting of new websites had to have been prepared before the public was aware of the invasion.[104] Likewise, cyberattacks were close in time to corresponding military operations. Just before Russian air attacks on the city of Gori, hackers attacked governmental and news websites.[105] Nonetheless, the Russian government denied involvement. Yevgeniy Khorishko, a spokesman for the Russian embassy in Washington, said that "it was possible individuals in Russia or elsewhere had taken it upon themselves to start the attacks."[106]

The lack of firm attribution to the Russian government does not change the legal classification of the cyber operations. Michael Schmitt and Liis Vihul find that "when cyber operations accompany kinetic hostilities qualifying as armed conflict (as with the conflict between Russia and Georgia in 2008), IHL [international humanitarian law] applies fully to all cyber operations that have a nexus to the conflict, whether they are launched by states, non-states groups or individual hackers."[107] For example, IHL prohibits injurious or destructive cyberattacks against civilians and civilian objects. This determination is consistent with Rule 80 of the *Tallinn Manual 2.0*, which delineates that "cyber operations executed in the context of an armed conflict are subject to the law of armed conflict."[108] The authors of the *Tallinn Manual 2.0* agreed that "the law of armed conflict applied to the cyber operations that occurred during the international armed conflict between Georgia and Russia in 2008 . . . because they were undertaken in furtherance of those conflicts."[109] The term *international armed conflict* is appropriate because there were hostilities between two or more states.[110]

The problem in the Georgian case is that in order to hold a state—in this matter, Russia—responsible for the cyberattacks under the law of armed conflict, it must be established that the cyberattacks can be directly connected with a particular state. Eneken Tikk points out that "the governing principle of state responsibility under international law has been that the conduct of private actors—both entities and persons—is not attributable to the state unless the state has directly and explicitly delegated a part of its tasks and functions to a private entity."[111] She also states that the rules governing state responsibility codified into the 2001 Draft Articles on Responsibility of States for Internationally Wrongful Acts can be considered as a reflection of customary international law. Tikk concludes that in Georgia in 2008, as in Estonia in 2007, it has not been possible "to prove support by any certain state behind the cyber attacks."[112] Therefore, the cyber operations alone in both cases do not constitute a breach of what can be regarded as a state's international duty so as to even qualify as an internationally wrongful act and justify the use of countermeasures in kind in response.

Investment Trends

The need to modernize the Russian military became obvious after its dismal tactical performance in Georgia in 2008. In direct-fire engagements, Georgian forces inflicted more damage on Russian units due to superior Georgian tanks and infantry fighting vehicles equipped with reactive armor and advanced radios and fire-control systems.[113] In 2010, Russia embarked on an ambitious State Armament Program (SAP), setting a goal of 30 percent share of modern equipment (i.e., with advanced technology) by 2015 and 70 percent by 2020. Russia reached an actual share of 60 percent before President Putin approved the SAP 2018–27 in December 2017.[114] The SAP emphasizes programs for the development of a viable twenty-first-century military, including the improvement of antiaccess capabilities.[115] The SAP also funds six new nuclear or hypersonic weapon systems designed to penetrate and evade US antimissile defenses.[116] However, the SAP is not just about new and more capable weapons but also "well trained, manned and equipped land, sea and air forces" for "rapid, high intensity conventional operations within a geographically limited zone."[117]

Russia has showcased the newest weapon platforms in displays and parades. For instance, a military show in August 2018 just outside Moscow featured the latest fighter jet, the Su-27, and the Armata battle tank.[118] A naval parade the previous month sent forty ships through waters near Saint Petersburg and anchored eleven more, including the guided-missile frigate *Admiral Gorshkov*, at parade formation.[119] Shows of military force are impressive but can be questionable on substance, while actual operations prove the existence of true capability. The commander of US European Command told lawmakers in March 2018 that "at sea, on land, in the air—frankly, every domain—Russia's increasingly modernized military is operating at levels not seen since the Cold War."[120] US Navy leaders concur by contending that "in terms of great power competition," Russia operates its newest attack submarines in the North Atlantic "at a pace not seen since the Cold War."[121]

Over a period of two years, Russia demonstrated the ability to strike into Syria from virtually all directions.[122] In the Caspian Sea, the frigate *Dagestan* and three Buyan-M-class corvettes launched twenty-six Kaliber subsonic cruise missiles more than nine hundred miles into Syria.[123] In the Mediterranean, Kaliber cruise missiles were launched by the frigate *Admiral Grigorovich* and the Kilo-class attack submarine *Rostov-on-Don*.[124] In addition, Russian strategic bombers flying from northern Russia released Kaliber cruise missiles at targets in Syria.[125] The Russian defense minister, Sergei Shoigu, said new Russian weapons have "proven their worth in the conflict."[126] Their impressive performance lends credence to a 2018 RAND Corporation report that "improvements in Russia's military forces over the last decade have reduced the once-gaping qualitative and technological gaps between Russia and NATO."[127] However, the display of military power in Syria was by a finite number of units.

New air and surface platforms with similar advanced capabilities have suffered technical issues and funding shortages that have delayed or limited production. For instance, the stealth frigate *Admiral Gorshkov* was commissioned in July 2018, two years later than expected due to periodic funding shortages for the entire program.[128] Also, it is uncertain whether compatibility problems with its Poliment-Redut air-defense missile system have been solved. The second ship in the *Admiral Gorshkov* class is delayed, and two more are uncertain to enter service since they depend on Ukrainian-made gas-turbine engines.[129] In the aviation sector, President Putin has announced intentions for a modest buy of seventy-six Su-57 fifth-generation fighters by 2028.[130] The aircraft is supposed to replace the MiG-29 and Su-27, with original plans to purchase 150 aircraft over a decade. The most likely reasons for the reduced acquisition are shifting defense priorities and budgetary deficits.

The hard reality is that while military modernization remains a priority, the Russian defense budget is severely constrained. While Russia seeks respect on the world stage with military forces that are comparable to those of the United States and NATO, President Putin reassures domestic audiences that defense spending will not rise at the expense of domestic priorities.[131] From 2012 to 2015, increases in defense expenditures averaged 12 percent a year, but defense spending fell by 15 percent from 2015 to 2018, reducing allocations for modernization of the armed forces.[132] Projections within the 2018–20 budget show defense expenditures falling from 3.8 percent of GDP in 2016 to 2.6 percent in 2020, their lowest level since 2008. While the SAP was ostensibly delayed for the last two years, the Kremlin shows no sign of abandoning modernization in approving $270 billion for the SAP 2018–27.[133] However, for an energy-dependent economy, fluctuating oil prices could hinder aspirations for armament modernization, as oil plunged to a fifteen-month low in December 2018.[134] While Russia will attempt to modernize its entire military, progress in 2019 will have been mostly "in its air defense, submarine and electronic warfare capabilities."[135] Consequently, the need for low-cost cyber operations will not necessarily fade away.

Conclusion

The restoration of Russia's great power status is clearly connected to military power in Russian strategic culture.[136] Therefore, conventional military and nuclear forces remain essential in the context of "Russian responses to perceived security challenges which are asymmetric in the broad sense."[137] Moscow has deployed antiaccess/area-denial (A2/AD) capabilities in the "strategic outposts" of the Kola Peninsula, Kaliningrad, and Crimea to dissuade, deter, or, if ordered, defeat third-party intervention.[138] Famed historian Stephen Blank agrees that military forces play a vital role in Moscow's strategic rivalry with Washington but not necessarily a primary role. He argues that "even as Moscow builds up its conventional and nuclear weapons . . . , it conducts an unrelenting asymmetric information and cyber warfare that targets key sociopolitical, infrastructural institutions and grids" and "uses energy, organized crime, media and intelligence subversion and subsidization of foreign politicians, movements and parties for its aims."[139] While Russia enjoys massed conventional superiority in Europe along its frontiers, the nonkinetic aspects of its asymmetric arsenal operate uninterrupted today without fear of legal reprisal.

The DDoS attacks against Estonia in 2007 constituted Moscow's first use of large-scale, coordinated cyber operations in an attempt to coerce a neighboring state into making a concession.[140] The unrest posed no immediate threat to the Russian Federation but to the interests of nearby Russian-minority populations. Throughout the cyber campaign, NATO member Estonia grappled with the decision to invoke Article 5 of the NATO charter for collective self-defense but could not decisively tie the Kremlin to the attacks. Seemingly, according to Jaak Aaviksoo, it was clear that "at present, NATO does not define cyber-attack as a clear military action."[141] Nonetheless, the DDoS attacks failed to reach the scale-and-effects threshold for classification of an armed attack, an essential condition of Article 5, which alone did not allow Estonia to defend itself with force. Likewise in the Georgia conflict, labeled by the international media as "cyber war," the effect of the cyber operation itself "was not serious enough to amount to severe economic damage or significant human suffering."[142] It was also difficult to distinguish the damage and suffering in Georgia caused by cyber operations from that caused by the traditional armed conflict. Even if the effects could be deemed as sufficiently severe, the role of the state on behalf of the hackers and criminals was questionable enough to avoid state responsibility for the cyber operations.

The use of proxies for misattribution prevented holding Russia responsible for the cyber operations in Georgia under the law of armed conflict—even though the cyber operations appeared to be a distinct component of the conflict. So did the deceptive use of patriotic hackers to divert or take the blame in Estonia stymie attribution, which gave Russia a viable option for cyber coercion while plausibly denying its involvement. In some ways, the two cyber campaigns represented the Russian theory of victory, for which leading Russian defense intellectual Andrei Kokoshin has "labeled as asymmetrical, as it is a competitive strategy playing one's strengths to opponent's weaknesses."[143] The Russian leadership recognizes that despite recent modernization of its armed forces, the state cannot compete with the West in conventional military terms. President Putin has said, "We must take into account the plans and directions of development of the armed forces of other countries. . . . Our responses must be based on intellectual superiority, they will be asymmetric, and less expensive."[144] Cyber operations fit well into this unique category.

Notes

1. Steven J. Lambakis, "Reconsidering Asymmetric Warfare," *Joint Forces Quarterly*, no. 36 (December 2004): 102.
2. Minority Staff, *Putin's Asymmetric Assault on Democracy in Russia and Europe: Implications for U.S. National Security*, report prepared for the US Senate Committee on Foreign Relations (Washington, DC: Government Publishing Office, January 10, 2018), iv.
3. Olga Oliker, "Unpacking Russia's New National Security Strategy," Center for Strategic and International Studies, January 7, 2016, 3.
4. Keir Giles, *Moscow Rules: What Drives Russia to Confront the West* (Washington, DC: Brookings Institution Press, 2019), 15.
5. Keir Giles et al., *The Russia Challenge* (London: Chatham House, June 2015), 21.
6. Brian Wang, "Russia Is Weak and Has a Rapidly Aging and Shrinking Population," Next Big Future, August 6, 2018.
7. DOD, *DOD Dictionary of Military and Associated Terms* (Washington, DC: Secretary of Defense, April 2018), 22.
8. Oliker, "Unpacking Russia's New National Security Strategy," 7.
9. Dmitri Trenin, "The Revival of the Russian Military: How Moscow Reloaded," *Foreign Affairs*, May/June 2016: 23–29.
10. Associated Press, "NATO Members Concerned about Russian 'Military Posturing,'" *Stars and Stripes*, September 11, 2018.
11. Mark Galeotti, "Here's the Real Message behind Russia's Big Far-East Wargame," Defense One, September 12, 2018.
12. Justin Doubleday, "New Cyber Strategy Etches Out DOD's More Prominent, Day-to-Day Role," Inside Defense, September 19, 2018.
13. Lionel Beehner et al., "Analyzing the Russian Way of War," US Army Modern War Institute, March 20, 2018, 4.
14. Steven Metz, "Strategic Asymmetry," *Military Review* (July/August 2001): 23.
15. Joseph S. Nye Jr., "Cyber Power," Belfer Center for Science and International Affairs, May 2010, 5.
16. Rebecca Slayton, "What Is the Cyber Offense-Defense Balance?," *International Security* 41, no. 3 (Winter 2016/17): 79.

17. Joseph L. Votel, "Operationalizing the Information Environment," *Cyber Defense Review* (Fall 2018): 1.

18. Everett C. Dolman, *Pure Strategy: Power and Principle in the Space and Information Age* (New York: Frank Cass, 2005), 6.

19. Lukas Milevski, "Asymmetry Is Strategy, Strategy Is Asymmetry," *Joint Force Quarterly*, no. 75 (Fourth Quarter, 2014): 79.

20. Roger W. Barnett, *Asymmetrical Warfare: Today's Challenge to U.S. Military Power* (Washington, DC: Potomac Books, 2003), 15.

21. Milevski, "Asymmetry Is Strategy," 79.

22. Milevski, 79.

23. Dmitry (Dima) Adamsky, "Cross-Domain Coercion: The Current Russian Art of Strategy," Proliferation Papers no. 54, IFRI Security Studies Center, November 2015, 25.

24. Andreas Jacobs and Guillaume Lasconjarias, "NATO's Hybrid Flanks: Handling Unconventional Warfare in the South and the East," in *NATO's Response to Hybrid Threats*, ed. Guillaume Lasconjarias and Jeffrey A. Larsen, Forum Paper no. 24 (Rome: NATO Defense College, 2015), 268.

25. Diego A. Ruiz Palmer, "Back to the Future? Russia's Hybrid Warfare, Revolutions in Military Affairs, and Cold War Comparisons," in Lasconjarias and Larsen, *NATO's Response to Hybrid Threats*, 49.

26. Palmer, 50, 51.

27. "The Russian Federation's National Security Strategy," Russian Federation Presidential Edict 683, full-text translation, December 31, 2015, http://www.ieee.es/Galerias/fichero/OtrasPublicaciones/Internacional/2016/Russian-National-Security-Strategy-31Dec2015.pdf.

28. Mark Galeotti, "Russia's New National Security Strategy: Familiar Themes, Gaudy Rhetoric," War on the Rocks, January 4, 2016.

29. Defense Intelligence Agency, "Russia Military Power: Building a Military to Support Great Power Ambitions," 2017, 17.

30. Roger McDermott, "Russia's 2015 National Security Strategy," *Eurasia Daily Monitor*, January 12, 2016.

31. Oliker, "Unpacking Russia's New National Security Strategy," 7.

32. Tracy German, "In with the Old: Russia's New National Security Strategy," Defense-in-Depth (blog), King's College London, January 27, 2016.

33. "Russian Federation's National Security Strategy," Presidential Edict 683.

34. German, "In with the Old."

35. "Russian Federation's National Security Strategy," Presidential Edict 683.

36. "Russian Federation's National Security Strategy."

37. Chris Miller, "How Russia Survived Sanctions," Foreign Policy Research Institute, May 14, 2018.

38. Richard Connolly, "Stagnation and Change in the Russian Economy," *Russian Analytical Digest*, no. 213 (February 7, 2018): 5.

39. Matt Rosenberg, "Population Decline in Russia," Thought Co., March 6, 2018, https://www.thoughtco.com/population-decline-in-russia-1435266.

40. Frank Holmes, "Which Has the Bigger Economy: Texas or Russia?," Great Speculations (blog), *Forbes*, April 17, 2018.

41. Polina Sinovets and Bettina Renz, "Russia's 2014 Military Doctrine and Beyond: Threat Perceptions, Capabilities and Ambitions," in Lasconjarias and Larsen, *NATO's Response to Hybrid Threats*, 75.

42. The Military Doctrine of the Russian Federation, Approved by the President, No. Pr.-2976, December 25, 2014, https://www.rusemb.org.uk/press/2029.

43. Military Doctrine of the Russian Federation.

44. Adamsky, "Cross-Domain Coercion," 31.

45. Thomas Schelling, *Arms and Influence* (New Haven, CT: Yale University Press, 1966), 71.

46. Schelling, 69–72.

47. Adamsky, "Cross-Domain Coercion," 33.

48. Brandon Valeriano, Benjamin Jensen, and Ryan C. Maness, *Cyber Strategy: The Evolving Character of Power and Coercion* (New York: Oxford University Press, 2018), 31.

49. Valeriano, Jensen, and Maness, 35.

50. Binoy Kampmark, "Cyber Warfare between Estonia and Russia," *Contemporary Review* (Autumn 2007): 288.

51. "Europe: A Cyber-Riot; Estonia and Russia," *The Economist* 383, no. 8528 (May 12, 2007): 42.

52. Rebecca Grant, *Victory in Cyberspace*, special report, Air Force Association, October 2007, 5.

53. Grant, 7.

54. Merike Kao, "Cyber Attacks on Estonia: Short Synopsis," Double Shot Security, 2007, 4.

55. "International: Newly Nasty; Cyberwarfare," *The Economist* 383, no. 8530 (May 26, 2007): 76.

56. Joshua Davis, "Hackers Take Down the Most Wired Country in Europe," *Wired*, August 21, 2017.

57. Andreas Schmidt, "The Estonian Cyberattacks," in *A Fierce Domain: Conflict in Cyberspace, 1986 to 2012*, ed. Jason Healey (Washington, DC: Cyber Conflict Studies Association, 2013), 176–77.

58. Schmidt, 176–77.

59. Eneken Tikk, Kadri Kaska, and Liis Vihul, *International Cyber Incidents: Legal Considerations* (Tallinn: NATO CCD COE Publications, 2010), 18.

60. Tikk, Kaska, and Vihul, 19.

61. Michael Connell and Sarah Vogler, "Russia's Approach to Cyber Warfare," CNA, March 2017, 14.

62. Jose Nazario, "DDoS Attacks: A Summary to Date," Arbor Networks, May 17, 2007.

63. Iain Thomson, "Russia 'Hired Botnets' for Estonia Cyber-War," Computing United Kingdom, May 31, 2007.

64. Rain Ottis, "Overview of Events," CCD COE Activation Team, May 15, 2007.

65. Schmidt, "Estonian Cyberattacks," 181.

66. Davis, "Hackers."

67. Mark Landler and John Markoff, "Digital Fears after Data Siege in Estonia," *New York Times*, May 29, 2017.

68. Tikk, Kaska, and Vihul, *International Cyber Incidents*, 22.

69. Tikk, Kaska, and Vihul, 23.

70. Patrick Jackson, "The Cyber Raiders Hitting Estonia," BBC News, May 17, 2007.

71. Charles Clover, "Kremlin-Backed Group behind Estonia Cyber Blitz," *Financial Times*, March 11, 2009.

72. Thomson, "Russia 'Hired Botnets.'"

73. Connell and Vogler, "Russia's Approach to Cyber Warfare," 15.

74. Christopher Rhoads, "Cyber Attack Vexes Estonia, Poses Debate," *Wall Street Journal*, May 18, 2007.

75. Michael N. Schmitt, *Tallinn Manual on the International Law Applicable to Cyber Warfare* (Cambridge: Cambridge University Press, 2013), 58.

76. Schmitt, 58.
77. Schmitt, "Cyber Operations in International Law," 156.
78. Schmitt, 157.
79. Michael N. Schmitt, ed., *Tallinn Manual 2.0 on the International Law Applicable to Cyber Operations*, 2nd ed. (Cambridge: Cambridge University Press, 2017), 382.
80. Tikk, Kaska, and Vihul, *International Cyber Incidents*, 27.
81. Tikk, Kaska, and Vihul, 27.
82. Paul Cornish et al., *On Cyber Warfare* (London: Chatham House, November 10, 2010), vii.
83. Cornish et al., vii.
84. East West Institute, "Russia: U.S. Bilateral on Cybersecurity; Critical Terminology Foundations," April 2011.
85. Gen. James E. Cartwright, USMC, vice chairman of the Joint Chiefs of Staff, "Joint Terminology for Cyberspace Operations," memorandum, 2011, 8.
86. Keir Giles, *Information Troops: A Russian Cyber Command?* (Tallinn: NATO CCD COE Publications, 2011).
87. Roy Allison, "Russia Resurgent? Moscow's Campaign to Coerce Georgia to Peace," *International Affairs* 84, no. 6 (2008): 1151–52.
88. Ariel Cohen and Robert E. Hamilton, "The Russian Military and the Georgia War: Lessons and Implications," Strategic Studies Institute, June 2011, 1–4.
89. Cohen and Hamilton, 13–18.
90. John Markoff, "Before the Gunfire, Cyberattacks," *New York Times*, August 12, 2008.
91. Stephen W. Korns, "Botnets Outmaneuvered," *Armed Forces Journal*, January 2009, 26.
92. Steven Adair, "Georgian Attacks: Remember Estonia?," Calendar (blog), Shadowserver Foundation, August 13, 2008.
93. Adair.
94. Beehner et al., "Analyzing the Russian Way of War," 38–42.
95. Beehner et al., 44–46.
96. David Smith, "How Russia Harnesses Cyber Warfare," American Foreign Policy Council, *Defense Dossier*, no. 4 (August 2012): 9.
97. Tikk, Kaska, and Vihul, *International Cyber Incidents*, 69–71.
98. Tikk, Kaska, and Vihul, 73.
99. Project Grey Goose, "Russia/Georgia Cyber War: Findings and Analysis," Phase I Report, October 17, 2008, 15.
100. Iftach Ian Amit, "Cyber[Crime/War]," Security and Innovation, April 2001, 4–5.
101. Beehner et al., "Analyzing the Russian Way of War," 61–62.
102. Beehner et al., 50.
103. John Bumgarner, "Overview by the US-CCU of the Cyber Campaign against Georgia in August of 2008," US Cyber Consequences Unit, August 2009, 2, http://static1.1.sqspcdn .com/static/f/956646/23401794/1377708642927/US-CCU+Georgia+Cyber+Campaig n+Overview.pdf?token=qsctl9f%2FMEKA8LrILGO%2B9EDlwYI%3D.
104. Bumgarner, 3.
105. Joseph Mann, "Expert: Cyberattacks on Georgia Websites Tied to Mob, Russian Government," *Los Angeles Times*, August 13, 2008.
106. Markoff, "Before the Gunfire, Cyberattacks."
107. Michael N. Schmitt and Liis Vihul, "The Nature of International Law Cyber Norms," *The Tallinn Papers*, no. 5, special expanded issue (Tallinn: NATO CCD COE Publications, 2014), 7–8.
108. Schmitt, *Tallinn Manual*, 375.
109. Schmitt, 376.

110. Schmitt, 379.
111. Eneken Tikk et al., *Cyber Attacks against Georgia: Legal Lessons Identified* (Tallinn: NATO CCD COE Publications, 2013), 21–22.
112. Tikk et al., 23.
113. Cohen and Hamilton, "Russian Military and the Georgia War," 28.
114. Julian Cooper, "The Russian State Armament Programme, 2018–2027," NATO Defense College, Research Division, Russian Studies, no. 01/18 (May 2018): 2.
115. Richard Connolly and Mathieu Boulègue, "Russia's New State Armament Programme," research paper, Chatham House, May 2018, 2, https://www.chathamhouse.org/pub lication/russia-s-new-state-armament-programme-implications-russian-armed -forces-and-military.
116. Cooper, "Russia's Invincible Weapons," 10.
117. Daniel Gouré, "A Competitive Strategy to Counter Russian Aggression against NATO," Lexington Institute, May 2018, 14.
118. Associated Press, "Russia Displays Its Latest Weapons," *Stars and Stripes*, August 21, 2018.
119. Brad Lendon, "Russia's Navy Parade: Big Show but How Much Substance?," CNN, July 29, 2018.
120. Thomas Watkins, "US Agencies Need to Join Efforts against Russia," Agence France-Presse, March 8, 2018.
121. Sam LaGrone, "Carrier USS *Harry S. Truman* Operating in the Atlantic as Russian Submarine Activity Is on the Rise," USNI News, June 29, 2018.
122. Rossiskoe Oruzhiye and Siriskom Konflikte, "Russian Weapons in the Syrian Conflict," NATO Defense College, Research Division, Russian Studies, no. 02/18 (May 2018): 4–10.
123. Jeremy Binnie and Neil Gibson, "Syria Strikes Showcase Russian Navy's Cruise Missile Capability," *Jane's Defence Weekly*, October 14, 2015, 4.
124. Tim Ripley, "Russia Ramps Up Syria Strikes," *Jane's Defence Weekly*, November 18, 2016, 4; Nicholas de Larrinaga, "Russian Submarine Fires Cruise Missiles into Syria," *Jane's Defence Weekly*, September 12, 2015.
125. Nicholas de Larrinaga, "Russia Launches Long-Range Air Sorties into Syria," *Jane's Defence Weekly*, November 17, 2015, 5.
126. Vladimir Isachenkov, "Russian Defense Minister Happy with Results of Syria Mission," Associated Press, February 22, 2017.
127. Scott Boston et al., "Assessing the Conventional Force Imbalance in Europe," research report, RAND Corp., 2018, 1, https://www.rand.org/pubs/research_reports/RR2402 .html.
128. Franz-Stefan Gady, "Russian Navy Commissions New Stealth Frigate," *The Diplomat*, August 1, 2018.
129. Gady.
130. Miko Vranic, "Russia to Acquire More Su-57s and Mi-28NMs," *Jane's Defence Weekly*, May 22, 2019, 13.
131. Tim Ripley, "Putin's Plans," *Jane's Defence Weekly*, April 17, 2019, 21.
132. Jane's Defence Budgets, "Russia Defense Budget," September 12, 2018, 2–3.
133. Jane's Defence Budgets, 6–7.
134. Stephanie Yang and Amrith Ramkumar, "Oil Plunges to 15-Month Low," *Wall Street Journal*, December 19, 2018.
135. Daniel R. Coats, director of national intelligence, "Worldwide Threat Assessment of the US Intelligence Community," statement for the record, Senate Select Committee on Intelligence, January 29, 2019, 38.

136. Sinovets and Renz, "Russia's 2014 Military Doctrine and Beyond," 78.
137. Keir Giles, "Conclusion: Is Hybrid Warfare Really New?," in Lasconjarias and Larsen, *NATO's Response to Hybrid Threats*, 326.
138. Keir Giles and Mathieu Boulègue, "Russia's A2/AD Capabilities: Real and Imagined," *Parameters* 49, nos. 1–2 (Spring/Summer 2019): 26–30.
139. Stephen Blank, "Moscow's Competitive Strategy," American Foreign Policy Council, July 2018, 1.
140. Connell and Vogler, "Russia's Approach to Cyber Warfare," 13.
141. Ian Traynor, "Russia Accused of Unleashing Cyberwar to Disable Estonia," *The Guardian*, May 17, 2007.
142. Tikk, Kaska, and Vihul, *International Cyber Incidents*, 81.
143. Adamsky, "Cross-Domain Coercion," 26.
144. Vladimir Putin, Annual Address to the Federal Assembly of the Russian Federation, May 11, 2006, cited in Keir Giles, *Handbook of Russian Information Warfare*, Fellowship Monograph no. 9 (Rome: NATO Defense College, November 2016), 3.

CHAPTER 3

Hybrid Warfare Element

The term *hybrid* in military affairs implies the coordinated and combined use of variants of warfare.[1] In hybrid warfare the adversary uses a unique combination of approaches that are intended to target its opponent's vulnerabilities. States or groups select from "a menu of tactics and technologies and blend them in innovative ways to meet their own strategic culture, geography, and aims."[2] The result is seen in twenty-first-century conflict that features multiple modes and methods of warfare, both military and nonmilitary, that converge in combinations of increasing frequency and lethality. Although *hybrid warfare* implies war, the individual elements do not necessarily rise to the level of armed conflict. The North Atlantic Treaty Organization recognizes the phenomenon exists in a dangerous, unpredictable, and fluid security environment that contains threats from all strategic directions and from cyber and hybrid attacks. In the 2018 Brussels Summit Declaration, the heads of state and government declared they "face hybrid challenges, including disinformation campaigns and malicious cyber activities."[3] They singled out Russia for "challenging Euro-Atlantic security and stability through hybrid actions."[4] In addition, they said the security environment has become "less stable and predictable as a result of Russia's illegal and illegitimate annexation of Crimea and ongoing destabilization of Eastern Ukraine."[5]

In the 2016 Warsaw Summit communiqué, the heads of state and government branded hybrid warfare as "where a broad, complex and adaptive combination of conventional and non-conventional means, and overt and covert military, paramilitary, and civilian measures are employed in a highly integrated design by state and non-state actors to achieve their objectives."[6] This broad definition reflected the consensus and negotiations of the twenty-eight member states of the alliance, which means it is primarily a Western interpretation of this type of warfare. The concept itself had emerged in US military thinking and evolved in European circles. In the aftermath of the Russian annexation of Crimea in 2014, "the idea of 'hybrid warfare' quickly gained prominence as a concept that could help to explain the success of Russian military operations."[7] Russia's swift victory contrasted with previous military adventures, such as in Chechnya and Georgia, which were fought primarily by conventional forces and were criticized for their brutality. The construct of hybrid warfare seemed appropriate "to explain how Russia's approach differed from previous, less successful wars."[8]

Moscow successfully employed a broad range of politico-military instruments to annex Crimea. Consequentially, the introduction to the 2015 edition of the authoritative *Military Balance* by the International Institute for Strategic Studies described Russia's hybrid warfare as "the use of military and non-military tools in an integrated campaign designed to achieve surprise, seize the initiative and gain psychological as well as physical advantages, utilizing diplomatic means; sophisticated and rapid information, electronic and cyber operations; covert and occasionally overt military and intelligence action; and economic pressure."[9] This form of warfare was arguably not new, but the means and methods, including the use of cyber operations, were quite innovative. Some Western observers have tried to understand if Russian methods in Crimea were just an application of the so-called Gerasimov Doctrine (discussed below) because, in reality, Russia does not formally recognize the Western concept of hybrid warfare, although limited academic writings exist on an interpretation translated as *gibridnaya voyna*. While the Western concept focuses mainly on military activities to achieve synergistic effects, the Russian counterpart involves all spheres of public life.[10] An alternative theory is that Russia has embarked on what is called new-generation warfare, as tested in its elusive support of organized separatists in a noninternational armed conflict with Ukraine in the Donbass region. This chapter will provide context for the gamut of theoretical assertions. It will also describe the role and usage of Russian cyber operations as an element of hybrid warfare in Crimea and of new-generation warfare in Eastern Ukraine.

Western Conception

The conceptual foundation of hybrid warfare can be traced to an American officer and scholar named Frank Hoffman. While at the Marine Corps Combat Development Command, Hoffman studied trends in the security environment seen in emerging threats and recent conflicts. Hoffman conducted historical analysis and drew in particular practical observations from the 2006 Second Lebanon War between Israel and Hezbollah. He determined that Hezbollah is "representative of the rising hybrid threat."[11] The militant group aptly portrayed his theory of the convergence of the modes of war. Hezbollah was a legitimate political party that initiated the 2006 war with the capture of Israeli soldiers for use in a prisoner exchange. When Israel retaliated in force, Hezbollah used a mixture of guerrilla tactics to hold ground for terrorizing civilians with rocket launches. Although Hezbollah sought concealment and employed roadside bombs, it stood like a conventional force in extended, close-range firefights.[12] Hezbollah also exploited access to lethal missiles to inflict extensive damage on Israeli Merkava tanks in ambushes and on the Israeli corvette *Hanit* at sea.[13] Hezbollah also used the Internet and sympathetic cable news networks in a form of information warfare to not only highlight military victories but also Lebanese suffering, which resulted in a UN-brokered cease-fire.

The complex array of alternative structures and strategies demonstrated by Hezbollah in 2006 appeared to lead Hoffman to conclude that hybrid threats (or more so, hybrid wars) incorporate a range of different modes of warfare involving "conventional capabilities, irregular tactics and formations, terrorist acts including indiscriminate violence and coercion, and criminal disorder."[14] This type of thinking apparently inspired defense secretary Robert Gates to first use the term *hybrid* in 2009.[15] Secretary Gates wrote that "the categories of warfare are blurring and no longer fit into neat, tidy boxes. One can expect to see more tools and tactics of destruction—from the sophisticated to the simple—being employed simultaneously in hybrid and more complex forms of warfare."[16] Likewise, the Capstone Concept for Joint Operations, produced by the Joint Chiefs of Staff, cited Hoffman in stating that "future conflicts will appear as hybrids comprising diverse, dynamic, and simultaneous combinations of organizations, technologies, and techniques that defy categorization."[17] The same year, NATO seemed to adopt the American view in its distribution of a working definition of hybrid threats that concentrated on conventional, irregular, terrorist, and criminal elements in mixed modes of operation.[18]

A number of ensuing NATO-sponsored workshops tempered the working definition to include consideration of the position held by Russell Glenn, a senior defense analyst with the RAND Corporation, that a hybrid threat not only simultaneously and adaptively employs methods of warfare but also employs "some combination of political, military, economic, social, and information means."[19] This position reflects the stance by Col. Margaret Bond at the US Army War College that "war of the next century will comprise a kind of hybrid war, projecting all elements of national power along a continuum of activities."[20] In an input to a New NATO Capstone Concept for the Military Contribution to Countering Hybrid Threats, the alliance provided a consensus description that "hybrid threats are those posed by adversaries, with the ability to simultaneously employ conventional and non-conventional means adaptively in pursuit of their objectives."[21] The concept paper recognized that hybrid threats "present a significant challenge for the Alliance . . . across non-physical domains," which may include "cyber, information/media and financial environments."[22] The capstone concept was published in 2010, and a series of experiments attempted to identify potential hybrid threats and effective strategies to counter them.[23] Although even with productive debate, NATO members were politically unwilling to devote resources to develop the capabilities necessary to meet these threats.[24]

That perception by NATO members changed after the 2014 Russian incursion into Ukraine. Russia's operational methods took NATO by surprise. After years of employing heavy conventional forces, the use of an approach that relied on "non-military armed force and instruments" was simply unexpected.[25] European scholars wrote papers, and institutions convened conferences to explain the phenomenon. Nicu Popescu, a senior analyst at the European Union Institute for Security Studies, argued that "hybrid tactics are neither new, nor exclusively (or primarily) a Russian invention. . . . Hybrid war encompasses a set of hostile actions . . . to undermine an opponent through a variety of acts."[26] Guillaume Lasconjarias and Jeffrey Larson, both researchers at the NATO Defense College, agreed that a "hybrid approach to war is not new,"[27] although they contended that "it looks as if old tools have been reinvented and used in innovative ways to bring to bear a new kind of pressure on an opponent, in order to achieve faster, quicker and sometimes dirtier political goals."[28]

Gen. Philip Breedlove, then supreme Allied commander Europe, stated in 2015 that "NATO's greatest challenge coming out of the Wales Summit is to take on two different forms of strategic challenge from the East and South simultaneously. These challenges are composed of very different actors, and various forms of modern hybrid warfare."[29] A conference sponsored by the NATO Defense College in April 2015 examined the scope and tools used by actors from both strategic directions. The conference report noted that "Russia's use of hybrid warfare is both strategic and ambitious; it involves and incorporates a planned mix of soft and hard power elements, as part of a preconceived and multilayered campaign."[30] These elements include "the use of conventional military force (including unmarked Special Forces), intimidation by the threatened use of nuclear forces . . . , employment of cyber to disrupt and destabilize Alliance societies, use of economic levers . . . , and massive propaganda and disinformation."[31] After watching the conflict in Ukraine unfold, Frank Hoffman realized that the construct developed by the Marine Corps a decade before was overly focused on "combinations of tactics associated with violence and warfare."[32] Written at the operational level, it did not capture nonviolent actions such as cyber operations. The elements articulated from the NATO Defense College conference help to better understand the range of means and measures used by Russia to achieve strategic ends.

Gerasimov Doctrine

Following the annexation of Crimea, scholars looked for evidence of hybrid warfare doctrine in the writings of respected military thinkers in Russia. A well-known article written in 2013 by Gen. Valery Gerasimov, the chief of the General Staff, identified the importance of nonmilitary tools in conflict. His views on the changing nature of war became known in the West as the Gerasimov Doctrine. In the article, General Gerasimov described new developments as a "new adaptive approach to the use of military force," for which he provided the following explicit articulation of its narratives:

> In the twenty-first century, there is a tendency to erase the differences between the state of war and peace. Wars are no longer declared, but when they do begin, they do not follow our usual pattern. . . . The emphasis of the methods used in the confrontation is shifting toward the widespread use of political, economic, information, humanitarian, and other nonmilitary measures implemented using the protest potential of the population. All this is complemented by covert military measures, including the implementation of information confrontation measures and the actions of special operations forces.[33]

Gerasimov argued that modern war focuses on intelligence and domination of the information space. He concluded that goals are achieved in a "remote, contactless" way and "differences between the strategic, operational, and tactical levels" are erased."[34] However, Gerasimov was espousing "what he thought the West was doing as much as he was prescribing a strategy for Russia."[35] His article highlighted a pattern of US-forced regime change, in particular in Afghanistan and Iraq, through an overt military invasion, which was supplanted by a new method of installation of political opposition.[36] The Russians had watched the perceived roles that Western agencies played in fostering social movement revolts against regimes in the "color revolutions" in Georgia, Serbia, and Ukraine, and during the Arab Spring, especially in Libya, although, admittedly, in Russia there is a "long established trend of discussing offensive strategies and capacities in Aesopian terms, by ascribing them to the other side."[37]

Gerasimov used his views on the operational environment to develop a model for modern warfare under the title of "The Role of Nonmilitary Methods in Interstate Conflict Resolution" (see fig. 3.1).[38] As he illustrated, war is "now conducted by a roughly 4:1 ratio of nonmilitary and military measures."[39] In particular, the conduct of information warfare permeates across all six phases of interstate conflict (covert origins, escalations, conflict activities, crisis, resolution, and restoration of peace), as depicted in the model.

Although born of Western conception, the Gerasimov model is a useful construct for analyzing the role of cyber operations in relation to other tools used in the Russian annexation of Crimea. Disruptive attacks occurred on Ukrainian websites but this time expanded to mobile phones and election systems. They were a decisive part of an armed intervention, which qualified as a violation of international law in the use of force.

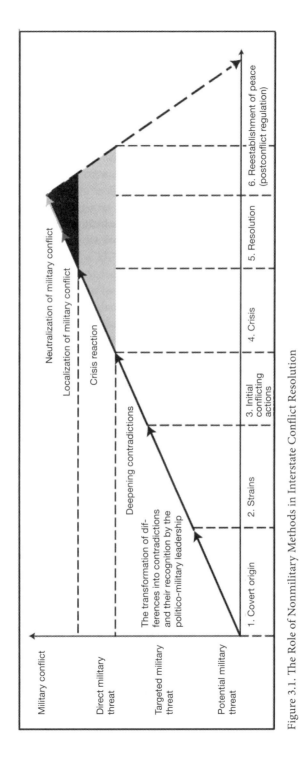

Figure 3.1. The Role of Nonmilitary Methods in Interstate Conflict Resolution

Source: Charles K. Bartles, "Getting Gerasimov Right," *Military Review,* January/February 2016, 35.

Map 3.1. Ukraine

Source: Central Intelligence Agency, "Europe: Ukraine," *The World Factbook,* https://www.cia.gov
/library/publications/resources/the-world-factbook/geos/up.html.

2014 Crimean Incursion

Each stage of the Gerasimov model is characterized by the primacy of nonmilitary measures, but features increased military involvement over time. The first stage of covert origins began in Ukraine with President Viktor Yanukovych's refusal to sign an association agreement with the European Union, which would have opened borders for trade. Yanukovych cited diplomatic pressure from Russia for his decision.[40] On December 1, 2013, a mass demonstration in Kiev attended by over 350,000 people marked the popularization of a political movement or opposition that became known as Euromaidan.[41] When it was clear that protesters were not going to leave the main square (known as the Maidan), cyberattacks began on the opposition's websites. They were targeted by DDoS attacks that originated mostly "from commercial botnets employing Black Energy and Dirt Jumper malware."[42] The covert-origins phase included economic moves by Russia. On December 16, Yanukovych signed a plan with Russia for a buyout of $15 billion in Ukrainian debt and reductions in the price of natural gas by one third, which only aggravated the Euromaidan protesters.[43]

The escalations phase was signaled on February 20, 2014, by a bloody crackdown on continued Euromaidan protests. Dozens were killed after police deployed snipers using live ammunition.[44] Moscow had threatened to withhold crucial aid unless Yanukovych cracked down hard on the unrest.[45] The most sophisticated cyberattacks to date coincided with the lethal shootings. The mobile phones of opposition-affiliated parliament members "were flooded with SMS [short message service] messages and telephone calls in an effort to prevent them from communicating and coordinating defenses."[46] On February 21, fifty thousand protestors at the Maidan commemorated those who had lost their lives and threatened an armed coup if Yanukovych did not resign.[47] The next day, he was gone. An interim president was appointed, and some of Yanukovych's allies were arrested, which sparked pro-Russian demonstrations in Crimea.[48] Russian president Vladimir Putin held a meeting with his security chiefs to deliberate next steps, which he closed by stating, "We must start working on returning Crimea to Russia."[49] His words invoked the strategic deployment of thirty to forty thousand troops and equipment to Russia's Western Military District, close to the Ukrainian border, for an unannounced large-scale military exercise (see map 3.1).[50]

At the start of conflict activities on February 27, 2014, armed men seized governmental buildings, airports, television stations, and military installations in Crimea. Border checkpoints were established on major roads into the Crimean Peninsula from mainland Ukraine.[51] These so-called little green men acted as "local security forces" without "national or other identification tags."[52] Although Moscow denied any involvement, analysts later concluded the men were Russian special and intervention forces, "especially Spetsnaz and troops of the 810th Independent Naval Infantry Brigade, a marine unit attached to the Black Sea Fleet."[53] The presence of the naval brigade in Ukraine for immediate covert deployment had been facilitated by a 2010 political deal to extend the stay of the Russian fleet in Sevastopol for another twenty-five years in exchange for significant discounts on the purchases of Russian natural gas.[54] On March 1, the crisis phase commenced when the Russian upper house of parliament formally authorized the deployment of Russian troops in Crimea, ostensibly to protect the lives of the Russian-speaking minority.[55] The deployed troops promptly seized the Kirovske air base and other sites.

From the start of their operation, Russian forces took action to control the peninsula's telecommunication infrastructure. They raided the local offices of the Ukrainian telecommunications company Ukrtelecom before severing phone and Internet cables.[56] In addition, they blocked physical access to media companies and shifted local television programming from Ukrainian to Russian channels.[57] Russian forces also interfered with the mobile phones of members of parliament, using equipment installed at the entrance to Ukrtelecom to block phones.[58] Russian actions to isolate and influence the Crimean population by physical sabotage or interference differed from the cyber playbook used in the 2008 Russo-Georgian conflict. Although two governmental websites in Crimea were taken down, it was not clear if foreign hackers were responsible.[59] Cyber warfare expert Jeffrey Carr has argued that Russia did not blind the Ukrainian government and society with DDoS attacks, for two reasons. First,

Nashi, the government-financed Russian youth group that orchestrated the Georgian DDoS attacks, had been disbanded, and second, the open forums that actively recruited patriotic volunteers for the Georgian attacks would not likely attract Russian hackers since most supported an independent Ukraine.[60] Instead, Russia relied on a nationalist hacking group named CyberBerkut to stir unrest with website defacements and disinformation.[61]

The resolution phase was heralded with a public referendum held by the interim Crimean government on March 16 regarding secession from Ukraine. With thousands of heavily armed Russian troops standing watch, exit polls showed more than 93 percent of voters favored secession.[62] Western leaders declared the vote to join Russia was illegal since it violated the Ukrainian constitution and international law. They attempted to declare the referendum invalid with a UN Security Council resolution that Russia promptly vetoed.[63] In addition, cyber operations were launched to stifle NATO opinions. The pro-Russian group CyberBerkut took down several public NATO websites. The main site, which posted a statement by Secretary-General Anders Fogh Rasmussen on the illegitimacy of the referendum, worked intermittently. DDoS attacks also struck the NATO Cooperative Cyber Defence Centre of Excellence in Estonia. Additionally, the network for NATO unclassified email was affected.[64] CyberBerkut claimed responsibility on its website for the assault, saying it was conducted by patriotic Ukrainians angry over NATO interference, although an alliance spokeswoman stated that "due to the complexities involved in attributing the attacks, NATO would not speculate about who was responsible or their motives."[65] Two days after the vote, Putin signed a treaty to annex Crimea into the Russian Federation.[66]

The final phase for restoration of peace began with a visit to Crimea on March 31, 2014, by Russian prime minister Dmitry Medvedev, who promised significant economic aid.[67] Yet as Russian business leaders worked to integrate Crimea into the Russian economy, coercive energy policies were employed to establish political control of the region,[68] for Russia had acquired not only the Crimean landmass but also a maritime zone with rights to trillions of dollars' worth of oil and gas. [69] The loss of potential energy independence made Ukraine more vulnerable to ensuing Russian pressure, which was promptly enacted on June 16 by Gazprom, in cutting off Ukraine's gas supply after Kiev failed to meet a deadline for the $2 billion it owed the Russian company.[70] Likewise in the cyber domain, the pro-Russian CyberBerkut continued operations to influence the political process in Ukraine. On May 21, during the Ukraine presidential election, CyberBerkut compromised "the Central Election Commission (CEC), disabling core CEC network nodes and numerous components of the election system."[71] For instance, the displays of real-time updates in the vote count did not work properly for nearly twenty hours. On

May 25, just minutes before the polls closed, the attackers "posted on the CEC website a picture of Ukrainian Right Sector leader Dmitry Yarosh, incorrectly claiming that he had won the election."[72] Later that night, Russian Channel One declared Yarosh as the victor, with 37 percent of the vote.[73]

Technical evaluation of the CEC hack by the Ukrainian computer emergency response team (CERT) revealed the attackers began reconnaissance two months prior to the election and eventually gained administrator privileges.[74] The CERT found sophisticated cyber espionage malware on the network, typically associated with APT28, which is often associated with the Russian government.[75] CyberBerkut itself claimed to have "discovered and exploited a 'zero-day' vulnerability in the CEC Cisco ASA software."[76] Nikolay Koval, who served as the CERT chief, stated that "if CyberBerkut really did exploit a zero-day, the group is likely supported by a nation-state."[77] Glib Pakharenko, a board member of ISACA (Information System Audit and Control Association) Kyiv, who investigated the aforementioned cyber operations at the Maidan and did not specify attacker identities, admits that "with cyber attacks, attribution and motive are not always clear, and the level of deception is high."[78] Although the assortment of documented cyber operations seen in the Russian annexation of Crimea might not be clearly attributable to Russia, the motive to disrupt and destabilize Ukraine is rather obvious.

Russia achieved a near bloodless coup de main in the annexation of Crimea. Cyber operations caused confusion and distractions but no injuries or deaths or destruction of, or damage to, property. They served as an element of hybrid warfare in line with the Western interpretation, along with political, economic, and information measures. All of these measures were complemented by military means of a hidden or overt character, closely in line with the components of the Gerasimov Doctrine. In regard to legal classification, Jan Stinissen, a military lawyer at the NATO Cooperative Cyber Defence Centre of Excellence, argues that "cyber activities conducted as part of a wider conflict are governed by that conflict's legal framework."[79] Stinissen finds the Euromaidan protests to be a conflict between governmental authorities and civilian groups. Although the protests resulted in violence that resulted in causalities, he states that, as an internal matter, they "could not be seen as an armed conflict."[80]

It is important to note that cyber operations occurred on both sides of the protests. Hackers from the group Anonymous Ukraine commenced Operation Independence on October 28 to promote Ukraine's independence from the EU, NATO, and Russia.[81] The operation consisted of DDoS attacks and website defacements on both Western and Russian sites.[82] Opposition activists also launched DDoS attacks on the Ukrainian government, including on the president's website.[83] Thus, while speculation of Russian governmental involvement in politically motivated cyberattacks on opposition websites and mobile phones during Euromaidan is reasonable, any potential role is lost in the myriad of internal disturbances or civilian uprisings, which fall nowhere near the thresholds of armed conflict. Ultimately the cyber incidents in the protests were merely a law enforcement issue since they violated Ukrainian criminal law.[84]

The Russian incursion by armed troops into Crimea was an entirely different legal matter. Secretary-General Rasmussen clearly stated that "Russia's military aggression in Ukraine is in blatant breach of its international commitments and it is a violation of Ukraine's sovereignty and territorial integrity."[85] Russian foreign minister Sergei Lavrov attempted to oppose that assertion in his presentation of a letter to the UN Security Council from former Ukrainian president Yanukovych, who had requested an armed intervention. However, Marc Weller, professor of international law at Cambridge University, upholds that "once Mr. Yanukovych had lost effective control over events in the country, he could no longer authorize intervention."[86] He concluded that Russia's actions "to displace the lawful public authorities of Ukraine" amounted to "a significant act of intervention" and that since Russian military units were involved, "it is a case of armed intervention."[87]

Jan Stinissen asks the pertinent question, "Was this armed intervention also a use of force, a violation of Article 2(4) of the UN Charter?"[88] The question is applicable since Stinissen asserts that "moving armed forces to the territory of another state, without the consent of that state, should definitely be considered a use of force."[89] Therefore, the answer is yes since, after all, unmarked Russian troops did leave their bases in Crimea and along with reinforcements secured strategic sites and blocked Ukrainian troops, although Russia's actions in their armed intervention could not be seen as an armed attack because hardly a shot was fired in Crimea. Therefore, Russian military operations in the annexation of Crimea, including any associated cyber operations, were at most a violation of international law in the use of force, which gave the international community the right to response with countermeasures. The United States and EU chose to impose economic sanctions on Russia.

Russian Perspectives

The Russian annexation of Crimea illustrates the various elements, including cyber operations, of the hybrid warfare concept made prominent by Western analysts, although, as previously mentioned, the Western version is not integral to Russian military thinking.[90] Keir Giles, an associate fellow at Chatham House, argues the term *hybrid warfare*, translated literally as *gibridnaya voyna*, is being described in Russian writing on warfare. Giles adds that the phrase usually appears "when referring to Western thinking, rather than Russian approaches."[91] The translation is important, as Giles notes that no original Russian phrase exists to describe the idea, which does not fit within a Russian conceptual framework.[92] Instead, Russian scholars have sought to broaden the concept within the context of Russian politico-military experience. In their view, according to Ofer Fridman, a researcher at King's College London, *gibridnaya voyna* is the "creation of external controlling mechanisms, an infiltration of subversive and destructive concepts, projects and programs, a formation of an agency of influence and promoting its representatives to power."[93]

For Russian proponents of the *gibridnaya voyna* approach, the main purpose of this type of war is to "avoid the traditional battlefield and destroy the adversary via a hybrid of ideological, informational, financial, political and economic methods that dismantle the socio-cultural fabric of society, leading to internal collapse."[94] Therefore, the aim of *gibridnaya voyna* is to destroy the political cohesion of the adversary from the inside. In this sense, the term shares more with the US concept of political warfare than hybrid warfare.[95] Subversion and information are primary in this new type of war. In fact, the context in which the term *gibridnaya voyna* appears is "the same as another direct translation, 'kibervoyna' for cyber war."[96] Despite the rise of the term *gibridnaya voyna* in Russian discourse, members of the Russian military are reluctant to adopt it.[97] Most believe they will be the target, not the master of it. Furthermore, their objection to usage of the term *hybrid warfare* to describe Russian operations is that it inaccurately reflects Russian military thinking on how a modern, full-scale conflict would unfold.

In 2011, retired colonel Sergey Chekinov and retired lieutenant general Sergey Bogdanov, from the highly influential Centre for Military and Strategic Studies of the General Staff of the Russian Federation Armed Forces, described the following blueprint for modern conflict: "A new-generation war will be dominated by information and psychological warfare that will seek to achieve superiority in troops and weapons control and depress the opponent's armed forces personnel and population morally and psychologically. In the ongoing revolution in information technologies, information and psychological warfare will largely lay the groundwork for victory."[98] However, the authors do describe a preconflict stage that appears to use the kind of operations envisaged in Western perceptions of Russian hybrid warfare: "Months before the start of a new-generation war, large-scale measures in all types of warfare—information, moral, psychological, ideological, diplomatic, economic, and so on—may be designed and followed under a joint plan to create a favourable military, political, and economic setting for the operations of the allies' armed forces."[99] Here the two authors place specific emphasis on nonmilitary measures in their conceptualization of new-generation war. However, in a later article they note that without the employment of armed forces, "the achievement of the new-generation war aims will be impossible,"[100] for once the information operations and cyberattacks and so forth occur, the war would move into a kinetic phase of devastating aerial attacks and decisive ground combat. Therefore, the conceptual distinction between *gibridnaya voyna* and "new-generation war" is that while nonmilitary means and methods are used in both cases, in *gibridnaya voyna* they are used for "stand-alone, nonviolent political confrontation," while in new-generation war these methods are intended to "prepare the ground for subsequent military actions."[101]

The new-generation brand of warfare originated in the Georgian conflict and has been perfected in Eastern Ukraine. It appears to be more holistic and integrated than hybrid warfare, although both forms do include political subversion, proxy sanctuary, and coercive deterrence.[102] In the concept of new-generation warfare, aspects of actual warfare appear to be more dominant. The concept is conducted across multiple domains at multiple levels and can be part civil war and part interstate conflict. New-generation warfare is fought with "conventional forces as well as unconventional proxies and unmarked mercenaries, integrating cyber, psychological, electronic, and information warfare."[103] In this form of warfare, cyber operations offer an effective asymmetric means to covertly shape the battlefield while more overt military options such as unmanned aerial systems, massed fires, heavy infantry fighting vehicles, and mobile air defense networks achieve more radical effects. While the US Army has certainly embraced the concept of new-generation warfare to categorize these observations, a refined Russian perspective emerged in 2015 in a speech by Lt. Gen. Andrey V. Kartapolov at the Russian Academy of Military Science that covered elements of the concept. He replaced the term *new-generation* with *new-type* warfare, while noting "the features of the preparation and conduct of new-type warfare are being used and 'asymmetric' methods of confronting the enemy are being developed."[104] These methods include cyber operations in the Donbass region by Russian-led separatists that shape the battlefield through disruption, interception, and disinformation. While Russia denies the presence of its troops in Ukraine, these cyber operations used in kinetic strikes could rise to the level of an armed attack.

Donbass Intervention

Mark Galeotti, at the Center for Global Affairs, has observed that "if in Crimea the aim was to create a new order, in the Donbass it was as much as anything else to create chaos, even if a controlled, weaponized chaos."[105] Here the concept of new-generation warfare is instantly recognizable, starting with the creation by Moscow of favorable conditions for the employment of its armed forces. Throughout March and April 2014, Russian special operations forces and intelligence agents staged a pro-Russian movement in the Donbass region. Militants, likely led by Russian agents, stormed public buildings in Donetsk and Slovyansk, seizing television stations and police headquarters.[106] In May 2014, self-rule referendums were held in the Donetsk and Luhansk regions. Propositions to create new, quasi-independent "peoples' republics" won a landslide 90 percent of the vote.[107] The proxy regimes deployed their own militias, stiffened and supported by elements from Russia, to confront large-scale "antiterrorism operations" by Kiev to retake state property, although Russia denied involvement in the conflict, stating that any Russian servicemen fighting in Ukraine were volunteers on vacation, "following their convictions to fight for freedom."[108] However, over time, Russia relied increasingly on direct deployments, and by February 2015, there were 14,400 Russian troops, equipped with the latest armor and artillery, backing up formations of separatists in Eastern Ukraine.[109]

At the onset of hostilities, physical attacks, like in Crimea, by Russian-supported separatists destroyed "cabling, broadcast infrastructure, and ATM networks" in order to "isolate the region from Ukrainian media, communication, and financial services,"[110] while cyber-enabled offensive operations targeted Ukrainian military communications and individual soldier's personal communications. The lack of sufficient encrypted communications equipment in the Ukrainian military at the unit level made the use of clear communications by mobile phones a necessity.[111] Intercepts of personal mobile phones, combined with analysis of social media posts, alerted separatist forces to the positions of Ukrainian soldiers.[112] This practice was facilitated by the majority of Ukrainian citizens using Russian social media services, most commonly VKontakte, and Russian online services such as Mail.ru.[113] Some Ukrainian conscripts made positioning even easier by posting geotagged selfies on the front lines.[114] In addition, the intercept of mobile phone messages via managed infrastructures and manipulation of device protocols enabled man-in-the-middle attacks on Ukrainian soldiers. Demoralizing SMS and MMS (multimedia messaging service) texts were sent directly to soldiers on the front lines, saying to them, for example, "Ukrainian soldier, what are you doing here? Your family needs you alive."[115] At home, their wives received similar demoralizing texts and even death threats. Although the use of mobile phones created an operational vulnerability, their presence was deemed essential by Ukrainian soldiers to call home, check email, or even watch movies.

Russian cyber operations did not exploit conventional weapon systems due to legacy hardware and equipment,[116] although from late 2014 to 2016, a malware implant on Android devices was used to track and target Ukrainian artillery units. The security firm CrowdStrike reported discovery of a suspicious Android Package file linked to a legitimate application developed by a Ukrainian officer of the Fifty-Fifth Artillery Brigade.[117] The officer claimed the application, used by over nine thousand artillery personnel in the Ukrainian military, reduced the time to fire the D-30 122-millimeter towed howitzer from minutes to seconds. CrowdStrike said the file contained a variant of X-Agent, a command-and-control protocol. The X-Agent malware had the ability to access Android phone communications and locational data, which could be used to identify and target the artillery for counterbattery fire.[118] CrowdStrike attributed the malware to Fancy Bear, a cyber-espionage group affiliated with Russian military intelligence. Its report stated that the malware deployment "extends Russian cyber capabilities to the front lines of the battlefield."[119] It argued that by "leveraging of a mobile application for military purposes," Russian forces are delivering on "the practical application of full-spectrum combat."[120]

While cyber warfare is a key component of new-generation war, other forms of warfare such as electronic have been just as prevalent in Eastern Ukraine. Russia has demonstrated the ability to "intercept and access any and all EM [electromagnetic] transmissions at their discretion in the areas of conflict."[121] A handbook on Russian new-generation warfare by the Asymmetric Warfare Group reports that in Eastern Ukraine, Russian electronic warfare systems have "proved devastating to Ukrainian radio communications, are capable of jamming unmanned aircraft systems (UAS), and can broadcast false GPS [Global Positioning System] signals (an effect called spoofing)."[122] The handbook says the systems also have the ability to find the directions of EM signals and, when combined with a fire-direction center, can result in accurate fire on enemy forces. It gives an example from a Ukrainian army unit in Eastern Ukraine that received accurate artillery fire when broadcasting a radio message. After incurring casualties, the unit received "text messages on their cell phones from the Russian led separatist commander asking how they liked the artillery."[123] Besides electronic warfare, Eastern Ukraine has become a test bed for the latest Russian tactics and equipment, such as unmanned aerial vehicles for target acquisition for massed fires of artillery and the multiple-launch rocket system, modern main battle tanks with integrated active-armor defense systems, and networked self-propelled air-defense systems.[124] Russia has dramatically increased the supply of modernized weapons to the units of the First and Second Army Corps, which are the designations of the separatist forces station in the Donbass region.[125]

On April 16, 2015, during a question-and-answer show, President Putin said defiantly, "Let me be clear: There are no Russian troops in Ukraine." This staunch position was consistent with his previous remark at an end-of-year press conference that "Russian soldiers in eastern Ukraine were volunteers."[126] The statement was hard to believe since eight battalion-level tactical groups were seen covertly entering Ukraine in August 2015, heading in armored columns to Luhansk and Donetsk.[127] Professor Michael Schmitt observed in 2017 that "with respect to its activities in Ukraine, Russia played on the legal margins by masking its direct involvement in the hostilities, which would have implicated the *jus ad bellum* [conduct of hostilities] use of force prohibition and openly initiated an international armed conflict between Russia and Ukraine under the *jus in bello* [resort to force]."[128]

Instead, the situation in Eastern Ukraine has been characterized by the International Committee of the Red Cross as a noninternational armed conflict between the armed forces of the government of Ukraine and the separatists.[129] The term *noninternational armed conflict* is appropriate because there is protracted armed violence, which may include cyber operations, between governmental armed forces and an organized armed group.[130] Although there is widespread belief that Russia actively supports the separatists by sending "volunteers" to the area, there is no compelling evidence it exercises overall control.[131] The extensive presence of Russian forces in Eastern Ukraine alludes to an act of aggression, which is by law an egregious use of force.[132] However, by exploiting the principles and rules of international law, Russia refocuses "attention on the complex questions of State responsibility for the actions of non-State actors."[133] Along with the challenges of attribution in cyber space, that attention misdirects any claim of state responsibility for cyber operations, although the existence of firm attribution to the GRU for the hack of Android devices to target Ukrainian artillery units would implicate the Russian state. In that case, Russian cyber operations used in kinetic strikes could rise to the level of an armed attack since the Ukrainian armed forces have suffered extensive losses, such as from 15 percent to 20 percent of their prewar inventory of D-30 howitzers.[134]

Conclusion

Experts use the terms *hybrid warfare* and *new-generation war* in different ways. Christopher Chivvis, a researcher at the RAND Corporation, testifies that they point to the same thing: "Russia is using multiple instruments of power and influence, with an emphasis on nonmilitary tools, to pursue its national interests outside its borders."[135] Vladimir Putin's strategic goal in Ukraine is to restore the unity of Ukrainians and Russians as one people. Putin has said, "Kiev is the mother of Russian cities. Ancient Rus is our common source and we cannot live without each other."[136] Not just Putin but also the majority of the Russian political class and population have always refused to accept Ukraine as a sovereign state. Russia has never considered the borders of Ukraine to be justified or natural and therefore inviolable.[137] When President Yanukovych fled the country, Putin decided to activate a prepared scenario for military intervention. As the leader of a revisionist state in competition with the West over the political orientation of Ukraine, Putin applied his own interpretation of international law to justify his actions. Scenarios abound where Russia could repeat the hybrid warfare model with an opaque and muddled assault on the Baltic states using proxy forces, disinformation, and cyberattacks.[138]

Chivvis also notes that Russia may "still use its conventional and even nuclear threats as part of a hybrid strategy, but in general terms it prefers to minimize the actual employment of a traditional military force."[139] Accordingly it appears that cyber operations in Ukraine have proved to be an optimal way for Russia to economize the use of overt military force. Researcher Mark Galeotti acknowledges that for Western scholars and practitioners alike, "hybrid war has become, in part by default, the accepted term for Russia's current approach."[140] However, for the Russians, the phenomenon is part of a new way of war, in which the use of direct force may not be the central element. Thus, Galeotti more recently argues that *hybrid war* applies only to a proportion of Russia's wider challenge that is best considered through the lens of political warfare.[141] The NATO Strategic Communications Centre of Excellence concurs that "hybrid threats, by their very nature, are about creating effects that influence political decision-making."[142] The effects can be diffuse, develop over a long period of time, and not be noticed until it is too late to respond. Yet to complicate matters, this form of political activity is often described as occurring in the "gray zone" between the traditional war-and-peace duality.[143]

Heidi Reisinger, a staff member of the German Ministry of Defense, and Alexander Golts, a columnist for the *Moscow Times*, recognize together that Russia's actions in "hybrid warfare" can "include all kinds of instruments such as cyber and information operations."[144] They find that the Russian approach, as demonstrated in the intervention in Crimea and the conflict in Donbass, consists of five key aspects—namely, actions with an appearance of legality, a military show of force, ambiguity and denials, local proxy forces, and a disinformation campaign.[145] Reisinger and Golts also find that in hybrid warfare "none of the single components is new; it is the combination and orchestration of different actions that achieves a surprise effect and creates ambiguity, making an adequate reaction extremely difficult."[146] Keir Giles points out that the challenge for NATO is that in order "to take action, foolproof attribution to a specific aggressor is essential."[147] Although the perpetrator of the cyber operations in Crimea and Donbass might seem obvious, the attribution is ambiguous. The use of proxy forces in Ukraine extends from the physical domain to the cyber domain. Cyber actors operating on behalf of the Russian cause include CyberBerkut, which is purported to be a front for Russian military intelligence.[148] Its tactics and results stay below the threshold of an armed attack, consistent with the other indirect applications of hybrid warfare or new-generation war by unidentifiable armed proxies, which have hampered a formidable response by the alliance under the guidelines of international law.

Notes

1. Frank G. Hoffman, *Conflict in the 21st Century: The Rise of Hybrid Wars* (Arlington, VA: Potomac Institute for Policy Studies, 2007), 8.

2. Frank G. Hoffman, "Hybrid Warfare and Challenges," *Joint Force Quarterly*, no. 52 (First Quarter 2009): 35.

3. NATO, "Brussels Summit Declaration," Public Diplomacy Division press release, PR/CP(2018)074, July 11, 2018, para. 2.

4. NATO, para. 6.

5. NATO, para. 6.

6. NATO, "Warsaw Summit Communiqué," Public Diplomacy Division press release, 2016, para. 72.

7. Bettina Renz, "Russia and 'Hybrid Warfare,'" *Contemporary Politics* 22, no. 3 (2016): 283.

8. Renz, 284.

9. "Complex Crises Call for Adaptable and Durable Capabilities," editor's introduction, *Military Balance* 115, no. 1 (2015): 5.

10. Ofer Fridman, "Hybrid Warfare or *Gibridnaya Voyna*?," *RUSI Journal* 162, no. 1 (2017): 42–49.

11. Hoffman, "Hybrid Warfare and Challenges," 37.

12. Stephen Biddle and Jeffrey A. Friedman, "The 2006 Lebanon Campaign and the Future of Warfare: Implications for Army and Defense Policy," Strategic Studies Institute, September 2008, 35–38.

13. Anthony H. Cordesman, "Preliminary 'Lessons' of the Israeli-Hezbollah War," Center for Strategic and International Studies, September 11, 2006: 22.

14. Hoffman, *Conflict in the 21st Century*, 8, 14.

15. John Arquilla, "Perils of the Gray Zone: Paradigms Lost, Paradoxes Regained," *Prism* 7, no. 3 (May 2018): 126.

16. Robert M. Gates, "A Balanced Strategy: Reprogramming the Pentagon for a New Age," *Foreign Affairs* 88, no. 1 (January/February 2009): 33.

17. DOD, Capstone Concept for Joint Operations, version 3.0, January 15, 2009, 8.

18. NATO, "Phase 1 Countering Hybrid Threat (CHT) IPT Report," 5000 TC-70/TT -4587/ Ser: NU0365, June 16, 2009, 1.

19. Russell W. Glenn, "Thoughts on 'Hybrid' Conflict," *Small Wars Journal* (2009): 2, https://smallwarsjournal.com/jrnl/art/thoughts-on-hybrid-conflict.

20. Margaret S. Bond, "Hybrid War: A New Paradigm for Stability Operations in Failing States," US Army War College, March 30, 2007.

21. NATO, "Bi-SC Input to a New NATO Capstone Concept for the Military Contribution to Countering Hybrid Threats," 5000 FXX 0100/TT-6051/ Ser: NU0040, August 25, 2010, 2.

22. NATO, 2.

23. Supreme Allied Commander Transformation, "Assessing Emerging Security Challenges: Countering Hybrid Threats (CHT) Experiment Overview," May 9, 2011.

24. Sascha-Dominik Bachman and Hikan Gunneriusson, "Hybrid Wars: The 21st-Century's New Threats to Global Peace and Security," *Scientia Militaria: South African Journal of Military Studies* 43, no. 1 (2015): 79.

25. Renz, "Russia and 'Hybrid Warfare,'" 283.

26. Nicu Popescu, "Hybrid Tactics: Neither New nor Only Russian," *European Union Institute for Security Studies*, Alert Issue no. 4 (January 2015): 1.

27. Guillaume Lasconjarias and Jeffrey A. Larsen, "Introduction: A New Way of Warfare," in *NATO's Response to Hybrid Threats*, ed. Guillaume Lasconjarias and Jeffrey A. Larsen, Forum Paper no. 24 (Rome: NATO Defense College, 2015), 1.

28. Lasconjarias and Larsen, 1.

29. Lasconjarias and Larsen, xxi.

30. Julian Lindley-French, "NATO and New Ways of Warfare: Defeating Hybrid Threats," NDC conference report no. 03/15, Research Division, NATO Defense College, May 2015, 4.

31. Lindley-French, 4.

32. Frank Hoffman, "On Not-So-New Warfare: Political Warfare vs Hybrid Threats," War on the Rocks, commentary, July 28, 2014, 3.

33. Valery Gerasimov, "Tsennost nauki v predvidenii [The value of science is in foresight]," *Voyenno-Promyshlennyy Kuryer*, no. 8 (February 27, 2013): 1–2.

34. Gerasimov, 2.

35. Sydney J. Freedberg Jr., "US Needs New Strategy to Combat Russian, Chinese 'Political Warfare': CSBA," Breaking Defense, May 31, 2018.

36. Charles K. Bartles, "Getting Gerasimov Right," *Military Review*, January/February 2016, 34.

37. Mark Galeotti, *Russian Political War: Moving beyond the Hybrid* (London: Routledge, 2019), 28.

38. US Army Special Operations Command, "'Little Green Men': A Primer on Modern Russian Unconventional Warfare, Ukraine 2013–2014," 2016, 18.

39. Bartles, "Getting Gerasimov Right," 34.

40. "Ukraine Protests after Yanukovych EU Deal Rejection," BBC News, November 30, 2013.

41. Elias Kuhn von Burgsdorff, "The Euromaidan Revolution in Ukraine: Stages of the Maidan Movement and Why They Constitute a Revolution," *Inquiries Journal* 7, no. 2 (2015).

42. Glib Pakharenko, "Cyber Operations at Maidan: A First-Hand Account," in *Cyber War in Perspective: Russian Aggression against Ukraine*, ed. Kenneth Geers (Tallinn: NATO Cooperative Cyber Defense Centre of Excellence, 2015), 61.

43. Von Burgsdorff, "Euromaidan Revolution in Ukraine."

44. Ian Traynor, "Ukraine's Bloodiest Day: Dozens Dead as Kiev Protesters Regain Territory from Police," *The Guardian*, February 21, 2014.

45. Traynor.

46. Pakharenko, "Cyber Operations at Maidan," 61.

47. Von Burgsdorff, "Euromaidan Revolution in Ukraine."

48. US Army Special Operations Command, "Little Green Men," 55.

49. Mark Galeotti, "Hybrid, Ambiguous, and Non-linear? How New Is Russia's 'New Way of War'?," *Small Wars and Insurgencies* 27, no. 2 (2016): 284.

50. Heidi Reisinger and Alexander Golts, "Russia's Hybrid Warfare: Waging War below the Radar of Traditional Collective Defense," in Lasconjarias and Larsen, *NATO's Response to Hybrid Threats*, 118.

51. Emmanuel Karagiannis, "The Russian Interventions in South Ossetia and Crimea Compared: Military Performance, Legitimacy and Goals," *Contemporary Security Policy* 35, no. 3 (September 29, 2014): 408.

52. Karagiannis, 119.

53. Galeotti, "Hybrid, Ambiguous, and Non-linear," 284.

54. Philip P. Pan, "Ukraine to Extend Russia Naval Base Lease, Pay Less for Natural Gas," *Washington Post*, April 22, 2010.

55. Kathy Lally, "Russian Parliament Approves Use of Troops in Ukraine," *Washington Post*, March 1, 2014.

56. John Leyden, "Battle Apparently Underway in Russia-Ukraine Conflict," *The Register*, March 4, 2014.

57. Pakharenko, "Cyber Operations at Maidan," 62.

58. Pavel Polityuk, "Ukraine Says Communications Hit, MPs Phones Blocked," Reuters, March 4, 2014.
59. Infosec Institute, "Crimea: The Russian Cyber Strategy to Hit Ukraine," General Security (blog), March 11, 2014.
60. Jeffrey Carr, "Rival Hackers Fighting Proxy War over Crimea," CNN Special, March 25, 2014.
61. CrowdStrike, "Global Threat Intel Report," 2014, 25–27; John Bumgarner, "A Cyber History of the Ukraine Conflict," Dark Reading, March 27, 2014; Doug Bernard, "Russia-Ukraine Crisis Could Trigger Cyber War," Voice of America, April 20, 2014.
62. David M. Herszenhorn, "Crimea Votes to Secede from Ukraine as Russian Troops Keep Watch," *New York Times*, March 16, 2014.
63. John B. Bellinger III, "Why the Crimean Referendum Is Illegitimate," Council on Foreign Relations, March 16, 2014.
64. Adrian Croft and Peter Apps, "NATO Websites Hit in Cyber Attack Linked to Crimea Tension," Reuters, March 15, 2014.
65. Croft and Apps.
66. Danielle Wiener-Bronner, "Putin Holds Treaty Signing to Annex Crimea," *The Atlantic*, March 18, 2014.
67. US Army Special Operations Command, "Little Green Men," 58.
68. Michael Ruhle and Julijus Grubliauskas, "Energy as a Tool of Hybrid Warfare," in Lasconjarias and Larsen, *NATO's Response to Hybrid Threats*, 189–94.
69. William J. Broad, "In Taking Crimea, Putin Gains a Sea of Fuel Reserves," *New York Times*, May 17, 2014.
70. Danielle Wiener-Bronner, "Russia Cuts Off Gas Supplies to Ukraine," *The Atlantic*, June 16, 2014.
71. Nikolay Koval, "Revolution Hacking," in Geers, *Cyber War in Perspective: Russian Aggression against Ukraine*, 56.
72. Koval, 56.
73. Mark Clayton, "Ukraine Election Narrowly Avoided 'Wanton Destruction' from Hackers," *Christian Science Monitor*, June 17, 2014.
74. Clayton.
75. FireEye, "APT28: A Window into Russia's Cyber Espionage Operations?," special report, 2014, 3.
76. Koval, "Revolution Hacking," 57.
77. Koval, 57.
78. Pakharenko, "Cyber Operations at Maidan," 63.
79. Jan Stinissen, "A Legal Framework for Cyber Operations in Ukraine," in Geers, *Cyber War in Perspective: Russian Aggression against Ukraine*, 124.
80. Stinissen, 125.
81. Eduard Kovacs, "Anonymous Ukraine Launches OpIndependence, Attacks European Investment Bank," *Softpedia News*, October 31, 2013.
82. Kovacs.
83. Pakharenko, "Cyber Operations at Maidan," 61.
84. Stinissen, "Legal Framework for Cyber Operations in Ukraine," 131.
85. Fred Dews, "NATO Secretary-General: Russia's Annexation of Crimea Is Illegal and Illegitimate," Brookings Now, March 19, 2014.
86. Marc Weller, "Analysis: Why Russia's Crimea Move Fails Legal Test," BBC News, March 7, 2014.
87. Weller.

88. Stinissen, "Legal Framework for Cyber Operations in Ukraine," 127.
89. Stinissen, 127.
90. Renz, "Russia and 'Hybrid Warfare,'" 285.
91. Keir Giles, *Russia's "New" Tools for Confronting the West: Continuity and Innovation in Moscow's Exercise of Power*, Chatham House, Russia and Eurasia Programme (London: Royal Institute of International Affairs, March 2016), 9.
92. Giles, 9.
93. Ofer Fridman, *Russian Hybrid Warfare: Resurgence and Politicisation* (London: Hurst, 2018), 93.
94. Fridman, 93.
95. Fridman, 96.
96. Giles, *Russia's "New" Tools*, 9.
97. Fridman, *Russian Hybrid Warfare*, 93.
98. Galeotti, *Russian Political War*, 43–44.
99. Galeotti, 44.
100. Sergey Chekinov and S. A. Bogdanov, "The Nature and Content of a New-Generation War," *Military Thought*, no. 4 (2013).
101. Fridman, *Russian Hybrid Warfare*, 135–36.
102. Phillip Karber and Joshua Thibeault, "Russia's New-Generation Warfare," Association of the US Army, May 20, 2016.
103. Lionel Beehner and Liam Collins, "Countering Russian Aggression in the Twenty-First Century," US Army Modern War Institute, March 20, 2018.
104. Timothy Thomas, "The Evolving Nature of Russia's Way of War," *Military Review*, July/August 2017, 39.
105. Galeotti, "Hybrid, Ambiguous, and Non-linear," 285.
106. US Army Special Operations Command, "Little Green Men," 59.
107. Shaun Walker, Oksana Grytsenko, and Howard Amos, "Ukraine: Pro-Russia Separatists Set for Victory in Eastern Region Referendum," *The Guardian*, May 12, 2014.
108. Reisinger and Golts, "Russia's Hybrid Warfare," 123.
109. Reuben F. Johnson, "Russia's Hybrid War in Ukraine 'Is Working,' Conference Concludes," *Jane's Defence Weekly*, February 25, 2015, 4.
110. Pakharenko, "Cyber Operations at Maidan," 63.
111. Pakharenko, 27.
112. Anna Reynolds, "Social Media as a Tool of Hybrid Warfare," NATO Strategic Communications Centre of Excellence, 2016.
113. Nicole Kobie, "Ukraine Banned Its Biggest Social Network over Fears of Russian Influence," Motherboard, May 16, 2017.
114. Aaron F. Brantley, Nerea M. Cal, and Devlin P. Winkelstein, "Defending the Borderland," Army Cyber Institute, 2017, 27.
115. Brantley, Cal, and Winkelstein, 36.
116. Brantley, Cal, and Winkelstein, 25.
117. Adam Meyers, "Danger Close: Fancy Bear Tracking of Ukrainian Field Artillery Units," CrowdStrike (blog), December 22, 2016.
118. Rafia Shaikh, "Russian-Linked DNC Hackers Used Android Malware to Track Ukrainian Military," WCCFTech Security (blog), December 22, 2016.
119. Dustin Volz, "Russian Hackers Tracked Ukrainian Artillery Units Using Android Implant: Report," Reuters, December 21, 2016.
120. Elias Groll, "In a Hacked Ukrainian App, a Picture of the Future of War," *Foreign Policy*, December 22, 2016.

121. Brantley, Cal, and Winkelstein, "Defending the Borderland," 32.
122. Asymmetric Warfare Group, "Russian New Generation Warfare Handbook," version 1, unclassified sections, December 2016, 17.
123. Asymmetric Warfare Group, 18.
124. Karber and Thibeault, "Russia's New-Generation Warfare."
125. Samuel Cranny-Evans, "Russia Sustains Pressure in East Ukraine, Tests Latest Weapons," *Jane's Defence Weekly*, May 15, 2019, 23.
126. Pamela Engel, "Putin: 'I Will Say This Clearly: There Are No Russian Troops in Ukraine,'" *Business Insider*, April 16, 2015.
127. Viktor Shydlyukh, "Eight Russia's Battalion-Level Tactical Groups Entered Ukraine a Year Ago: General Staff," Central Research Institute of the Armed Forces of Ukraine, August 13, 2015.
128. Michael N. Schmitt, "Grey Zones in the International Law of Cyberspace," *Yale Journal of International Law Online* 42, no. 2 (2017): 1.
129. Noelle Quenivet, "Trying to Classify the Conflict in Eastern Ukraine. . . . ," IntLaw-Grrls (blog), August 28, 2014.
130. Michael N. Schmitt, ed., *Tallinn Manual 2.0 on the International Law Applicable to Cyber Operations*, 2nd ed. (Cambridge: Cambridge University Press, 2017), 385.
131. Stinissen, "Legal Framework for Cyber Operations in Ukraine," 130.
132. M. Dovbenko, "International Legal Classification of the Russian Federation's Actions in the East of Ukraine as an Act of Aggression," Borysfen Intel, November 30, 2015.
133. Schmitt, "Grey Zones," 2.
134. Meyers, "Danger Close."
135. Christopher S. Chivvis, *Understanding Russian "Hybrid Warfare" and What Can Be Done about It*, testimony before the House Committee on Armed Services, March 22, 2017 (Santa Monica, CA: RAND Corp., 2017), 1, https://www.rand.org/content/dam/rand/pubs/testimonies/CT400/CT468/RAND_CT468.pdf.
136. Marcel H. Van Herpen, *Putin's Wars: The Rise of Russia's New Imperialism* (New York: Rowman & Littlefield, 2015), 268.
137. Van Herpen, 269.
138. Kyle Rempfer, "Hybrid Warfare," *Defense News*, May 20, 2019, 10–11.
139. Rempfer, 2.
140. Galeotti, "Hybrid, Ambiguous, and Non-linear," 287.
141. Galeotti, *Russian Political War*, 13.
142. NATO Strategic Communications Centre of Excellence, "Hybrid Threats: A Strategic Communications Perspective," April 2019, 18.
143. Philip Kapusta, "The Gray Zone," *Special Warfare*, October–December 2015.
144. Reisinger and Golts, "Russia's Hybrid Warfare," 116.
145. Reisinger and Golts, 116.
146. Reisinger and Golts, 116.
147. Keir Giles, "Conclusion: Is Hybrid Warfare Really New?," in Lasconjarias and Larsen, *NATOs Response to Hybrid Threats*, 329.
148. Sara Moore, "Russian Federation," intelligence report, Anomali, August 2017, 3, https://www.anomali.com/resources/whitepapers/russian-federation-cybersecurity-profile.

CHAPTER 4

Information Warfare Component

Russian official references to cyberspace (*kiberprostranstvo*) and cyber warfare (*kibervoyna*) occur mostly in translations of foreign texts, approaches, and activities.[1] Instead, Russians conceptualize cyber operations within the broader rubric of information warfare (*informatsionnaya voyna*).[2] Russian writings express a "holistic and integrated view of information warfare as a distinct, but unified and complete discipline."[3] The term *information warfare* as employed by Russian military theorists "includes computer network operations, electronic warfare, psychological operations and information operations."[4] In other words, cyberspace is considered to be a "mechanism for enabling the state to dominate the information landscape."[5] According to prominent Russian strategists retired colonel Sergey Chekinov and retired lieutenant general Sergey Bogdanov, "information could be used to disorganize governance, organize anti-government protests, delude adversaries, influence public opinion, and reduce an opponent's will to resist."[6] Cyber-enabled information operations give Moscow a covert means to achieve these objectives while maintaining a degree of plausible deniability.

Keir Giles, an associate fellow at Chatham House notes that the conflict in Ukraine demonstrates how "Russia sees cyber activity as a subset, and sometimes facilitator, of the much broader domain of information warfare."[7] For instance, at the onset of hostilities, cyber-enabled interference with Ukrainian parliament members' mobile phones and the National Security and Defense Council's Internet infrastructure attempted to influence their decision-making,[8] while concurrent information operations spread propaganda through Russian television content and media outlets to influence the population with false news and ideological narratives.[9] The techniques seen in Ukraine illustrate that Russian information warfare has evolved in practice by reviving and adapting well-established Soviet techniques for subversion and destabilization to the Internet age.[10] Distinct doctrinal assumptions about information warfare drawn from the 2014 Military Doctrine depict "a clinging to old methods (sabotage, diversionary tactics, disinformation, state terror, manipulation, aggressive propaganda, exploiting the potential for protest among the population)."[11] The current Russian practice of information warfare combines these "tried and tested tools of influence with a new embrace of modern technology and capabilities."[12]

Russian military doctrine indicates that information warfare and information operations "are peacetime affairs and not just wartime activities."[13] Sergei Ivanov, the former Russian deputy premier and defense minister, has openly "admitted that IW and IO allowed Moscow to find a new weapon to use in what might be called purely political warfare."[14] In this fashion Moscow uses information as a weapon to shape political narratives in countries of interest. Cyber operations play a key role in the theft of valuable information to be used in influence operations. This chapter will articulate further the concepts and terminology of Russian IW used in strategic competition with the United States and its allies and partners. It will examine their application in the Russian interference in the 2016 US presidential election using the technical and legal framework. The chapter will finish by explaining the role of cyber operations in Russian political warfare, as seen in elections in European countries.

Information Concepts

Notable scholar Stephen Blank claims that "Russia's assault upon the entire Western information space, both civilian and military may be the most important weapon in its arsenal and the one where it has clearly garnered a comparative advantage."[15] Blank notes that Russian power structures understand completely the capabilities of information weapons. His observation is evident in the stated priority "to enhance capacity and means of information warfare" in the 2014 Military Doctrine.[16] Russia expert Dmitry Adamsky agrees, in stating, "It is difficult to overemphasize the role that Russian official doctrine attributes to . . . information struggle in modern conflicts."[17] Keir Giles believes Russia considers itself to be "engaged in full-scale information warfare."[18] Giles explains that Russian IW can cover "a vast range of different activities and processes seeking to steal, plant, interdict, manipulate, distort or destroy information."[19] In this sense, information acts as a tool or a target. Giles contends that the channels and methods of Russian IW are equally vast, including computers, smartphones, news media, and online troll campaigns.

Russian IW provides a means for victory in armed conflict. Long-term IW campaigns in peacetime prepare the battlefield for the manifestation of conflict, as seen in Georgia and Ukraine. Chekinov and Bogdanov, at the Centre for Military and Strategic Studies of the General Staff of the Russian Federation Armed Forces, wrote,

> Wars will be resolved by a skillful combination of military, nonmilitary, and special nonviolent measures that will be put through by a variety of forms and methods and a blend of political, economic, informational, technological, and environmental measures, primarily by taking advantage of information

superiority. Information warfare in the new conditions will be the starting point of every action now called the new type of warfare, or hybrid war, in which broad use will be made of the mass media and, where feasible, global computer networks (blogs, various social networks, and other resources).[20]

Giles asserts that this "blending and coordination between different information tools is a distinct feature of how Russia aspires to prosecute information warfare."[21] Officially the Russian Ministry of Defense has defined IW as "the ability to . . . undermine political, economic, and social systems; carry out mass psychological campaigns against the population of a State in order to destabilize society and the government; and force a State to make decisions in the interest of their opponents."[22]

Another term in the Russian lexicon for conflict in the information sphere is information confrontation (*informatsionnoye protivoborstvo*). The concept aims primarily to shape the perception and manipulate the behavior of target audiences. Information confrontation encompasses two measures for influence: informational-technical effect, which is "analogous to computer network operations," and informational-psychological effect, which "refers to attempts to change people's behavior or beliefs."[23] In either measure, cyber operations are part of an attempt to control the information environment. Blank asserts there is "no real distinction in Moscow's concept of information confrontation between attacking cyber networks like civilian power grids and networks, or attacking military ones such as space-based and civilian ISR [intelligence, surveillance, and reconnaissance] networks, or the saturation of the social and other media spaces with pro-Russian narratives."[24] Each approach entails the influence of the transfer and storage of information. The intent of information confrontation during peacetime or wartime is the assurance of information superiority, although peacetime measures are mostly covert, whereas wartime measures are overt.

IO, which incorporate all the uses of information and disinformation, are a key part of Russia's way of contemporary war.[25] Before the invasion of Ukraine, an emphasis on "information operations, which may encompass broad, socio-psychological manipulation . . . [resided] comfortably in the mainstream of Russian military thought."[26] Christopher Chivvis testifies that Russia uses IO to shape political discussion and cast doubt on objective truths.[27] Information is the "object of operations, independent of the channel through which the information is transmitted."[28] Russia used IO during the Cold War, but the volume and ambition today are "far greater and facilitated by the existence of the Internet, cable news, and especially social media."[29] In addition, the existence of cyber tools offers Russia "new means of exerting both direct and indirect influence over the Western political scene."[30] The most recent Department of Defense Cyber Strategy asserts that "Russia has used cyber-enabled information operations to influence our population and challenge our democratic processes."[31] This assertion is in line with the definition of IO offered by A. A. Strel'tsov, a prominent Russian theorist, as "activities coordinated in terms of time, efforts, and objectives performed by agents to implement government information policy over a relatively long period of time that are directed at carrying out mid-term or short-term political tasks."[32]

A key aspect of Russian IW is the weakening and undermining of adversary societies. The underlying approaches of activities and principles are "broadly recognizable as reinvigorated aspects of subversion campaigns from the Cold War era and earlier."[33] The most radical thinker on the topic, Evgenii Messner, defined subversion war (*myatezhevoina*) as "psychological warfare aimed to conquer the mind and soul of people."[34] Soviet intelligence and security services concentrated on subversion, using methods known as active measures (*aktivnyye meropriyatiya*).[35] The concept of active measures was "predominately used in Western literature on Soviet influence operations during the 1980s."[36] By definition in a study published in 1984, active measures are "certain overt and covert techniques for influencing events and behavior in, and the actions of, foreign countries."[37] Soviet agencies used active measures during the Cold War to divide NATO, subvert governments not aligned with the USSR, and shape the thinking of societies to accept the communist agenda.[38]

Today Russia employs the same logic in the use of active measures to influence the policies of another government, undermine confidence in their leaders and institutions, disrupt relations between other nations, and discredit opponents.[39] The most common subcategory of active measures is *dezinformatsiya*, or disinformation.[40] During the Cold War, the KGB considered disinformation to be "the heart and soul of Soviet intelligence."[41] In Soviet terminology, disinformation is described as "a carefully constructed, false message that is secretly introduced into the opponent's communication system to deceive either his decision-making elite or public opinion."[42] Accordingly, Giles claims that a key element of subversion campaigns is "spreading disinformation among the population about the work of state bodies, undermining their authority, and discrediting administrative structures."[43] Russia has enhanced and augmented the spread of disinformation by adapting principles of subversion to the Internet age. Its new investments in technologies and organizations resulted in targeted and consistent information and disinformation campaigns for which Western society was entirely unprepared.

Influence Operations

In 2017, former director of national intelligence James Clapper testified that "Russian has used cyber tactics and techniques to seek to influence public opinion across Europe and Eurasia."[44] In addition, Clapper asserted that "Russian cyber operations will likely target the United States . . . to conduct influence operations to support Russian military and political objectives."[45] The concept of IW carries within it computer network operations alongside disciplines such as psychological operations, influence, deception (*maskirovka*), and disinformation.[46] Taken together, this collective of disciplines forms "a whole of systems, methods, and tasks to influence the perception and behavior of the enemy, population, and international community on all levels."[47] Therefore, conceptually and practically, the Russian approach to IW is "much broader than simply sowing lies and denials."[48]

Instead, Russian state and nonstate actors have "exploited history, culture, language, nationalism, disaffection and more to carry out cyber-enhanced disinformation campaigns with much wider objectives."[49] The advance of digital technology and communication have allowed Russia to spread disinformation during influence operations at high speed via "massive and unsecured points of influence."[50] The Russian approach to disinformation is manifested in overt foreign propaganda, social media infiltration, and cyber hacks and leaks. Kremlin-linked media, such as Russia Today (RT) and Sputnik, convey purposeful misinformation and distortion, while trolls infiltrate and manipulate social media to mount and mask disinformation. Trolls are individuals who bait reactions, similar to drawing a line through water for fish, by posting rude, inflammatory, derogatory, misleading, or controversial comments online.[51] Finally, Russian hackers steal and leak emails and information in order to spin and distribute disinformation narratives.[52]

2016 US Presidential Election

The US Intelligence Community assessed with high confidence that "Russian President Vladimir Putin ordered an influence campaign in 2016 aimed at the US presidential election."[53] Russia's efforts represented its "longstanding desire to undermine the US-led liberal democratic order" but were an escalation in scope compared to previous influence operations.[54] The Russian influence campaign was multifaceted, blending "covert intelligence operations—such as cyber activity—with overt efforts by Russian Government agencies, state-funded media, third-party intermediaries, and paid social media users or trolls."[55] The IO components conveyed selected information and indicators to American audiences to influence their emotions, motives, reasoning, and behavior in a manner favorable to Russia's objectives.[56] It appeared successful in sowing discord and dividing the country.

Overt Foreign Propaganda

A striking but subtle aspect of the influence campaign was the broadcast of propaganda. Scholars define propaganda as "the organized attempt through communication to affect belief or action or inculcate attitudes in a large audience in ways that circumvent or suppress an individual's adequately in-formed, rational, reflective judgment."[57] Russia's state-run propaganda machine seeks to subvert reality through messages that challenge the idea of an objec-tive, impartial truth. Russia does not lead with a facts-based narrative but with novel, emotionally appealing stories that are often false.[58] The Russian strategy to subvert reality also includes the provision of multiple, contradictory narra-tives or alternatives to the truth, to undermine trust in objective reporting.[59] Official state propaganda is disseminated abroad via foreign-language news channels as well as Western media. Most notable is the government-financed television news channel RT. The channel initially aimed to improve Russia's image abroad by stressing its unique culture and ethnic diversity. It eventually shifted to cover the negative aspects of the West—for instance, topics of mass unemployment, social inequality, and the banking crisis.[60] Broadcast on Rus-sian state television, in English in the United States, and around the world in multiple languages, RT was well positioned, along with government-funded Sputnik, a television, radio, and online outlet, to attempt to influence the 2016 US presidential election with fake news.

The US Intelligence Community assessed that "state-owned Russian media made increasingly favorable comments about President-elect Donald Trump as the 2016 U.S. general and primary election campaigns progressed, while consistently offering negative coverage of Secretary Clinton."[61] RT and Sput-nik cast President-elect Trump as the object of biased reporting by traditional American media channels they claimed were sympathetic to the views of cor-rupt politicians, while their coverage of Secretary Hillary Clinton focused on leaked emails and accused her of poor physical and mental health and corrup-tion. Popular English-language videos by RT that echoed these themes were titled "Trump Will Not Be Permitted to Win" and "How 100% of the Clintons' Charity Went to . . . Themselves."[62] These videos were also broadcast on so-cial media platforms with millions of views. Blinded by passion and prejudice, people are susceptible to this type of fake news and other forms of disinforma-tion since the outlandish or demonstrably false claims "often align with their political ideology."[63]

Social Media Infiltration

Media stories to denigrate Secretary Clinton and vindicate President-elect Trump during the election were amplified by a Russian army of professional trolls. The trolls were IW troops assigned primarily to the Internet Research Agency (IRA) based in Saint Petersburg. The IRA is financed by "a close Putin ally with ties to Russian intelligence."[64] Each troll at the agency is expected to "post 50 news articles daily and maintain six Facebook and 10 Twitter ac-counts, with 50 tweets per day."[65] They employ bots, which are automated accounts, along with impersonation accounts on social media platforms. Their work is no different from the use of active measures by Soviet agents, who would "try to weave propaganda into an existing narrative."[66] Trolls seize command of an ongoing news trend to spread disinformation, often with links to RT reports within their tweets. They take advantage of an existing network of true believers who are willing to spread the message.[67] During the 2016 US presidential election, the trolls amplified the voices of the American true believers while inserting propaganda into social media accounts and trends, which many Americans monitor for most of their breaking news. For instance, right after the first presidential debate, "the #TrumpWon hashtag quickly became the number one trend globally. Using the TrendMap application, one quickly noticed that the worldwide hashtag seemed to originate in Saint Petersburg, Russia."[68]

The IRA assigned more than eighty trolls to the "translator project," which focused on the American population during the election. The stated goal of the project was to "spread distrust toward the candidates and the political system in general."[69] The trolls created fictitious social media accounts on Facebook, Twitter, YouTube, and Instagram that appeared to be operated by US persons. The accounts were registered and monitored through hundreds of email accounts hosted by US providers. The trolls used election-related account names such as "March for Trump" on Twitter and "Clinton FRAUDation" on Facebook, in addition to election-related hashtags such as "#Trump2016," "#MAGA," and "#Hillary4Prison."[70] The account pages and groups addressed divisive US political and social issues, such as gun rights and immigration.

In particular, the IRA trolls promoted allegations of voter fraud by the Democratic Party in Iowa, North Carolina, and Florida. Similarly, they posted messages encouraging African Americans and American Muslims not to vote or to vote for a third-party candidate.[71] To amplify messaging, the organization produced, purchased, and posted advertisements on social media. Facebook later disclosed in congressional testimony that it had shut down 470 pages linked to the IRA that "shared divisive content and then promoted it using targeted political ads" in the run-up to the 2016 election.[72] Likewise, Twitter revealed that Russia-linked accounts "generated approximately 1.4 million automated, election-related tweets."[73] A research report for the Senate Intelligence Committee revealed that the Russians posted more than one thousand YouTube videos and that Instagram posts generated more than twice the engagement rate among users than either Facebook or Twitter.[74] Although it may never be known how much of an influence the Russian posts, ads, tweets, and videos had on the 2016 US presidential election, what is known is that "the combination of Trump support and anti-Clinton rhetoric made for a potent combination."[75]

Cyber Hacks and Leaks

The Russian influence campaign was bolstered by the hack of Democratic Party organizations and individuals followed by the leak of compromising information. Two Russian state–sponsored hacker groups used spear-phishing campaigns to obtain employee credentials and steal the information. The hacks and leaks of private data did not qualify as an armed attack but just might qualify as prohibited intervention, which is an internationally wrongful act. To release sensitive communications and private documents, the perpetrators used a variety of platforms and personas, including WikiLeaks, DCLeaks, and Guccifer 2.0. They falsely claimed "that DCLeaks was started by a group of American hackers and that Guccifer 2.0 was a lone Romanian hacker."[76] According to Herbert Lin and Jaclyn Kerr, researchers at the Center for International Security and Cooperation at Stanford University, the strategic release of "compromising material" concerning political rivals was not unusual since Russia has used so-called kompromat for years to "tarnish reputations and undermine opponent messages."[77] Historically, materials for kompromat are real or forged, in the form of documents, photographs, recordings, or videos. In the early days, the KGB used kompromat on Eastern bloc defectors and dissidents, and more recently the Russian Federal Security Service (FSB) has used it on Russian opposition activists and corrupt officials and also on American diplomats.[78] In the modern world, the advent of computer technology and digital cameras amplifies the range of materials and victims, as clearly seen in the Russian campaign to influence the 2016 US presidential election.

Headlines in June 2016 reported that Russian governmental hackers had penetrated the computer network of the Democratic National Committee and gained access to opposition research on presidential candidate Donald Trump.[79] DNC officials acknowledged that the intruders had gone deep into the DNC system and were able to read all email and chat traffic. The DNC had actually become aware of the hack in April when its IT team noticed unusual network activity. Within twenty-four hours, the security firm CrowdStrike installed software on the DNC computers to analyze data. A day after news of the breach, CrowdStrike published a report of analysis and findings, stating that two separate Russian intelligence–affiliated adversaries were present in the DNC network.[80] Later that day, a blog post on the site WordPress by an individual using the moniker Guccifer 2.0 claimed credit for penetrating the DNC by himself. The hacker mocked the security firm's assessment "that he was a sophisticated hacker group" and noted the hack "was easy, very easy."[81] Guccifer 2.0 then leaked several stolen documents, including the full 235-page opposition memo on presidential candidate Trump. The hacker stated, "The main part of the papers, thousands of files and mails, I gave to WikiLeaks. They will publish them soon."[82] CrowdStrike issued a statement that it stood by its conclusions and openly questioned whether the blog post was part of a Russian disinformation campaign.

Also starting in June 2016 and continuing throughout the US presidential campaign, the website DCLeaks released emails and documents stolen from the individuals associated with the Clinton campaign. Then, in late July 2016, WikiLeaks dumped almost twenty thousand emails from top DNC officials, which revealed their irritation with the Bernie Sanders campaign.[83] The release was timed to occur just days before the Democratic National Convention in Philadelphia, where party leaders aimed to unify behind their nominee, Hillary Clinton. The most damaging emails showed that DNC officials, who were supposed to remain neutral during the primary contest, were clearly in favor of Clinton.[84] The emails outraged Sanders's supporters, who repeatedly interrupted and booed the DNC chairwoman, Debbie Wasserman Schultz, as she sought to speak to Florida's delegation at a breakfast meeting.[85] Schultz decided not to gavel in the convention and formally stepped down as leader of the committee, while protests continued throughout the weeklong convention.[86] Finally, in October 2016, WikiLeaks released installments of hacked emails from John Podesta, the chairman of Clinton's campaign. Although most were benign, some reflected poorly on the campaign and relationships—for example, an email exchange had negative things to say about Catholicism and evangelical Christians. The flood of stolen emails dominated the news stations and fueled condemnation by candidate Trump all the way to Election Day.

The DNC system was penetrated long before detection by their tech team. In the summer of 2015, the hacker group called Cozy Bear broke in and monitored email and chat communication. In the spring of 2016, another hacker group, named Fancy Bear, breached the network and targeted the opposition research files. CrowdStrike stated the two groups did not appear to be working together.[87] Both groups had previously hacked various governmental agencies, commercial firms, and defense contractors. For instance, Cozy Bear, also called APT29, had breached the unclassified computer networks of the State Department, the White House, and the Joint Chiefs of Staff,[88] whereas Fancy Bear, also called APT28, had targeted ministries in Georgia and the Caucasus, Eastern European governments and militaries, and security-related organizations such as NATO and the Organization for Security and Co-operation in Europe.[89] It is widely believed that APT29 is actually part of the FSB and that APT28 is part of the GRU.[90] The use of these dubious advanced persistent-threat groups in the Russian influence campaign represents the "intensification of warfare by proxy."[91] Russia seems to realize that proxies offer certain political and economic advantages, such as "minimizing the risk of escalation, providing plausible deniability, and avoiding the costs of direct involvement."[92]

CrowdStrike was not sure at the time of its report how the two hacker groups intruded into the DNC network. Analysis by Special Counsel Robert Mueller revealed a surprising amount of technical information on the intrusion techniques used by Fancy Bear. The APT group or, more accurately, the GRU, hacked into the DNC's computers through its initial access to the Democratic Congressional Campaign Committee (DCCC).[93] The GRU had sent a spear-phishing email to a DCCC employee who entered her password after clicking on the link. The GRU used these stolen credentials to access the DCCC network and install its X-Agent malware on at least ten DCCC computers, which allowed it to capture employee keystrokes and take pictures of employee computer screens. Eventually, the GRU used the keylog and screenshot functions to steal credentials of a DCCC employee who was authorized to access the DNC network. It entered the DNC network with the stolen credentials and gained access to thirty-three DNC computers. The GRU then used word searches to find key documents. To avoid detection, it used a publicly available tool to gather and compress the documents and moved them outside the networks through encrypted channels.[94] The GRU also compromised the DNC Microsoft Exchange Server and stole thousands of DNC employee emails. While in both the DCCC and DNC networks, the GRU evaded detection by intentionally deleting logs and computer files.[95]

The GRU also used a variety of means to hack the email accounts of volunteers and employees of the Hillary Clinton campaign in March 2016. The most infamous was the intrusion into the account of the campaign chairman, John Podesta. The GRU used the Uniform Resource Locator (URL)–shortening service named Bitly to mask a link in a spear-phishing email, which directed the recipient to a GRU-created website.[96] The GRU spoofed the sender email address to appear to come from Google. The email looked like a security notification that instructed the user to change his password by clicking the embedded link.[97] An aide for Podesta spotted the email and sent it to a computer technician. However, the aide mistakenly wrote, "This is a legitimate email. John needs to change his password immediately."[98] That mistake gave the GRU access to over fifty thousand emails in Podesta's private Gmail account. Moscow gave the entire email cache to WikiLeaks.[99]

The joint analysis report issued by the Department of Homeland Security (DHS) and the Federal Bureau of Investigation (FBI) revealed the basics of the intrusion techniques used by Cozy Bear. The APT group, or more appropriately the FSB, executed a spear-phishing campaign with emails that contained a malicious link.[100] The FSB used legitimate domains associated with real American organizations and educational institutions to hide their origin. Eventually they compromised the systems of the Democratic Party when one targeted individual activated the link to malware hosted on operational infrastructure.[101] Once Cozy Bear was inside the DNC network, CrowdStrike reported that it relied primarily on an implant named SeaDaddy and another

PowerShell backdoor, which allowed them to launch malware automatically on a specific schedule. The PowerShell code was obfuscated to avoid detection and run persistently.[102] The code also established an encrypted connection to a command-and-control channel to download additional modules. Cozy Bear also used a PowerShell version of Mimikatz, a credential theft tool, to facilitate acquisition of credentials for lateral movement.[103]

Despite the precise execution of the hacks and leaks, there is no allegation in the Mueller investigation that the GRU hacking team changed the outcome or altered the vote count of the 2016 US presidential election,[104] although other Russian hackers did breach the electoral systems of at least thirty-nine states prior to Election Day.[105] From a technical perspective, their attacks relied on employees clicking and opening MS Word documents that ran VBScript. Disabling VBScript within Word would have prevented the malware from executing. Investigators discovered evidence in one state that the perpetrators attempted without success to delete or alter voter data.[106] The Russians also planted malware at election equipment manufacturer VR Systems of Tallahassee, Florida. The company makes electronic poll books and other devices that help officials conduct elections but does not make voting machines.[107] Without the ability to directly manipulate the vote count, the Russians had to rely on an aggressive influence campaign to indirectly manipulate the minds of voters. Just like in the Cold War, the Russians spread disinformation to targets strong in prejudice, who sought to gain their information from biased sources without critical skepticism.[108] Although tolerated during that era, did the apparent meddling in the 2016 US presidential election qualify as armed conflict?

Michael Schmitt, introduced previously as general editor of the *Tallinn Manual* and professor of international law at the University of Exeter, stated definitively that Moscow hacks and leaks are "not an initiation of armed conflict. It's not a violation of the U.N. Charter's prohibition on the use of force."[109] Nonetheless, Schmitt said the apparent attempt "to influence the outcome of the election by its release of emails through WikiLeaks probably violates the international law barring intervention in a state's internal affairs."[110] Rule 66 of the *Tallinn Manual 2.0* declares, "A State may not intervene, including by cyber means, in the internal or external affairs of another State."[111] The authors of the *Tallinn Manual 2.0* agreed that "the prohibition of intervention is a norm of customary international law."[112] This customary norm is derived from the foundational principle of sovereignty. The obligation not to intervene is "the corollary of every State's right to sovereignty, territorial integrity and political independence."[113] Thus, states must respect the rights of others to exercise control over certain activities occurring on their territory. Cyber operations qualify as an unlawful intervention if they "are intended to coerce (as distinct from lawfully influence) the targeted state's government in matters reserved to that state (e.g., by using cyber means to interfere with election results)."[114]

Schmitt explains that "two elements must be satisfied before a cyber operation qualifies as wrongful intervention. The operation must affect a State's *domaine réservé* and it must be coercive. Absent one of these elements, the operation may constitute interference, but it will not rise to the level of unlawful intervention."[115] The International Group of Experts agreed that "the matter most clearly within a State's *domaine réservé* appears to be the choice of both the political system and its organization, as these issues lie at the heart of sovereignty."[116] Therefore, Schmitt asserts that cyber operations that "affect either the process by which elections are conducted or their outcome qualify as prohibited intervention, so long as the second prong of the intervention test, coercion, is satisfied."[117] The constituent element of coercion refers to "an affirmative act designed to deprive another State of its freedom of choice, that is, to force that State to act in an involuntary manner or involuntarily refrain from acting in a particular way."[118] In regard to the 2016 US presidential election, Schmitt claims that "slanted reporting by Russian controlled media" and "the purchasing of advertising" on social media are not coercive and do not qualify as a prohibited intervention. The "cyber activities that feigned American citizenship and the hacking and release of private data" just might qualify.[119]

The deceptive nature of the troll operation deprived Americans of freedom of choice by manipulating their decision-making, thus weakening their ability to control their governance. Likewise, the hacks and leaks tainted the election process by introducing information that, albeit true, was obtained illegally under US domestic law. Catherine Lotrionte, the director of Georgetown University's Cyber Project, decided that Russia's efforts to influence the presidential election "don't rise to the level of an armed attack—or even a use of force. They were, however, still forbidden under a provision of international law that bans 'coercive interference.'"[120] If that is true, the United States would have had the grounds to undertake countermeasures that would otherwise be unlawful. The DNC hack represented an effort by Moscow to further test national responses and the limits of acceptable behavior in cyberspace, given "the absence of any real chance of provoking an armed (or any kind of significant) response."[121]

Political Warfare

Seventy years ago, George Kennan, the State Department's first director of policy planning, defined political warfare as "the employment of all the means at a nation's command, short of war, to achieve its national objectives. Such operations are both overt and covert."[122] Keenan had revived and reinterpreted the concept for the Cold War after its use in Allied psychological warfare campaigns in World War II. Today, Mark Galeotti argues that the Kremlin has embarked on "a campaign against the West that it considers to be equivalent to a war—and yet which it is determined to keep within the realms of the political, to keep it short of war."[123] Alina Polyakova and Spencer Boyer at the Brookings Institution add that Russian influence operations "do not focus on isolated events. Rather, taken as whole, they are at the core of a political strategy—honed in Europe's East and deployed against the West—to weaken Western institutions and undermine trans-Atlantic consensus."[124] The Russian strategy of political warfare is designed to achieve foreign policy objectives at the expense of US and allied interests. The main characteristics of political warfare are its focus on the targeted population, ever-present conflict, and economy of kinetic force.[125] Russia employs multiple instruments in political warfare, including outlets for IO, cyber tools for espionage or direct attacks, proxy groups, economic coercion, covert action, political pressure, and military intimidation.[126]

Kennan's definition points to the use of coercion in political warfare to alter adversary behavior. Russia engages in political warfare to discourage inimical foreign narratives, generate support for favorable policies, distract rivals from restraining freedom of action, and mitigate pushback over their overt acts of revisionism.[127] Moscow relies heavily on influence campaigns in an aggressive form of political warfare with very few self-imposed limitations. Political warfare serves as a less ambitious alternative to military conflict, where the "main goal is not hard victories, but simply sowing doubt, creating confusion, and imposing costs."[128] Political warfare is comparable to hybrid warfare but not quite identical. There is a great deal of overlap in the methods, but the primary difference is the role of the military instrument. Hybrid warfare clearly includes the use of military force, whereas there is no violence or lethal force in political warfare.[129] Instead, the military is used primarily for "heavy-metal diplomacy" in acts of brinkmanship and intimidation. The buzzing of NATO warships and airplanes, the sending of bombers near European and US airspace, and the war-gaming of thinly veiled offensives against neighbors are all part of a coherent attempt to use the threat of military force as a diplomatic instrument.[130] Likewise, there is a great deal of overlap in the players—for instance, both use special operations forces, mercenaries, and intelligence agencies—but political warfare extends into deeper realms, using criminal gangsters, religious patriarchs, ethnic warlords, diaspora communities, and political fronts.[131]

Since Vladimir Putin's return to power in 2012, there is no doubt that the Kremlin has worked to resurrect its arsenal of active measures. They can be seen as "tools of political warfare once used by the Soviet Union that aimed to influence world events through the manipulation of media, society, and politics."[132] Polyakova and Boyer argue that the Kremlin's strategy of influence includes disinformation campaigns, the cultivation of political allies, and cyberattacks.[133] For Malcolm Nance, evidence that Putin's intelligence agencies, as well as state-sponsored organizations and state-run news media, used "well cultivated espionage methods developed under the Soviet Union to carry out the cyber-attack on the 2016 United States election is overwhelming."[134] The espionage methodology that these entities used for these operations is a form of active measures.[135] Mark Galeotti claims that Russia sees active measures "from supporting populist parties through disinformation and espionage campaigns . . . as an essential part of its efforts to influence Europe."[136] Galeotti notes that active measures are a regular part of the work of Russia's intelligence agencies. They undertake a "broad range of political missions," from computer hacking to obtain compromising material, through spreading disinformation, all the way to actively fomenting unrest and direct sabotage.[137]

The US Intelligence Community assessed that "Moscow will apply lessons learned from its Putin-ordered campaign aimed at the US presidential election to future influence efforts worldwide, including against US allies and their election processes."[138] Although the election interference might have come as a big surprise to the Americans, it was nothing new for many European nations. Roy Godson, a professor from Georgetown University and longtime authority on Soviet disinformation efforts, testified that "they have a history of doing this."[139] Moscow has stepped up this type of activity by targeting the political process in the United Kingdom, France, and Germany, among other nations. For instance, in the run-up to the 2016 Brexit referendum, the IRA executed an extensive social media campaign to sway the vote toward the #LeaveEU camp. More than 156,000 Russia-based accounts posted and amplified #Brexit rhetoric on Twitter, while RT advertised divisive messages. As tens of millions of UK citizens turned out to vote on the referendum, Russian hackers targeted the UK power supply to disrupt the result.[140] While the impact of hacks, fake news, and disinformation is uncertain, the Leave campaign beat the Remain campaign with just over 51 percent of the vote. In the 2017 German federal elections, a cyberattack blamed on Fancy Bear / APT28 stole sixteen gigabytes of emails from the Bundestag and the state offices of Chancellor Angela Merkel's party, although they were never released. German-language Russian media stoked domestic tensions with fake stories and magnified issues, such as on immigration, along with Russian-controlled social media accounts that amplified right-wing rhetoric.[141] In the outcome of the election, Merkel's party won the majority of the vote, but the far-right, anti-immigration party made significant gains.

In addition, Moscow has bolstered the ambitions of far-right and far-left political parties in Europe that have adopted a pro-Kremlin stance. Many have signed cooperation agreements with Putin's United Russia Party, including the French National Front, the Austrian Freedom Party, Germany's Alternative for Germany and The Left, and the Italian League.[142] Other parties, such as the Spanish Podemos, the Hungarian Jobbik, and the Dutch Party for Freedom make frequent pro-Putin and pro-Kremlin statements. Collectively, the Kremlin's strategy of influence in European nations appears to be working to sow division and discord. The Russian regime would like to see the demise of both the European Union and NATO. The encouragement of these competing camps is an attempt to coax some of these countries to side with Russia against their neighbors. In addition, the Kremlin's ongoing influence campaign in the United States serves to delegitimize that nation's status as a credible partner for the allies. The aim is to paint the United States as a country in decline and distracted, led by an administration that is incompetent, erratic, and distrusted.[143]

Conclusion

The Russian hack of the 2016 US presidential election polarized public opinions more than Vladimir Putin could have ever imagined. The leaks and stories sowed doubt in voters' minds of the physical stamina and moral standing of Secretary Clinton enough to swing the election in favor of candidate Trump. Dan Coats, the director of national intelligence, assessed that Russian use of influence operations, mainly through cyber means, will "remain a significant threat to US interests as they are low-cost, relatively low-risk, and deniable ways to retaliate against adversaries, to shape foreign perceptions, and to influence populations."[144] Researchers Lin and Kerr also posited they are ideal to use against liberal democracies that are "inherently open societies."[145] Elections and political campaigns in open societies are especially lucrative targets for influence operations. Director Coats testified that "the 2018 US mid-term elections are a potential target for Russian influence operations."[146] Six months later, his prediction that Russia would continue to employ "means of influence to try to exacerbate social and political fissures in the United States" materialized. In October 2018, a Russian national named Elena Khusyaynova was charged with interfering in the US political system as well as the 2018 US mid-term elections.[147]

The indictment revealed that Khusyaynova acted as the chief accountant in the Project Lakhta finance department of the IRA. Allegedly the project's actors sought to conduct what they called "information warfare against the United States of America" through "fictitious U.S. personas on social media platforms and other Internet-based media."[148] They managed pages and groups designed to address divisive issues and advocate for the election or defeat of specific candidates in the 2018 US midterm elections.[149] Assistant Attorney General John Demers summed up the potential impact by saying that "unlawful foreign interference with these debates debases their democratic integrity."[150] Although no indications of compromise to election infrastructure were detected on Election Day, social media firms spotted deliberate disinformation attempts, including false claims of voter fraud.[151] A week later, Russian hackers—namely, Cozy Bear / APT29—attempted to break into the DNC in a targeted spear-phishing campaign.[152] In citing attempts to sow distrust within society and disrupt elections, Gen. Paul Nakasone, the head of US Cyber

Command, stated that American adversaries are "looking to really take us on below that level of armed conflict." Nakasone contended that "this is what great power competition looks like today."[153] Dan Coats would probably agree in his assessment that Russia is probably looking ahead "to the 2020 US elections as an opportunity to advance their interests," with influence toolkits—disinformation, hacks and leaks, and data manipulation.[154]

IW is firmly entrenched in the official Russian Military Doctrine and in the unofficial Gerasimov Doctrine, which appears here to stay despite some pushback by Mark Galeotti on coherency.[155] Catherine Harris and Mason Clark at the Institute for the Study of War argue that "Russian officers of all ranks do not doubt either its existence or its dominance."[156] Lessons learned from operations in Ukraine and Syria that put Gerasimov's ideas into practice are being articulated in Russian military journals and integrated into military doctrine. Russian scholar Timothy Thomas reiterates that Valery Gerasimov says the principal tactic in contemporary war is "noncontact or remote engagement, since information technology has greatly reduced the spatial and temporal distances between opponents."[157] In a speech in March 2019, Gerasimov reiterated that "the information sphere provides capabilities for remote, covert effect not only on critically important information infrastructures, but also on a country's population by directly affecting the state of national security of the state."[158] He invariably is referring, first, to cyber operations and, second, to cyber-enabled IO to remotely engage opponents below the level of armed conflict.

Notes

1. Keir Giles and William Hagestad II, "Divided by a Common Language: Cyber Definitions in Chinese, Russian and English," in *Proceedings of 5th International Conference on Cyber Conflict* (Tallinn: NATO CCD COE Publications, 2013), 419–20.
2. Michael Connell and Sarah Vogler, "Russia's Approach to Cyber Warfare," CNA, March 2017, 3.
3. Giles and Hagestad, "Divided by a Common Language," 422.
4. Connell and Vogler, "Russia's Approach to Cyber Warfare," 3.
5. Connell and Vogler, 3.
6. Connell and Vogler, 4.
7. Keir Giles, "The Next Phase of Russian Information Warfare," NATO Strategic Communications Centre of Excellence, May 20, 2016, 4.
8. Keir Giles, "With Russia and Ukraine, Is All Really Quiet on the Cyber Front?," Ars Technica, March 11, 2014.
9. Kateryna Kruk, "Analyzing the Ground Zero: What Western Countries Can Learn from Ukrainian Experience of Combating Russian Disinformation," Kremlin Watch Report, European Values, December 2017, 13.
10. Keir Giles, "Russia's Toolkit," in *The Russian Challenge* (London: Chatham House, June 2015), 45.
11. Jolanta Darczewska, *The Devil Is in the Details: Information Warfare in the Light of*

Russia's Military Doctrine, Point of View, no. 50 (Warsaw: Centre for Eastern Studies, May 2015), 7.

12. Keir Giles, *Russia's "New" Tools for Confronting the West: Continuity and Innovation in Moscow's Exercise of Power* (London: Chatham House, Russia and Eurasia Programme, March 2016), 27.

13. Stephen Blank, "Moscow's Competitive Strategy," American Foreign Policy Council, July 2018, 9.

14. Blank, 10.

15. Blank, 36.

16. The Military Doctrine of the Russian Federation, Approved by the President, No. Pr.-2976, December 25, 2014.

17. Dmitry (Dima) Adamsky, "Cross-Domain Coercion: The Current Russian Art of Strategy," Proliferation Papers 54, IFRI Security Studies Center, November 2015, 26–27.

18. Giles, "Russia's Toolkit," 46.

19. Keir Giles, *Handbook of Russian Information Warfare*, Fellowship Monograph no. 9 (Rome: NATO Defense College, November 2016), 4.

20. S. G. Chekinov and S. A. Bogdanov, "Forecasting the Nature and Content of Wars of the Future: Problems and Assessments," *Military Thought*, no. 10 (2015): 44–45.

21. Chekinov and Bogdanov, 7.

22. Timothy Thomas, "Russia's 21st Century Information War: Working to Undermine and Destabilize Populations," *Defense Strategic Communications* 1, no. 1 (Winter 2015): 11.

23. Defense Intelligence Agency, "Russia Military Power: Building a Military to Support Great Power Ambitions," 2017, 38.

24. Blank, "Moscow's Competitive Strategy," 37.

25. T. S. Allen and A. J. Moore, "Victory without Casualties: Russia's Information Operations," *Parameters* 48, no. 1 (Spring 2018): 60.

26. Stephen Blank, "Signs of New Russian Thinking about the Military and War," *Eurasia Daily Monitor*, February 13, 2014.

27. Christopher S. Chivvis, Testimony presented before the House Committee on Armed Services, published by the RAND Corp., March 22, 2017, 3.

28. Giles, "Next Phase of Russian Information Warfare," 6.

29. Christopher S. Chivvis, "Hybrid War: Russian Contemporary Political Warfare," *Bulletin of the Atomic Scientists* 73, no. 5 (2017): 316.

30. Chivvis, 316.

31. DOD, "Summary: Department of Defense Cyber Strategy," 2018, 1.

32. Timothy L. Thomas, *Recasting the Red Star: Russia Forges Tradition and Technology through Toughness* (Fort Leavenworth, KS: Foreign Military Studies Office, 2011), 143.

33. Giles, "Russia's Toolkit," 47.

34. Ofer Fridman, *Russian Hybrid Warfare: Resurgence and Politicisation* (London: Hurst, 2018), 67.

35. Allen and Moore, "Victory without Casualties," 61.

36. Katri Pynnoniemi and Andras Racz, *Fog of Falsehood: Russian Strategy of Deception and the Conflict in Ukraine*, Report no. 45 (Helsinki: Finnish Institute of International Affairs, May 11, 2016), 37.

37. Pynnoniemi and Racz, 38.

38. Allen and Moore, "Victory without Casualties," 61.

39. Pynnoniemi and Racz, *Fog of Falsehood*, 38.

40. Natasha Bertrand, "It Looks like Russia Hired Internet Trolls to Pose as Pro-Trump Americans," *Business Insider*, July 27, 2016.

41. Aristedes Mahairas and Mikhail Dvlyanski, "Disinformation (Dezinformatsiya)," *Cyber Defense Review* (Fall 2018): 21.
42. Pynnoniemi and Racz, *Fog of Falsehood*, 37.
43. Giles, "Handbook of Russian Information Warfare," 24.
44. James R. Clapper, "Foreign Cyber Threats to the United States," Joint Statement for the Record, Senate Armed Services Committee, January 5, 2017, 5.
45. Clapper, 5.
46. Khatuna Mshvidobadze, "The Battlefield on Your Laptop," Radio Free Europe / Radio Liberty, March 21, 2011.
47. A. J. C. Selhorst, "Russia's Perception Warfare," *Militaire Spectator* 185, no. 4 (2016): 151.
48. Giles, "Handbook of Russian Information Warfare," 12.
49. Giles, 12.
50. Daniel Fried and Alina Polyakova, "Democratic Defense against Disinformation," Atlantic Council, February 2018, 2.
51. Zoe Williams, "What Is an Internet Troll?," *The Guardian*, June 12, 2012.
52. Williams, 3–4.
53. Office of the Director of National Intelligence, "Assessing Russian Activities and Intentions in Recent US Elections," Intelligence Community assessment, January 6, 2017, 1.
54. Office of the Director of National Intelligence, 1.
55. Office of the Director of National Intelligence, 2.
56. Joint Chiefs of Staff, *Military Information Support Operations*, Joint Publication 3-13.2 (January 2010), vii.
57. Randal Marlin, *Propaganda and the Ethics of Persuasion* (Calgary: Broadview Press, 2002), 22.
58. Allen and Moore, "Victory without Casualties," 65–67.
59. Giles, *Russia's "New" Tools*, 37.
60. Media Ajir and Bethany Vailliant, "Russian Information Warfare: Implications for Deterrence Theory," *Strategic Studies Quarterly* (Fall 2018): 78.
61. Office of the Director of National Intelligence, "Assessing Russian Activities," 3.
62. Office of the Director of National Intelligence, 4.
63. Gordon Pennycook and David Rand, "Why Do People Fall for Fake News?," *New York Times*, January 19, 2019.
64. Neil MacFarquhar, "Yevgeny Prigozhin: Russian Oligarch Indicted by U.S. Is Known as Putin's Cook," *New York Times*, February 16, 2018.
65. Ajir and Vailliant, "Russian Information Warfare," 76.
66. Jarred Prier, "Commanding the Trend: Social Media as Information Warfare," *Strategic Studies Quarterly* (Winter 2017): 66.
67. Prier, 67.
68. Prier, 74.
69. United States v. Internet Research Agency, US District Court, District of Columbia, Criminal Complaint, February 16, 2018, 6.
70. United States v. Internet Research Agency, 17.
71. United States v. Internet Research Agency, 18–19.
72. Natasha Bertrand, "DOJ Says Russian Trolls Are Interfering Online with the Midterms," *The Atlantic*, October 19, 2018.
73. Bertrand.
74. New Knowledge, "The Tactics and Tropes of the Internet Research Agency," December 2018, 7.

75. Todd Neikirk, "Massive Twitter Data Dump Shows How Russians Came to Support Trump," *Hill Reporter*, October 17, 2018.
76. Department of Justice, "Deputy Attorney General Rod J. Rosenstein Delivers Remarks," July 13, 2018.
77. Herbert Lin and Jaclyn Kerr, "On Cyber-Enabled Information/Influence Warfare and Manipulation," *Oxford Handbook of Cybersecurity* (Oxford: Oxford University Press, forthcoming), 14.
78. Malcolm Nance, *The Plot to Destroy Democracy* (New York: Hachette, 2018), 106–9.
79. Ellen Nakashima, "Russian Government Hackers Penetrated DNC, Stole Opposition Research on Trump," *Washington Post*, June 14, 2016.
80. Dmitri Alperovitch, "Bears in the Midst: Intrusion into the Democratic National Committee," CrowdStrike (blog), June 15, 2016, 1.
81. Steve Ragan, "DNC Hacker Slams CrowdStrike, Publishes Opposition Memo on Donald Trump," CSO News, June 15, 2016.
82. Ragan.
83. Alana Abramson and Shushannah Walshe, "The 4 Most Damaging Emails from the DNC Wikileaks Dump," ABC News, July 25, 2016.
84. Julian Routh, "Emails Show DNC Taking Aim at Sanders," *Wall Street Journal*, July 26, 2016.
85. Ben Kamisar, "Wasserman Schultz Booed off Stage in Philadelphia," *The Hill*, July 25, 2016.
86. Jeff Zeleny, M. J. Lee, and Eric Brader, "Dems Open Convention without Wasserman Schultz," CNN Politics, July 25, 2016.
87. Nakashima, "Russian Government Hackers."
88. Ellen Nakashima, "Hackers Breach Some White House Computers," *Washington Post*, October 28, 2014; Craig Whitlock and Missy Ryan, "U.S. Suspects Russia in Hack of Pentagon Computer Network," *Washington Post*, August 6, 2015.
89. FireEye, "APT28."
90. Anomali, "Russian Federation," 3.
91. Joint Chiefs of Staff, "Joint Operating Environment," July 14, 2016, 6.
92. Joint Chiefs of Staff, 6.
93. US District Court for the District of Columbia, criminal indictment, United States of America v. Viktor Borisovich Netyksho et al., received July 13, 2018, 10.
94. US District Court, 11.
95. US District Court, 11.
96. Micha Lee, "What Mueller's Latest Indictment Reveals about Russian and U.S. Spycraft," *The Intercept*, July 18, 2018, 3.
97. US District Court, criminal indictment, United States of America v. Viktor Borisovich Netyksho et al., 6.
98. Luke Harding, "Top Democrat's Email Hacked by Russia after Aide Made Typo, Investigation Finds," *The Guardian*, December 14, 2016.
99. Harding.
100. DHS and FBI, "Joint Analysis Report," JAR-16-20296, December 29, 2016.
101. DHS and FBI, 3.
102. Alperovitch, "Bears in the Midst," 4.
103. Alperovitch, 6.
104. Department of Justice, "Grand Jury Indicts 12 Russian Intelligence Officers for Hacking Offenses Related to the 2016 Election," July 13, 2018.
105. Robert Abel, "Russian Election Hackers Breached 39 U.S. States," *SC Magazine*, June 13, 2017.

106. Abel.
107. Michael Wines, "Russians Breached Florida County Computers before 2016 Election, Mueller Report Says," *New York Times*, April 18, 2019.
108. Nance, *Plot to Destroy Democracy*, 101–2.
109. Ellen Nakashima, "Russia's Apparent Meddling in U.S. Election Is Not an Act of War, Cyber Expert Says," *Washington Post*, February 7, 2018.
110. Nakashima.
111. Michael N. Schmitt, ed., *Tallinn Manual 2.0 on the International Law Applicable to Cyber Operations*, 2nd ed. (Cambridge: Cambridge University Press, 2017), 312.
112. Schmitt, 312.
113. Robert Jennings and Arthur Watts, *Oppenheim's International Law*, 9th ed. (Oxford: Oxford University Press, 1992), 428.
114. Michael N. Schmitt, "The Law of Cyber Warfare: *Quo Vadis*?," *Stanford Law and Policy Review* 29 (2014): 275.
115. Michael Schmitt, "Virtual Disenfranchisement: Cyber Election Meddling in the Grey Zones of International Law," *Chicago Journal of International Law* 19, no. 1 (August 16, 2018): 48.
116. Schmitt, *Tallinn Manual 2.0*, 315.
117. Schmitt, "Virtual Disenfranchisement," 49.
118. Schmitt, *Tallinn Manual 2.0*, 317.
119. Schmitt, "Virtual Disenfranchisement," 50, 51.
120. Byard Duncan, "When Does a Cyberattack Mean War? Experts Say There's No Clear Line," Reveal News, January 30, 2017.
121. Matthijis Veenendall et al., *DNC Hack: An Escalation That Cannot Be Ignored* (Tallinn: NATO CCD COE Publications, 2016).
122. Department of State, "The Inauguration of Organized Political Warfare," Policy Planning Staff memorandum, May 4, 1948.
123. Mark Galeotti, *Russian Political War: Moving beyond the Hybrid* (London: Routledge, 2019), 53.
124. Alina Polyakova and Spencer P. Boyer, "The Future of Political Warfare: Russia, the West, and the Coming Age of Global Digital Competition," Brookings Institution, Robert Bosch Foundation Transatlantic Initiative, March 2018, 3.
125. Chivvis, "Hybrid War," 316.
126. Chivvis, 316.
127. Thomas G. Mahnken, Ross Babbage, and Toshi Yoshihara, "Countering Comprehensive Coercion: Competitive Strategies against Authoritarian Political Warfare," Center for Strategic and Budgetary Assessments, 2018, 4.
128. Mahnken, Babbage, and Yoshihara, 6.
129. Frank Hoffman, "On Not-So-New Warfare: Political Warfare vs Hybrid Threats," War on the Rocks, commentary, July 28, 2014, 3.
130. Galeotti, *Russian Political War*, 71.
131. Galeotti, 73–99.
132. Alina Polyakova et al., "The Kremlin's Trojan Horses," Atlantic Council, November 2016, 3.
133. Polyakova and Boyer, "Future of Political Warfare," 4.
134. Nance, *Plot to Destroy Democracy*, 95.
135. Nance, 95.
136. Mark Galeotti, "Controlling Chaos: How Russia Manages Its Political War in Europe," policy brief, European Council on Foreign Relations, August 2017, 1.

137. Galeotti, 4.
138. Office of the Director of National Intelligence, "Assessing Russian Activities," iii.
139. Ann M. Simmons, "Russia's Meddling in Other Nations' Elections Is Nothing New. Just Ask the Europeans," *Los Angeles Times*, March 20, 2017.
140. Laura Galante and Shaun Ee, "Defining Russian Election Interference: An Analysis of Select 2014 to 2018 Cyber Enabled Incidents," issue brief, Atlantic Council, September 2018, 8–9.
141. Galante and Ee, 12–13.
142. Polyakova and Boyer, "Future of Political Warfare," 6.
143. Mahnken, Babbage, and Yoshihara, "Countering Comprehensive Coercion," 18.
144. Coats, "Worldwide Threat Assessment," 11.
145. Lin and Kerr, "On Cyber-Enabled Information/Influence," 17.
146. Coats, "Worldwide Threat Assessment," 11.
147. Elizabeth Zwirz, "Russian National Charged with Interfering in US Political System, 2018 Elections," Fox News, October 19, 2018.
148. United States v. Elena Alekseevna Khusyaynova, US District Court, Eastern District of Virginia, criminal complaint, September 28, 2018, 6.
149. United States v. Elena Alekseevna Khusyaynova, 32–37.
150. Alfred Ng, "Justice Department Charges Russian Troll's Chief Accountant," CNET, October 19, 2018.
151. Dustin Volz, "No Major Vote Interference Detected," *Wall Street Journal*, November 7, 2018.
152. Catalin Cimpanu, "DNC Says Russia Tried to Hack Its Servers Again in November 2018," ZDNeT, January 19, 2019.
153. Julian E. Barnes, "U.S. Begins First Cyber Operation against Russia Aimed at Protecting Elections," *New York Times*, October 23, 2018.
154. Coats, "Worldwide Threat Assessment," 7.
155. Mark Galeotti, "I'm Sorry for Creating the 'Gerasimov Doctrine,'" *Foreign Policy*, March 5, 2018.
156. Mason Clark and Catherine Harris, "Russia in Review: The Gerasimov Doctrine Is Here to Stay," Institute for the Study of War, October 30, 2018.
157. Timothy Thomas, "The Evolving Nature of Russia's Way of War," *Military Review*, July/August 2017, 36.
158. Bill Gertz, "Russian Military Chief Outlines Aggressive Anti-U.S. War Strategy," *Free Beacon*, March 12, 2019.

PART II
Security Dynamics

CHAPTER 5

Rational State Behavior

The term *rational* denotes "behavior that is appropriate to specified goals in the context of a given situation."[1] President Vladimir Putin's goal is to restore "Russia to greatness and a respected position on the world stage."[2] However, the given situation for Russia is perceived containment and encroachment by the West, particularly in the former Soviet states along its borders. Cyber operations offer a covert means to achieve political utility for the leader of the state. The utility in this case is defined "in the ability to covertly alter an adversary's policy positions."[3] A rational individual weighs the value of alternative courses of action, creates a preference order, and chooses the preference with the highest expected utility. The leader of Russia knows covert actions can convey a foreign policy message without attribution from the sender. He has used cyber operations against critical infrastructure to signal that Russia "can do significant damage to your information and economic infrastructure if you engage in policy behaviors we deem hostile."[4] Therefore, based on the potential to achieve political utility, Putin chooses to use cyber operations to intervene secretly in the affairs of foreign states even if they violate international law or disrupt international order.

The Group of Seven (G7) nations expressed at their 2018 ministerial meeting in Toronto their commitment to "a rules-based international order."[5] They acknowledged that certain foreign actors "seeking to undermine democratic institutions and processes through coercive, corrupt, covert or malicious means constitute a strategic threat."[6] Russia represents a strategic threat in the form of a revisionist power. Moscow wants to revise the status quo by actively shaping "a world antithetical to U.S. values and interests."[7] Russia appears "dissatisfied with the current Western-derived notion of international order."[8] The Western view of order is delineated by the current set of international rules, norms, and agreements. Staunch dissatisfaction causes Russia to attempt to change or challenge international order. In particular, Russia has tried to shape international views on responsible state conduct and behavior in cyberspace through participation in multinational forums. Meanwhile, Russia contests international order with a military or cyber dimension short of traditional armed conflict.

Putin once remarked that "uncontested Western leadership means an international environment in which . . . no one can feel that international law is like a stone wall that can protect them."[9] In response to an apprehension of Western encroachment, Russia uses sources of power to establish or reestablish local spheres of influence, create buffer states, and disconnect neighboring states from the broader global economic and political system. As a rational state actor, Putin uses a maximizing strategy in choosing how best to achieve state goals. That strategy includes the fracturing of weaker states as a way to alter regional balances of power in a manner unfavorable to Western interests.[10] Nowhere has that strategy been applied more than in Ukraine. The country has been the target and testing ground for Russian cyber operations that disrupt or damage critical infrastructure. The goal of Russian interference "appears to be to weaken Ukraine to the point that it becomes a failed state, rendering it incapable of joining Western institutions in the future."[11] Practically every sector of society and economy has been the target of Russian proxies or agencies without any concern over the impact. The chance to alter policy positions outweighs adherence to international norms for responsible state behavior in cyberspace. This chapter will explore whether Russia or other states establish and circumvent norms in rational decisions to use cyber operations to achieve political utility. It will examine that type of decision in the NotPetya mock-ransomware attack that undermined established norms. The chapter will conclude with options and initiatives to bring states, in particular Russia, closer to compliance with promulgated norms.

International Norms

Norms are defined as "a collective expectation for the proper behavior of actors with a given identity."[12] Norms are based upon shared beliefs within a group that actors relate to. Thus, a norm "exists only when some relevant group agrees with and holds particular beliefs about expected behavior."[13] That means the group must buy in to the norm and recognize that the behavioral instructions apply to it. Actors may not agree fully with a norm but conform anyway to maintain their standing in the group or because they value the goals of the group.[14] Failure to comply with norms brings a bad reputation. Norms, and also rules that promote order and peace, differ from principles, which are "statements of fact, causation, or rectitude" that guide action.[15] Principles can serve as the foundation for formal treaties. For example, the so-called Outer Space Treaty of 1967 is actually the Treaty on Principles Governing the Activities of States in the Exploration and Use of Outer Space, Including the Moon and Other Celestial Bodies. States that are parties to the treaty agree upon articles pertaining to the exploration and use of outer space for peaceful purposes, including arms control provisions to restrict activities.

Part of the reason that organizations have pursued voluntary, nonbinding norms, rules, or principles of responsible behavior of states in cyberspace is widespread doubts about the applicability of formal treaties for the domain. Cyber expert James Lewis has remarked that "legally binding commitments have serious drawbacks."[16] Treaties regarding cybersecurity face definitional, compatibility, compliance, and verification problems in implementation.[17] For instance, what defines a cyber weapon, in particular in regard to dual-use technologies for security testing or intelligence purposes? How can malware be controlled when it is widely available, easy to use, and relatively inexpensive? How is verification of compliance even possible when no state would probably allow the scanning of its computers and devices, especially those in classified systems?[18] Norms offer a better alternative than treaties, which are not well suited for "the rapid and unpredictable pace of technological innovation in the cyber domain," where "attack vectors and offensive capabilities are continuously evolving."[19]

The United States 2011 International Strategy for Cyberspace declares, "We will build and sustain an environment in which *norms of responsible behavior* guide states' actions, sustain partnerships, and support the rule of law in cyberspace."[20] To establish a stable environment of expectations, the United States commits to building "a consensus on what constitutes acceptable behavior."[21] Adherence to norms brings not just stability but also predictability in states' actions, which could prevent conflict. Principles serve as a basis for norms in regard to traditional obligations or duties of states.[22] The Office of the Coordinator for Cyber Issues led initiatives on cyber norms for the United States, including engagements with China and Russia, until shuttered in August 2017.[23] The work has continued through officials at the level of deputy assistant secretary.[24] In June 2018, Senate lawmakers voted to advance the Cyber Diplomacy Act, which would restore the functions of the cyber policy office under a new name.[25]

Russia has initiated or participated in international partnerships to shape rules for international order in the cyber domain. In January 2015, Russia, along with China and four Central Asian states, submitted to the UN a letter that recognized "an international consensus is now emerging on the need . . . to formulate relevant international norms, in order to address common challenges in the sphere of information security."[26] To that end, they proposed a revised "international code of conduct for information security," after considering comments on a previous version.[27] Although adherence is voluntary, each state subscribing to the revised code of conduct would pledge to comply with universally recognized norms governing "sovereignty, territorial integrity, and political independence of all States" and not to use information and communication technologies "to interfere in the internal affairs of other States or with the aim of undermining their political, economic and social stability."[28]

Oddly, the provisions appear opposite to the alleged Russian usage of covert action in the form of cyber operations to achieve perceived benefits.

In July 2015, Russia participated with the United States, China, and seventeen other nations in the fourth meeting of the UN Group of Governmental Experts on Information Security (GGE). The origin of the UN body can be traced to a resolution introduced by Russia in 1998 to examine the issue of information security.[29] The first GGE in 2004 failed to reach consensus on recommendations because of divergent positions taken by Russia and China compared to the United States and its European allies.[30] The next two GGE sessions were able to submit reports in 2010 and 2013; the first recommended dialogue on norms, and the latter affirmed that international law applies in cyberspace. The 2015 GGE agreed that there are norms in cyberspace that nations should respect. The agreement was a breakthrough for US diplomats, who had been pushing for norms as an alternative to formal treaties.[31] The consensus document of the 2015 GGE states that norms "reflect the expectations of the international community, set standards for responsible State behaviour and allow the international community to assess the activities and intentions of States."[32] Taking into account existing and emerging threats, risks, and vulnerabilities, the 2015 GGE offered a number of recommendations for consideration by states for voluntary, nonbinding norms of responsible behavior of states, including the following:

- States should not knowingly allow their territory to be used for internationally wrongful acts using ICTs [information and communication technologies];
- A State should not conduct or knowingly support ICT activity contrary to its obligations under international law that intentionally damages critical infrastructure or otherwise impairs [its] use and operation;
- States should encourage responsible reporting of ICT vulnerabilities and share associated information on available remedies to such vulnerabilities to limit and possibly eliminate potential threats to ICTs.[33]

The 2015 GGE also offered non-exhaustive views on how international law applies to the use of ICTs by states, to include,

- States must observe, among other principles of international law, State sovereignty, sovereign equality, the settlement of disputes by peaceful means and non-intervention in the internal affairs of other States.
- States must not use proxies to commit internationally wrongful acts using ICTs, and should seek to ensure that their territory is not used by non-State actors to commit such acts.[34]

In December 2015, the UN General Assembly adopted a resolution that calls upon member states "to be guided in their use of information and communication technologies by the 2015 report of the Group of Governmental Experts."[35] While this resolution reflects progress, rapporteur James Lewis said that "the world's a long way from agreeing on basic principles of cyber sovereignty."[36] He added that the Russian delegation had requested that another GGE be held in 2016, under the pretext that "they think they can dominate another GGE and get it to endorse what they want,"[37] which is, according to Lt. Gen. Vincent R. Stewart at the Defense Intelligence Agency, to ensure "a state's ability to govern the information space as a means of maintaining state sovereignty," using the term *sovereignty* to "denounce other nations meddling in their internal affairs."[38]

Pseudo Ransomware

Although Russia has submitted or supported norms of responsible state behavior under the auspices of the UN, a mock ransomware campaign targeting Ukraine in 2017 demonstrated an intent to circumvent or undermine them. The NotPetya campaign intentionally damaged critical infrastructure in direct violation of the subject norm endorsed by the Russian representative on the 2015 GGE. The campaign appeared consistent with Russian objectives to maintain "long-term influence over Kyiv" and frustrate "Ukraine's attempts to integrate into Western institutions."[39] The Kremlin used cyber operations to weaken the nation's fragile economic and political systems. The destructive and costly cyber campaign, at the top of the ladder of covert action, was an attempt to not only influence political decisions but also to destabilize and punish the nation.[40] The use of ransomware malware and tactics was a deliberate effort at deception to mislead investigators on the source of the attack. Furthermore, employment of multiple methods for propagation across networks, including by stolen NSA exploits, displayed evolving technical complexity in Russian cyber operations.

NotPetya Campaign

In June 2017, national media headlines in the United States boldly announced a global ransomware attack by the NotPetya worm. Ransomware is typically a form of malware that threatens to perpetually block access to computers or encrypted files on computers unless a ransom is paid, usually with a virtual currency such as bitcoin, while a worm automatically executes on a remote machine without user involvement and self-replicates to spread from host to host. The majority of NotPetya infections, around three quarters, occurred in Ukraine. Symantec Threat Intelligence reported infections in 150 organizations in Ukraine, compared to under fifty in the United States.[41] The rest struck Russia, Germany, Poland, Serbia, and about sixty other countries. NotPetya took code from a well-known ransomware strain, referred to as Petya, to make it look like the same tool.[42] It also borrowed features from the WannaCry ransomware—for instance, use of the EternalBlue exploit—although NotPetya did not scan the whole Internet, like WannaCry, to jump from one network to the other. Instead, after the first infection, NotPetya buried itself deep into local corporate networks, taking out multinational firms whose internal networks were large enough for the worm to travel far from Ukraine.[43]

In the NotPetya outbreak, the typical ransomware demand for money to provide a key to decrypt files proved to be a ruse. Security researcher The Grugq wrote, "If this well engineered and highly crafted worm was meant to generate revenue, [the] payment pipeline was possibly the worst of all options." The attackers carelessly provided an email address (wowsmith123456@posteo .net) to the victims to send proof of payment, and that address was promptly and simply blocked by the provider, which made it impossible for victims to recover a decryption key for their files. The attackers also discarded the key used for encryption of the hard disk. This negligence supports the theory that the real aim of the operation was to cause economic losses and sow chaos or perhaps test cyber capabilities. However, the perpetrators did install a simple kill switch in the malware, which indicates they wanted to be able to control the spreading of the malware and the extent of the damage it caused.[44]

Researchers discovered that NotPetya was designed to wipe out data on infected computers by encrypting the master file table (a database the operating system uses to retrieve a file) and master boot record (the information for loading the operating system to start the computer). Microsoft's Malware Protection Center recorded infections in 12,500 machines in Ukraine.[45] From there it then spread unabated across Europe and into the United States. Maersk, the world's largest container-ship company, reported a significant interruption in business operations that resulted in a $300 million loss.[46] For well over a week, trucks lined up at ports to load ships and were turned away.[47] The American pharmaceutical giant Merck suffered more staggering losses of $870 million, but more concerning was its shutdown of production of vital vaccines for human papillomavirus (HPV) and hepatitis B.[48] The Russian state-controlled oil and gas company Rosneft was also infected, but that situation was quickly controlled, and neither oil production nor preparation processes were stopped.[49]

The primary method for installation of the NotPetya malware on victims' computers was a software supply-chain attack through customer updates of M.E.Doc tax and accounting software—the equivalent of TurboTax or Quicken—from the Ukrainian firm Linkos Group.[50] NotPetya was also spread via drive-by exploit kits, emails with malicious attachments, and embedded URL links. After initial infection, NotPetya leveraged multiple propagation methods to spread through internal networks. First, NotPetya attempted lateral movement using internal evasion techniques. NotPetya employed a modified version of the Mimikatz password-cracking tool to steal users' Windows credentials and hand off the credentials to the legitimate Windows administration tool PsExec or the legitimate Windows Management Instrumentation Command-line (WMI) tool to access other local systems.[51] Arbor Networks believes that in many enterprises this typical remote-administration activity would likely not be blocked.[52] For the second promulgation method, NotPetya leveraged the EternalBlue and EternalRomance exploits stolen from the NSA to infect systems that were not patched for a Microsoft vulnerability (identified as CVE-2017-0144) in the Server Message Block (SMB) protocol used for file sharing.[53] Since NotPetya was designed to avoid the snowball effect of spreading through the Internet, it was most likely intended to be used in a targeted fashion to influence one particular country: Ukraine. However, some cybersecurity experts assume the attackers underestimated the contagiousness of the worm.[54]

Ukraine quickly blamed NotPetya on the special services of the Russian Federation, while noting "the main purpose of the virus was the destruction of important data, disrupting the work of public and private institutions."[55] Six months later, the Central Intelligence Agency (CIA) attributed the NotPetya cyberattack to the GRU, specifically to hackers in its Main Center for Special Technology. Various cybersecurity experts attributed the attack to Sandworm, said to be a subunit of APT28 (associated with the GRU), which means essentially all the same group.[56] The CIA noted that the use of malware that looked like ransomware was an attempt to "make it appear as though criminal hackers or some group other than a nation state were the culprits."[57] In effect, NotPetya was a cyber form of *maskirovka*, the Soviet deception tactic to mislead adversaries about the true source of the attack.[58] Any deception attempt aside, ultimately in February 2018, the Five Eyes Nations (the United States, the United Kingdom, Canada, Australia, and New Zealand) united in statements that blamed the Russian military for NotPetya.[59] Multiple security researchers had previously suggested that NotPetya was launched by Russian attackers connected to the military, but "that's different from governments formally stating attribution as fact."[60]

The UK Foreign Office minister of state said, "The attack showed a continued [Russian government] disregard for Ukrainian sovereignty."[61] Tomas Minarik, a researcher at the NATO Cooperative Cyber Defense Centre of Excellence's Law Branch, agreed in his analysis, stating that "there is a lack of a coercive element with respect to any government in the campaign, so prohibited intervention does not come into play. As important government systems have been targeted, then in case the operation is attributed to a state [which it was] this could count as a violation of sovereignty."[62] Professor Michael Schmitt and Jeffrey Biller, a military professor at the US Naval War College's Stockton Center for the Study of International Law, agreed, based on the two different ways that breaches of the obligation to respect a state's sovereignty occur—namely, infringement on territorial integrity and interference with inherently governmental functions. For the first basis, they argued, "NotPetya seriously degraded or blocked the capability of cyber infrastructure in a manner exceeding that of temporary denial of service."[63] For the second basis, they determined that "the effects on government ministries may have qualified depending on whether the services interfered with fall within the exclusive competency of States."[64]

Schmitt and Biller noted that "cyber operations causing more than minor injury or physical damage are incontrovertibly uses of force." However, they stated, "There is no evidence that NotPetya caused such consequences. Operations resulting in permanent or extended loss of cyber functionality also rise, in our view, to the level of a use of force, but as noted, the available facts on this issue vis-à-vis NotPetya are sketchy."[65] Likewise, the cyber operation did not result in consequences comparable to an armed attack, which could have triggered Article 5 of the North Atlantic Treaty and allowed for forceful responses with military means. This determination indicates that NotPetya did not reach the threshold of armed conflict. Lauri Lindström of the NATO Cooperative Cyber Defense Centre of Excellence's Strategy Branch concluded that the "NotPetya campaign is a declaration of power—a demonstration of the acquired disruptive capability and the readiness to use it."[66] Thus, the demonstration was more an act of strategic competition by Russia, which once again challenged international order through harmful cyber operations.

Defense of Sovereignty

It is important to note that the argument by Professors Schmitt and Biller that NotPetya could count as a violation of sovereignty, based on infringement on territorial integrity and interference with inherently governmental functions, might not be valid in the future. Sovereignty is an area of legal ambiguity that has emerged outside of UN GGE deliberations. Rule 4 of the *Tallinn Manual 2.0* states, "A State must not conduct cyber operations that violate the sovereignty of another State."[67] The International Group of Experts, the author of the *Tallinn Manual 2.0*, agreed that sovereignty is "both a principle of international law from which certain rules, such as the prohibition of intervention into the external or internal affairs of other states, derive, and a primary rule of international law susceptible to violation."[68] The experts set out to identify the types of cyber operations that cross the violation line. Soon after the release of the *Tallinn Manual 2.0*, an internal memo addressed to military judge advocates general in the United States questioned the treatment of sovereignty as a primary rule of international law. The alternative approach, laid out in a symposium article, argues that sovereignty serves as a principle of international law that guides state interactions, but is not itself a binding rule that dictates results under international law. While this principle of sovereignty, including territorial sovereignty, should factor into the conduct of every cyber operation, it does not establish an absolute bar against individual or collective state operations that affect cyberinfrastructure within another state, provided that the effects do not rise to the level of an unlawful use of force or an unlawful intervention.[69]

Part of the reasoning for the alternative approach is that the concept of territorial sovereignty has been confused "with the more precise concepts of territorial integrity and the inviolability of borders" protected through Article 2(4) of the UN Charter, where "prescriptions against violating territorial integrity or borders" involve a much higher threshold of harm.[70] Under this reasoning, the sovereignty-as-a-principle-but-not-a-rule approach would permit cyber operations that do not qualify as an unlawful use of force or an unlawful intervention. Furthermore, if the cyber operations are not deemed to be unlawful, the injured state would not be entitled to use countermeasures. The real problem under this narrow approach is that "the vast majority of cyber operations that are directed against states would not violate international law."[71] In the case of NotPetya, while the cyber operation met both bases for a breach of the obligation to respect state sovereignty, NotPetya did not rise to the level of a use of force and under the alternative approach would not have qualified for countermeasures.

Therefore, in the case of NotPetya, the sovereignty-as-a-principle-but-not-a-rule approach would be beneficial to Russia. Other states that desire "a greater margin of appreciation within which to conduct operations they deem crucial" might also find the approach to be attractive.[72] Yet the alternative approach goes both ways, for it would allow other states to conduct similar operations against Russia. In essence, the alternative approach hampers the imposition of cost through countermeasures. To date, the alternative approach has not been formally adopted by the US government but might well persist in the UN GGE debate on international norms. Russia is sure to push for adoption if given the chance, since higher thresholds of harm are beneficial for its cyber operations.

National Interest Pursuit

Not just Russia in the case of NotPetya but also all states act as unified rational actors in their national interest. They make rational decisions in their interpretation and application of international norms. If an alternative course of action offers a higher utility, that option would be a rational choice, even if the choice is for self-interest over the common interest. For instance, the United States uses a Vulnerabilities Equities Policy and Process to make determinations "regarding disclosure or restriction when the USG [US government] obtains knowledge of newly discovered and not publicly known vulnerabilities in information systems and technologies."[73] The intent of the policy and process parallels the 2015 GGE-proposed norm that "states should encourage responsible reporting of ICT vulnerabilities," since the focus of the policy and process is to disclose vulnerabilities, "absent a demonstrable, overriding interest in the use of the vulnerability for lawful intelligence, law enforcement, or national security purposes."[74] The United States made a deliberate decision to not promptly reveal the Microsoft vulnerability used in the NotPetya attack. That decision is debatable since equity considerations include "Are threat actors likely to exploit this vulnerability?" and "Is exploitation of this vulnerability alone sufficient to cause harm?"[75] Given the extent of harm incurred by exploitation in the NotPetya attack, the calculus used by the US government to assess the broader economic impact of a vulnerability is questionable.[76]

It turns out the NSA had "used the [Microsoft] flaw for 5 years."[77] Officials had discussed "whether the flaw was so dangerous they should reveal it to Microsoft."[78] Yet they continued using it since the exploit was so powerful in harvesting intelligence. One former employee even said, "It was like fishing with dynamite."[79] When the NSA learned that EternalBlue, along with a trove of other exploits and backdoors, was stolen, it warned Microsoft of the vulnerability in January 2017.[80] That disclosure led to the release of a critical patch (identified as MS17-010) by Microsoft to fix the flaw in March 2017. The very next month, in April 2017, the mysterious group named Shadow Brokers leaked the EternalBlue exploit. The global WannaCry ransomware attack in May 2017 that occurred a month before NotPetya realized fears of exposure when the exploit was repackaged and unleashed on the world. WannaCry infected and shut down hospitals, banks, industries, and governmental agencies in over 150 countries. Samir Jain, a former White House cyber official, described the balancing act in using or reporting vulnerabilities found in widely used software by saying that "they may enable access to a larger number of targets," while the fact that "harm could be broad should be a significant factor."[81]

Microsoft responded to the WannaCry attack with a strongly worded blog post "criticizing governments for 'stockpiling' information about cybersecurity vulnerabilities,"[82] in effect using vulnerabilities to achieve political utility. Brad Smith, the president and chief legal officer for Microsoft, called on governments "to consider the damage to civilians that comes from hoarding these vulnerabilities and the use of these exploits."[83] Smith repeated the necessity outlined in proposed Microsoft norms "for governments to report vulnerabilities to vendors, rather than stockpile, sell, or exploit them."[84] Regardless of the damage, the NSA did eventually report the vulnerability to Microsoft, which issued a patch before the hacking tools went public. Therefore, companies and agencies had almost two months to install the patch before the WannaCry campaign struck. An argument can be made the United States did not neglect its obligation under international or commercial norms since "it informed the software manufacturer in due time of the vulnerability" after using the flaw in pursuit of national interests, albeit in self-interest.[85]

Norm-Compliance Options

Scott Charney, corporate vice president of Microsoft, sums up the primary challenge in verification of compliance with norms in stating that "anonymity and lack of traceability make the attribution of cyberattacks particularly difficult and allow actors to make blanket denials and assert lack of proof."[86] Russia denied involvement in the mock ransomware attack that targeted Ukraine, while the United States was never traced to its use of the EternalBlue exploit. Both nations made rational decisions intended to achieve political objectives, but the one by Russia borders on an act of war, even if meant to be a component of competition. Verification of compliance with norms is difficult but is compounded by state efforts to circumvent or undermine them. Nonetheless, the UN GGE did convene in 2016 and 2017 for another round of deliberations on the viability of international law in cyberspace. The GGE included once again representatives from Russia, China, the United States, and other nations.

According to Michele Markoff, the American representative, "The reluctance of a few participants [Russia and China] to seriously engage on the mandate on international legal issues" prevented conclusion of a consensus report.[87] Few options exist for the United States and other like-minded nations to engage Russia, or for that matter China, on acceptable and lasting norms of responsible state behavior in cyberspace. One is to embark on a new round of GGE talks that would "revive the same questions that plagued previous discussions, namely how best to apply international law."[88] Another is to follow the thinking behind the 2015 US-China Cyber Agreement to pursue a specific state commitment with Russia through "narrowly tailored deal-making."[89] However, Russia outmaneuvered the United States to bring forward its own plan to the UN to serve its interests while stymieing those of the West.

New Round of Talks

The 2016–17 GGE was tasked to continue to study norms, rules, and principles of responsible behavior of states.[90] In addition, the group was asked to study "how international law applies to the use of information and communications technology by states."[91] The United States pursued explicit statements to codify the application of international law to the cyber domain, specifically on the "inherent right of self-defense and the law of State responsibility, including countermeasures."[92] The Cuban representative argued for provisions "on how certain international law applies to states' use of ICTs" that would "legitimize . . . unilateral punitive force actions."[93] In 2015, Russia and China rebuffed a similar US proposal to spell out the implications of how international law applies in cyberspace, arguing, "the move would institutionalize U.S. hegemony in cyberspace."[94] In testimony, cyber expert James Lewis said, "The Chinese are opposed to anything that would appear to legitimize U.S. attack or U.S. retaliation upon them," which includes by countermeasures.[95]

China and Russian did participate in the 2015 Group of Twenty (G20) summit in Antalya, Turkey, where "leaders affirmed that international law applies to state conduct in cyberspace."[96] At the 2018 RSA Conference of cybersecurity industry experts, Lewis stated that Russia resisted US attempts to lay out the law of armed conflict in the limited structure of the 2016–17 GGE proceedings.[97] More than likely, Russia and China followed their pledge in May 2015 to cooperate with each other in international legal norms to stymie the interests of the West.[98] The 2018 G7 Ise-Shima Cyber Group expressed regret about the outcome of the GGE talks, while noting "some countries' experts walked back from previous reports' statements on the applicability of international law to states' activities in cyber space."[99] It emphasized that regardless of the outcome, the "recommendations contained in the 2010, 2013 and 2015 UN GGE reports remain valid."[100]

The position reached by Michele Markoff after the meetings of the 2016–17 GGE speaks to the difficulty of a new round of talks with Russia and China. Specifically, she came to the unfortunate conclusion that "those who are unwilling to affirm the applicability of these international legal rules and principles believe their States are free to act in or through cyberspace to achieve their political ends with no limits or constraints on their actions."[101] Markoff unequivocally rejected this "dangerous and unsupportable view."[102] Even Karsten Geier, the chair of the last group, was "less than enthused about reviving the UN GGE process, considering its failure" during his speech to the Global Conference on Cyber Space held in New Delhi in November 2017.[103] After all, the freedom to act in or through cyberspace without limits or constraints fits well with Russian cyber operations designed to achieve political objectives. So, why would the Kremlin accommodate the West?

Narrowly Tailored Deals

In 2015, Russia signed a Cyber Nonaggression Pact with China. In one provision, the two nations "pledge to refrain from computer attacks against each other."[104] Furthermore, the pact delineates that "each party has an equal right to the protection of the information resources of their state against misuse and unsanctioned interference."[105] The prospect of the United States enacting a similar narrow deal with Russia should be enticing. After all, the United States reached a historic deal with China in 2015 when President Barack Obama and President Xi Jinping agreed during a state visit in Washington that "neither country's government will conduct or knowingly support cyber-enabled theft of intellectual property, including trade secrets or other confidential business information, with the intent of providing competitive advantage to companies or commercial sectors."[106] The agreement was significant progress because never before had China even acknowledged that the cyber "theft of intellectual property for commercial gain was off limits."[107] The United States had accused China of stealing billions of dollars' worth of intellectual property from American companies. The so-called US-China cyber deal was a first step in a more aggressive posture with China's government on computer theft.[108]

While agreeing the pact was a step in the right direction, Jay Kaplan, a security firm executive, noted, "It is completely unenforceable given the non-attributable nature of state-sponsored cyber activities."[109] Initially, Chinese cyber theft seemed to decrease. A report by the security firm FireEye claimed that network compromises by the China-based hacking groups it tracks dropped from sixty to fewer than ten a month.[110] However, Assistant Attorney General John Carlin "confirmed the company's findings that attacks were less voluminous but more focused and calculated."[111] The attacks have become more targeted, "in accordance with national objectives for economic development and military modernization."[112] Evidence for that assertion resides in the indictment in September 2017 of employees of the Chinese cybersecurity firm Boyusec. The three defendants were charged with cyber intrusions of Moody's Analytics, Siemens AG, and Trimble Inc. to steal hundreds of gigabytes of sensitive data and trade secrets.[113] Boyusec has been linked to a hacker group known as APT3, attributed to the Chinese Ministry of State Security.[114] In November 2018, Rob Joyce, at the NSA, reaffirmed that Beijing's commitment has eroded: "It is clear they are well beyond the bounds of the agreement today that was forged between our two countries."[115] His allegation was confirmed in another indictment in December 2018 of two members of APT10, who acted in association with the Chinese Ministry of State Security to target more than forty-five technology companies in at least a dozen US states.[116] Intelligence officials and private security researchers have concluded that "the 2015 agreement appears to have been unofficially canceled amid the continuing trade tension between the United States and China."[117]

The Chinese ministry exploited ambiguity in the Obama-Xi agreement, specifically in what is cyber theft for commercial advantage versus cyber espionage to advance state interests, inducing doubt on prospects for future state-level deals. For instance, the basis for a cyber nonaggression pact–like deal between Russia and the United States on "protection of the information resources of their state against misuse and unsanctioned interference" could also face ambiguity.[118] In the US-China cyber deal, the Obama administration argued "that the theft of intellectual property is distinct from the work of the NSA and other U.S. intelligence agencies."[119] When arguing against Russian interference campaigns, the United States is on less firm ground since the US supposedly engages in cyber operations "to conduct covert action . . . to influence political, economic, or military conditions abroad."[120] The case can be made that there is no difference between the US influencing political conditions in authoritarian countries and Russia subverting the democratic process of a stable and free society.[121] Any tailored deal will be harder to make with the Russians than it was with the Chinese and just as difficult to enforce.

Nonetheless, the Russian business daily *Kommersant* reported in August 2018 that Moscow had offered to cooperate with the United States to prevent "cyberattacks on critical infrastructure."[122] Furthermore, the Kremlin desired to express words to that effect in a communiqué issued at the conclusion of the summit of the US and Russian presidents in Helsinki in July 2018.[123] The Helsinki summit did occur, but no communiqué was issued. Instead, the two leaders pledged in a joint press conference to pursue talks on an array of arms control and regional issues.[124] The absence of an agreed-upon public statement left secret the status and extent of any practical agreement,[125] though toward the end of the press conference, President Putin proposed to have American investigators go to Russia to observe interviews of the individuals the United States accused of hacking the Democratic Party during the presidential election.[126] President Trump praised the offer as an "incredible" deal, which was later rejected by the FBI director.[127] Moving forward, Russia will most likely aim for a leaders-level cyber agreement in order to bypass "an intransigent 'deep state'" in the United States bent on stymieing efforts at rapprochement.[128]

Latest Developments

In December 2019, the UN General Assembly adopted two separate resolutions regarding responsible state behavior in cyberspace. The first, sponsored by the United States, confirms the conclusions of the two previous GGE reports that international law and the UN Charter are applicable to cyberspace.[129] The resolution creates a new working group on the basis of equitable geographic distribution to study once again how international law applies to state actions in cyberspace. The second, sponsored by Russia, convenes an open-ended working group to further develop existing, and identify additional, rules, norms, and principles of responsible state behavior.[130] The Russian representative said the lack of consensus in the latest GGE was proof that a new model was necessary, omitting the truth that Russia blocked the report. By advocating for the open group, Russia positioned itself as a champion for inclusivity over the US quest for exclusivity in a limited group study. In essence, Russia masterfully framed itself as a "defender of the rules-based international order."[131] However, several passages in the preamble of the Russian proposal are contrary to their observed practices in the cyber domain. One section reaffirms "the right and duty of States to combat . . . the dissemination of false or distorted news, which can be interpreted as interference in the internal affairs of other States,"[132] while another section expresses concern that "embedding harmful hidden functions in ICTs could be used in ways that would affect secure and reliable ICT use and the ICT supply chain for products and services, erode trust in commerce and damage national security."[133]

The US representative claimed the Russian proposal "imposes a list of unacceptable norms and language that is broadly unacceptable to many states," while the Russian representative said the US version was crafted to "take the international community backwards."[134] This now leaves the UN split between two dueling working groups.[135] The US resolution has thirty-six sponsor nations, including the United Kingdom, Germany, Japan, and Israel. One hundred and thirty-eight nations voted to adopt it, while twelve voted against it. The new working group has three years to study measures to address threats in cyberspace and submit a report that does not imply consensus of all participants. The Russian version has the backing of thirty nations, including China, Iran, North Korea, and Pakistan. One hundred and nineteen countries voted in favor of it, with forty-six against it. The open-ended working group will involve all interested UN member states and hold consultative meetings with businesses, nongovernmental organizations, and academia. The group has two years to produce a consensus-based report.[136] Representatives from Australia and Canada claim the Russian version distorts previous findings on norms. Time will tell if Russia will reject again the applicability of cyber-relevant legal principles and rules—specifically the right to respond to internationally wrongful acts (with countermeasures), the right to self-defense, and international humanitarian law—in an attempt to intentionally politicize well-accepted international norms for cyberspace.[137]

Conclusion

US senator John McCain said in his memoir that Vladimir Putin is "intent on evil deeds, which include the destruction of the liberal world order that the United States has led and that has brought more stability, prosperity, and freedom to humankind than ever existed in history."[138] President Putin and his inner circle would most likely argue that Russia is just resuming its rightful position on the world stage while the West plots to blunt its great power aspirations. Russia competes in political, economic, and military arenas to change the balance of power and the Western version of international order that accompanies it. As a revisionist state, Russia wants to challenge the elements of international order, including alliances, institutions, and rules. It will inevitably use all available means to shift the hierarchy of authority and prestige. Cyber operations offer Russia a formidable and covert means for revising the status quo in its favor.

Covert action is seen as "a tool of rational states."[139] State leaders, as unitary actors, determine the political utility of covert action, including by cyber means. Covert action plays a role in the divide between overt diplomacy and overt war. The utility of covert action is "derived from its ability to alter the policy relationships of states in international relations."[140] Hence, the decision for Russia to use cyber operations that undermine or circumvent international norms is a rational decision made by a unitary state actor. There are no indications that Russia will change this stance or abide closer to the norms of responsible state behavior in cyberspace it helped to establish. After all, an argument can be made that "Who would believe that Putin would abide by a norm (really it's an arms control 'pledge'—not a norm, since it is not mutually practiced today) *not* [sic] to do something that he can do covertly and largely get away with?"[141] The NotPetya campaign "illustrates the complexity of applying international law to factually ambiguous cyber scenarios."[142] Without causing deaths or injuries and without timely attribution to the state, the right of self-defense through the use of force was not justified.

The audacious conduct of the NotPetya campaign indicates that in contrast to scholarly claims, the West is not "making significant headway in its competition with Russia over the former Soviet space."[143] Despite the prevailing argument that Russia is declining as a power due to economic and demographic problems, with little investment the leader of the state, President Putin, "punches above his weight."[144] Russia will revise the status quo by exploiting cyber vulnerabilities, sowing uncertainty in countries on its borders, and "contorting international rules and norms toward its will."[145] Russia has shown a willingness to provoke and push the boundaries of international order. The nation seeks to "shape the international system and regional security dynamics and exert influence over the politics and economies of states in all regions of the world."[146] In particular, Russia will continue to "sow a level of chaos within states it considers part of its zone of privileged interest [in particular Ukraine] to prevent them from joining Western clubs."[147] In sowing disorder, Russia will undoubtedly choose cyber operations as the preference with the highest expected utility. Any hope that Russia will acquiesce to an "international legal framework in which cyberwars take place," as envisioned by the UN secretary-general, is not rational.[148]

Notes

1. Herbert A. Simon, "Human Nature in Politics: The Dialogue of Psychology with Political Science," *American Political Science Review* 79 (1985): 294.

2. Minority Staff, *Putin's Asymmetric Assault on Democracy in Russia and Europe: Implications for U.S. National Security*, report prepared for the use of the US Senate Committee on Foreign Relations (Washington, DC: Government Publishing Office, January 10, 2018), 1.

3. Aaron Franklin Brantly, *The Decision to Attack* (Athens: University of Georgia Press, 2016), 44.

4. Brantly, 57.

5. G7 Foreign Ministers, "Defending Democracy: Addressing Foreign Threats," Ministerial Meeting, Toronto, April 22–24, 2018.

6. G7 Foreign Ministers.

7. Donald Trump, *National Security Strategy of the United States of America* (Washington, DC: White House, December 2017), 25.

8. Joint Chiefs of Staff, *Joint Operating Environment: JOE 2035; The Joint Force in a Contested and Disordered World* (Washington, DC: Joint Chiefs of Staff, July 14, 2016), 28.

9. Joint Chiefs of Staff, 28.

10. Joint Chiefs of Staff, 28.

11. Minority Staff, *Putin's Asymmetric Assault on Democracy*, 67.

12. Peter J. Katzenstein, ed., *The Culture of National Security: Norms and Identity in World Politics* (New York: Columbia University Press, 1996), 5.

13. Martha Finnemore, "Cybersecurity and the Concept of Norms," Carnegie Endowment for International Peace, November 30, 2017.

14. Finnemore.

15. Stephen D. Krasner, *International Regimes* (Ithaca, NY: Cornell University Press, 1983), 2.

16. James A. Lewis, "US International Strategy for Cybersecurity," testimony to Senate Foreign Relations Committee, March 12, 2015, 3–4.

17. Scott Jasper, *Strategic Cyber Deterrence: The Active Cyber Defense Option* (New York: Rowman & Littlefield, 2017), 144.

18. Dorothy Denning, "Obstacles and Options for Cyber Arms Controls," Heinrich Boll Foundation Conference, Berlin, Germany, June 29–30, 2001, 3.

19. Adam Segal, "Why Are There No Cyber Arms Control Agreements?," blog post, Council on Foreign Relations, January 16, 2018.

20. Barack Obama, "International Strategy for Cyberspace," White House, May 2011, 8.

21. Obama, 9.

22. Obama, 10.

23. Nick Wadhams and Nafeesa Syeed, "Tillerson to Shut Cyber Office in State Department Reorganization," Bloomberg News, July 19, 2017.

24. Sean Lyngaas, "The Uphill Battle to Relaunch State Department's Cybersecurity Policy Office," Cyberscoop, May 7, 2018.

25. Derek B. Johnson, "Senate Panel Votes to Revive State Cyber Office," *Federal Computing Weekly*, June 26, 2018.

26. UN General Assembly, "International Code of Conduct for Information Security," Document 69/723, January 13, 2015, 1.

27. UN General Assembly, 1.

28. UN General Assembly, 4–5.

29. Cherian Samuel, *Cybersecurity: Global, Regional and Domestic Dynamics*," Monograph Series no. 42 (New Delhi: Institute for Defense Studies and Analyses, 2014), 24.
30. Samuel, 24.
31. Joseph Marks, "U.N. Body Agrees to U.S. Norms in Cyberspace," *Politico*, July 9, 2015.
32. UN General Assembly, "Group of Governmental Experts on Developments in the Field of Information and Telecommunications in the Context of International Security," A/70/174, July 22, 2015, 7.
33. UN General Assembly, 8–9.
34. UN General Assembly, 12.
35. UN General Assembly, "Resolution Adopted by the General Assembly on 23 December 2015," A70/237, December 2015, 3.
36. Marks, "U.N. Body Agrees to U.S. Norms in Cyberspace."
37. Marks.
38. Defense Intelligence Agency, "Russia Military Power," 41.
39. Daniel R. Coats, "Worldwide Threat Assessment of the US Intelligence Community," statement for the record, Senate Select Committee on Intelligence, January 29, 2019, 18.
40. Brantly, *Decision to Attack*, 54–55.
41. Danny Palmer, "Petya Ransomware Attack: How Many Victims Are There Really?," ZDNet, June 28, 2017.
42. Catalin Cimpanu, "Before NotPetya, There Was Another Ransomware That Targeted Ukraine Last Week," Bleeping Computer, June 28, 2017.
43. Alex Hern, "WannaCry, Petya, NotPetya: How Ransomware Hit the Big Time in 2017," *The Guardian*, December 30, 2017.
44. Kadri Kutt, "NotPetya and WannaCry Call for a Joint Response from International Community," NATO Cooperative Cyber Defense Centre of Excellence, June 30, 2017.
45. Palmer, "Petya Ransomware Attack."
46. Doug Olenick, "NotPetya Attack Totally Destroyed Maersk's Computer Network: Chairman," *SC Magazine*, January 29, 2018.
47. Eduard Kovacs, "Maersk Reinstalled 50,000 Computers after NotPetya Attack," *Security Week*, January 26, 2018.
48. Paul Roberts, "NotPetya Infection Left Merck Short of Key HPV Vaccine," Security Ledger, November 1, 2017.
49. "Maersk, Rosneft Hit by Cyberattack," Offshore Energy Today, June 28, 2017.
50. Radware, "Petya/Petrwrap," threat alert, June 28, 2017.
51. US-CERT, "Petya Ransomware," alert TA17-181A, July 28, 2017.
52. Kirk Soluk, "Patching Not Enough to Stop Petya," Arbor Networks (blog), June 27, 2017, https://www.arbornetworks.com/blog/asert/patching-not-enough-stop-petya/.
53. US-CERT, "Petya Ransomware."
54. Risk and Resilience Team, "Addendum to Cyber and Information Warfare in the Ukrainian Conflict," version 2, Cyber Defense Project, Center for Security Studies, October 2018, 41.
55. Chantal Da Silva, "Russia Was behind Global Cyber Attack, Ukraine Says," *The Independent*, July 2, 2017.
56. Risk and Resilience Team, "Addendum to Cyber and Information Warfare," 38.
57. Ellen Nakashima, "Russian Military Was behind 'NotPetya' Cyberattack in Ukraine, CIA Concludes," *Washington Post*, January 12, 2018.
58. Alina Polyakova and Spencer P. Boyer, "The Future of Political Warfare: Russia, the West, and the Coming Age of Global Digital Competition," Brookings Institution, Robert Bosch Foundation Transatlantic Initiative, March 2018, 14.

59. Phil Muncaster, "Five Eyes Nations United in Blaming Russia for NotPetya," *Infosecurity Magazine*, February 19, 2018.
60. Sean Gallagher, "In Terse Statement, White House Blames Russia for NotPetya Worm," Ars Technica, Tech-Policy, February 15, 2018.
61. National Cyber Security Centre, "Russian Military 'Almost Certainly' Responsible for Destructive 2017 Cyber Attack," February 15, 2018.
62. Kutt, "NotPetya and WannaCry."
63. Michael Schmitt and Jeffery Biller, "The NotPetya Cyber Operation as a Case Study of International Law," EJIL: Talk! (blog), July 11, 2017.
64. Schmitt and Biller.
65. Schmitt and Biller.
66. Kutt, "NotPetya and WannaCry."
67. Michael N. Schmitt, ed., *Tallinn Manual 2.0 on the International Law Applicable to Cyber Operations*, 2nd ed. (Cambridge: Cambridge University Press, 2017), 17.
68. Michael Schmitt, "In Defense of Sovereignty in Cyberspace," Just Security, May 8, 2018.
69. Gary P. Corn and Robert Taylor, "Sovereignty in the Age of Cyber," *AJIL Unbound* 111 (2017): 208.
70. Corn and Taylor, 210.
71. Robert McLaughlin and Michael Schmitt, "The Need for Clarity in International Cyber Law," Asia and the Pacific Policy Society, Policy Forum, September 18, 2017.
72. McLaughlin and Schmitt.
73. White House, "Vulnerabilities Equities Policy and Process for the United States Government," November 15, 2017.
74. White House.
75. White House.
76. Cybersecurity Tech Accord, "Governments Need to Do More, and Say More, on Vulnerability Handling," September 10, 2018, https://cybertechaccord.org/government-vulnerability-handling/.
77. Bogdan Popa, "NSA Reported WannaCry Vulnerability to Microsoft after Using It for 5 Years," Softpedia, May 18, 2017.
78. Ellen Nakashima and Craig Timberg, "NSA Officials Worried about the Day Its Potent Hacking Tool Would Get Loose. Then It Did," *Washington Post*, May 16, 2018.
79. Nakashima and Timberg.
80. Dan Goodin, "Fearing Shadow Brokers Leak, NSA Reported Critical Flaw to Microsoft," Ars Technica, May 17, 2017.
81. Goodin.
82. Rich McCormick, "Microsoft Says Governments Should Stop 'Hoarding' Security Vulnerabilities after WannaCry Attack," The Verge, May 15, 2014.
83. Brad Smith, "The Need for Urgent Collective Action to Keep People Safe Online: Lessons from Last Week's Cyberattack," official Microsoft blog, May 14, 2017.
84. Smith.
85. Kadri Kutt, "WannaCry Campaign: Potential State Involvement Could Have Serious Consequences," NATO Cooperative Cyber Defense Centre of Excellence, May 16, 2017.
86. Scott Charney et al., "From Articulation to Implementation: Enabling Progress on Cybersecurity Norms," Microsoft Corp., June 2016, 1.
87. Charney et al., 1.
88. Tim Maurer and Kathryn Taylor, "Outlook on International Cyber Norms: Three Avenues for Future Progress," Just Security, March 2, 2018.
89. Maurer and Taylor.

90. UN General Assembly, "Resolution Adopted by the General Assembly on 23 December 2016," A/RES/70/237, December 30, 2015.

91. UN General Assembly.

92. Michele G. Markoff, "Explanation of Position at the Conclusion of the 2016–2017 UN Group of Governmental Experts (GGE) on Developments in the Field of Information and Telecommunications in the Context of International Security," Department of State, posted remarks, New York, June 23, 2017.

93. Elaine Korzak, "UN GGE on Cybersecurity: The End of an Era?," *The Diplomat*, July 31, 2017.

94. Marks, "U.N. Body Agrees to U.S. Norms in Cyberspace."

95. James A. Lewis, "U.S.-China Economic and Security Review Commission: Hearing on China's Information Controls, Global Media Influence, and Cyber Warfare Strategy," oral testimony, May 4, 2017.

96. White House, Office of the Press Secretary, "FACT SHEET: The 2015 G-20 Summit in Antalya, Turkey," November 16, 2015.

97. Jeff Lewis, "Bringing Order to Chaos: The Development of Nation-State Cyber-Norms," 2018 RSA Conference, San Francisco, April 17, 2018.

98. Elaine Korzak, "Russia and China Have a Cyber Nonaggression Pact," Defense One, August 20, 2015.

99. G7 Foreign Ministers, "Chair's Report of the Meeting of the G7 Ise-Shima Cyber Group," Toronto, April 22–24, 2018.

100. G7 Foreign Ministers.

101. Markoff, "2016–2017 UN Group of Governmental Experts."

102. Markoff.

103. Cherian Samuel, "Why Wait for the Elusive Tipping Point in Cyber?," Institute for Defence Studies and Analysis, India, March 21, 2018.

104. Korzak, "Russia and China."

105. Korzak.

106. White House, Office of the Press Secretary, "President Xi Jinping's State Visit to the United States," fact sheet, September 25, 2015.

107. David E. Sanger, "Limiting Security Breaches May Be Impossible Task for U.S. and China," *New York Times*, September 25, 2015.

108. Damian Paletta, "Cyberattack Deal Seen as First Step," *Wall Street Journal*, September 26–27, 2015.

109. Sheera Frenkel, "Nobody Thinks the U.S. and China's New Cyber Arms Pact Will Fix Much of Anything," BuzzFeed, September 25, 2015.

110. "RedLine Drawn: China Recalculates Its Use of Cyber Espionage," special report, FireEye, June 2016, 11.

111. Adam Segal, "The U.S.-China Cyber Espionage Deal One Year Later," Net Politics, September 28, 2016.

112. Elsa Kania, "Careful What You Wish For: Change and Continuity in China's Cyber Threats," The Strategist, Australian Strategic Policy Institute, April 5, 2018.

113. US District Court, Western District of Pennsylvania, criminal indictment no. 17-247, September 13, 2017.

114. Thomas Fox-Brewster, "Chinese Trio Linked to Dangerous APT3 Hackers Charged with Stealing 407GB of Data from Siemens," *Forbes*, November 27, 2017.

115. Dustin Volz, "China Violated Obama-Era Cybertheft Pact, U.S. Official Says," *Wall Street Journal*, November 8, 2018.

116. Department of Justice, "Two Chinese Hackers Associated with the Ministry of State

Security Charged with Global Computer Intrusion Campaigns Targeting Intellectual Property and Confidential Business Information," December 20, 2018.

117. Nicole Perlroth, "Chinese and Iranian Hackers Renew Their Attacks on U.S. Companies," *New York Times*, February 18, 2019.

118. Korzak, "Russia and China."

119. Timothy Edgar, "Indicting Hackers Made China Behave, but Russia Will Be Harder," Lawfare, February 18, 2018.

120. Edgar.

121. Edgar.

122. Alex Grigsby, "Russia Wants a Deal with the United States on Cyber Issues. Why Does Washington Keep Saying No?," blog post, Council on Foreign Relations, August 27, 2018.

123. Grigsby.

124. Michael R. Gordon and Ann M. Simmons, "Many Pledges but No Big Advances," *Wall Street Journal*, July 17, 2018.

125. Patrick Wintour, "Helsinki Summit: What Did Trump and Putin Agree?," *The Guardian*, July 17, 2018.

126. Chris Megerian, "Putin Offered to Help with the Russia Investigation. Don't Expect Mueller to Take Him Up on It," *Los Angeles Times*, July 16, 2018.

127. Chris Strohm, "FBI Chief Dismisses Putin Offer for Investigation Cooperation," *Bloomberg Politics*, July 18, 2018.

128. Grigsby, "Russia Wants a Deal."

129. UN General Assembly, "Resolution Adopted by the General Assembly on 22 December 2018," A/RES/73/266, January 2, 2019.

130. Alex Grigsby, "The UN Doubles Its Workload on Cyber Norms, and Not Everyone Is Pleased," blog post, Council on Foreign Relations, November 15, 2018.

131. Grigsby.

132. UN General Assembly, "Resolution Adopted by the General Assembly on 5 December 2018," A/RES/73/27, December 11, 2018.

133. UN General Assembly.

134. Derek B. Johnson, "U.S., Russia Jockey to Shape New Global Cyber Norms," FCW, cybersecurity section, November 9, 2018.

135. Derek B. Johnson, "Moving the Needle on Cyber Norms," FCW, cybersecurity section, February 1, 2019.

136. Ilona Sadnik, "Discussing State Behavior in Cyberspace: What Should We Expect?," Diplo (blog), March 20, 2019.

137. Michael Schmitt and Liis Vihul, "International Cyber Law Politicized: The UN GGE's Failure to Advance Cyber Norms," Just Security, June 30, 2017.

138. John McCain, "Putin Is an Evil Man," *Wall Street Journal*, May 12–13, 2018.

139. Brantly, *Decision to Attack*, 44.

140. Brantly, 44.

141. James Van De Velde, "Why Cyber Norms Are Dumb and Serve Russian Interests," Cipher Brief, June 6, 2018.

142. Schmitt and Biller, "NotPetya Cyber Operation."

143. Emil Avdaliani, "Russia vs. the West: The Beginning of the End," Perspectives Paper no. 832, Begin-Sadat Center for Strategic Studies, May 13, 2018, 1.

144. Gerald F. Seib, "In New Era, Putin Punches above His Weight," *Wall Street Journal*, May 7, 2019.

145. Lionel Beehner et al., "Analyzing the Russian Way of War," U.S. Army Modern War Institute, March 20, 2018, 6.

146. Coats, "Worldwide Threat Assessment," 4.
147. Beehner et al., "Analyzing the Russian Way of War," 6.
148. Antonio Guterres, "Address at the Opening Ceremony of the Munich Security Conference," UN Secretary-General speeches, February 16, 2018, https://www.un.org/sg/en/content/sg/speeches/2018-02-16/address-opening-ceremony-munich-security-conference.

CHAPTER 6

Unconvincing Responses

Lt. Gen. Paul Nakasone, the commander of US Cyber Command, told the Senate Armed Services Committee in March 2018 that adversaries including Russia are "willing to continue launching cyberattacks against the U.S. on account of the administration's subdued reaction to the alleged Kremlin-ordered hacking campaign waged against the 2016 White House race."[1] Nakasone said that "right now, they do not think that much will happen. They don't fear us."[2] Moreover, the US response to Russian interference has had no deterrent effect, since "it has not changed their behavior."[3] The achievement of a deterrent effect is largely a function of perception. Deterrence works in the mind of the adversary to change its decision-making calculus. If successful, the adversary believes that any attack will be futile or will result in unacceptable costs imposed on it. The deputy assistant secretary of defense for cyber policy, Aaron Hughes, testified that costs may be imposed on adversaries "through a variety of mechanisms including economic sanctions, diplomacy, law enforcement, and military action."[4]

The 2018 National Cyber Strategy of the United States explicitly states that while continuing "to promote consensus on what constitutes responsible state behavior in cyberspace, [the nation] must also work to ensure that there are consequences for irresponsible behavior that harms the United States and our partners."[5] In addition, the strategy emphasizes the use of all instruments of national power "to prevent, respond to, and deter malicious cyber activity."[6] It makes clear that when actors do harm in or through cyberspace, the United States will use "integrated strategies that impose swift, costly, and transparent consequences."[7] Although the new cyber strategy presents a formidable approach to attribute and deter malicious cyber activities, the responses of the United States to date have been unconvincing in the minds of adversaries, particularly the Russians. This chapter will describe the theories of deterrence and the subdued methods chosen by the United States in response to Russian interference in the 2016 US presidential election. It will then analyze subsequent Russian cyber operations during the 2017 French presidential election. The chapter will finish with the insufficiency of preferred deterrence mechanisms to impose cost for irresponsible Russian behavior in cyberspace.

Deterrence Theories

The great thinkers of our time have theorized "about the purpose and role of deterrence in national security strategy."[8] Thomas Schelling defined the theory of deterrence as "to prevent from action by fear of consequences."[9] Deterrence attempts to persuade adversaries not to take actions that threaten "vital interests by means of decisive influence over their decision making."[10] Decisive influence is attained by "credibly threatening to deny benefits and/or impose costs while ensuring restraint."[11] For deterrence to change behavior, it must "instill a belief in an adversary that a threat of retaliation actually exists, the intended action cannot succeed, or the costs outweigh the benefits of acting."[12] Therefore, effective deterrence requires capability (the means to influence behavior), credibility (that proposed actions may actually be employed), and communication (sending the intended message to the desired audience).[13] Dominant capability must be matched with commensurate credibility and communication.[14] Deterrence fails if a state has the capability necessary to respond but does not have the will to act or the reputation that it would. Even if a state has the capability and credibility (will and reputation) to act, it must communicate its position, for unless others receive the message clearly, they will not fully comprehend probable repercussions.[15]

Lawrence Freedman stated that deterrence is concerned with "deliberate attempts to manipulate the behaviour of others through conditional threats."[16] Patrick Morgan added that the essence of deterrence is that "one party prevents another from doing something the first party does not want by threatening to harm the other party seriously if it does."[17] In other words, deterrence is simply the prevention of undesired action by an adversary.[18] Therefore, with deterrence the objective is inaction, primarily obtained through the threat of retaliation. However, Ned Lebow opined that intimidation through threat-based strategies is risky since they can provoke instead of prevent behavior because restraint can be interpreted as weakness. Hence, deterrence in some cases uses aspects of soft power. Glenn Snyder affirmed that the concept of deterrence is not limited to military factors, given "its fundamental affinity to the idea of political power."[19] Joe Nye advanced this suggestion by identifying the political mechanism of norms of responsible state behavior as a means of dissuasion. However, Morgan noted that when "fear of the consequences of violating certain norms" is internalized, deterrence is at work.[20]

Robert Jervis affirmed that "in the most elemental sense, deterrence depends on perceptions" and therefore "unless statesmen understand the ways in which their opposite numbers see the world, their deterrence policies are likely to misfire."[21] Jervis postulated that for deterrence to work, an actor has to be convinced "that the expected value of a certain action is outweighed by the expected punishment."[22] That value, or risk, calculation resides ultimately in "the eye of the beholder"—that is "of the party being—it is hoped—deterred."[23] Thus, a key requirement for successful deterrence is viewing it through the eye of the adversary and not one's own.[24] An adversary's intentions are too often viewed by decision-makers from perceptual biases and organizational interests rather than credible signals.[25] Understanding the "rational value-maximizing mode of behavior of adversaries" requires perceptions of risk from "the eye of the beholder."[26] Thus, Freedman stated, deterrence "is about setting boundaries for actions and establishing the risks associated with the crossing of those boundaries."[27]

Contemporary scholars such as Aaron Brantly ask and examine the proverbial question, "Do conventional frameworks of deterrence maintain their applicability and meaning against state actors in cyberspace?"[28] A prevalent argument is that the inherent characteristics of cyberspace impact the viability of traditional approaches to deterrence. For instance, Kamal Jabbour and Paul Ratazzi point out that deterrence through threat of retaliation is challenged by the low probability of detection, lack of attribution, low cost of aggression, high payoff for success, and conflicting laws.[29] Another common argument is that the threat of unacceptable counteraction rooted in the Cold War has no actionable basis for deterrence. Dorothy Denning has noted the success of nuclear deterrence relies on the weapon itself, which by design restricts usage.[30] Denning argues the use of the weapon would be a rare occurrence and attribution for any attack is most certainly assured. Richard Harknett agreed that the nuclear deterrence framework was "a specific strategic response to a specific strategic environment, and it does not hold that it would be universally effective across all weapon types."[31] Harknett contends that deterrence does not map well to the "offense-persistent strategic environment" of cyberspace. However, Martin Libicki has contended that if "countries understand the United States is capable of impressive cyberspace operations then the threat that it will use them in reprisal is inevitably part of the U.S. deterrence package."[32]

Subdued Reaction

As previously delineated, before the breach of the Democratic National Committee, Russian hackers successfully penetrated unclassified networks at the State Department, the White House, and the Joint Chiefs of Staff. The cybersecurity firm CrowdStrike claimed the hackers were APT29, or Cozy Bear, a Russian proxy group.[33] At the State Department, the entire email system was shut down for days after traces of suspicious activity were found in its network.[34] Despite efforts to lock out the hackers, they were able to reenter the State Department system and use a compromised email account to launch a phishing attack upon the White House.[35] The hackers fought back when exposed at the White House by installing new malware when old versions were mitigated.[36] A public report in April 2015 openly accused Russia of infiltrating the unclassi-fied networks at the White House. The report was apparently designed to send "a message to the Kremlin: We know what you're up to, and how you're doing it."[37] While this veiled threat to Moscow was intended to convey that there could be consequences for malicious hacking, none followed. That proved to be a huge mistake and a missed precedent. If President Vladimir Putin thought there was no price to be paid for invading White House systems, why would he not hack the DNC?[38]

In October 2016, the United States officially accused Russia of interfering in the presidential election. The DHS and the Office of the Director of National Intelligence stated with confidence, "The Russian Government directed the recent compromises of e-mails from US persons and institutions, including from US political organizations."[39] Furthermore, the agencies said they be-lieved, "based on the scope and sensitivity of these efforts, that only Russia's senior-most officials could have authorized these activities."[40] US lawmakers welcomed the announcement but quickly noted they expected the Barack Obama administration to punish the Kremlin. Sen. Ben Sasse, a member of the Homeland Security Committee, said, "Russia must face serious consequences. The United States must upend President Putin's calculus with a strong diplo-matic, political, cyber and economic response."[41] President Obama affirmed this assertion by saying, "We need to take action and we will—at a time and place of our own choosing."[42]

American intelligence agencies and aides assembled a menu of options for President Obama to consider for action. The options were obvious and in-novative. One idea was to expose President Putin's financial links to oligarchs, but that was discarded after arguments that it would not shock the Russians.[43] Another option was to expose Russian hacking tools, but concern was raised that would also expose software implants used by the United States.[44] Other options included invoking economic sanctions or indicting the hackers be-hind the attacks. The administration also contemplated covert cyber action against Russia, but the prospect of hitting back that way caused trepidation at agency meetings. There were worries over escalation in cyber warfare and that the United States would have more to lose than the Russians. "If we got into a tit-for-tat on cyber with the Russians, it would not be to our advantage," a participant in the debate later remarked. "They could do more to damage us in a cyber war or have a greater impact."[45] The deeper concern was Russia had a playbook ready to respond with cyberattacks against America's critical infrastructure—and could possibly shut down the electrical grid.[46] The United States could not ensure escalation dominance in cyberspace and the ability to end any potential conflict.[47]

The United States did eventually respond but not in the cyber domain. In late December 2016, President Obama signed off on a package of punitive measures. The measures consisted of sanctions, expulsions, and closures. The president stated, "These actions follow repeated private and public warnings that we have issued to the Russian government, and are a necessary and appropriate response to efforts to harm U.S. interests in violation of established international norms of behavior."[48] The sanctions targeted the GRU for "tampering, altering or causing the misappropriation of information with the purpose or effect of interfering with the 2016 U.S. election processes."[49] The sanctions also cited the FSB for assisting the GRU in conducting the activities, four individual officers of the GRU, and three other Russian entities that provided material support to the GRU's cyber operations. The sanctions imposed travel bans and asset freezes, although the main targets had few known holdings abroad or vulnerable assets to freeze. The economic sanctions were "so narrowly targeted that even those who helped design them describe their impact as largely symbolic."[50]

In addition, the State Department expelled thirty-five intelligence operatives acting under diplomatic status from the Russian embassy in Washington and the Russian consulate in San Francisco. The officials and their families were given seventy-two hours to leave the country. The State Department also notified Moscow that it would lose access to two Russian government-owned recreational compounds, one on Maryland's Eastern Shore and one on Long Island, considered to be summer homes for Russian diplomats.[51] However, the expulsions and seizures had originally been devised to retaliate for harassment of American diplomatic personnel in Russia by security personnel and police. The measures were adopted and included in the election-related package, watering down the intent.[52] Finally, the US government released declassified technical information on Russian cyber activity to help defenders "identify, detect and disrupt Russia's global campaign of malicious cyber activity."[53] President Putin said Russia would not act in response to the US moves, in a public show of restraint that appeared aimed at embarrassing the Obama administration. Instead, Putin invited the children of US envoys to a New Year's celebration held on the grounds of the Kremlin.[54] Undeterred in his behavior, Putin proceeded to hack the French presidential election.

2017 French Presidential Election

Admittedly, the reason why President Putin declined to retaliate for the package of punitive measures is probably debatable. Charging documents in a case against former national security adviser Michael Flynn for lying to the FBI reveal that Flynn falsely stated that "he did not ask Russia's Ambassador to the United States . . . to refrain from escalating the situation in response to sanctions that the United States had imposed against Russia" and falsely stated that he did not remember the ambassador told him that "Russia had chosen to moderate its response to those sanctions as a result of Flynn's request."[55] What is not contentious is the reality that the US sanctions must not have induced a fear of significant consequences, for only four months later the NSA warned its French counterparts that Russian cyber actors were meddling in their presidential election.[56] On May 6, 2017, the political party of French presidential candidate Emmanuel Macron, En Marche, announced that its computer systems had been hacked and leaks had occurred, after nine gigabytes of data, including documents and emails, were posted online on the sharing website Pastebin.[57] The timing of the massive dump suggested the hackers meant to inflict maximum political damage two days before the French presidential election.

The leaked files were obtained from the personal and work email accounts of En Marche officials. The security firm Trend Micro identified the pro-Kremlin hacking group Pawn Storm, another alias for APT28, as the likely source of a multipronged phishing campaign that had started in March.[58] The group set up domains mimicking those of the party and sent emails with malicious links and fake login pages designed to lure campaign staffers to click a link or divulge their usernames and passwords. Simultaneously with the phishing attacks, the Russian media attacked the Macron campaign with fake news.[59] As part of the Russia-linked influence campaign, intelligence agents created bogus Facebook personas and accounts that spread disinformation. In addition, agents used bots to amplify the messaging and rhetoric around the Macron leaks, and the Twitter campaign #MacronLeaks reached forty-seven thousand tweets in just over three hours.[60] Far-right-wing activists in the United States, who supported Marine Le Pen, the primary opposing candidate, also spread the hashtag. Within three and a half hours, the document dump was viewed by millions.

While mindful of what happened in the American presidential campaign, the technology team for En Marche decided to make it hard for the Russians. They developed "unorthodox methods to confuse detected attackers."[61] One of their policies was "to flood [fake site forms] with multiple passwords and logins, true ones, false ones, so the people behind them [the attacks] use up a lot of time trying to figure them out."[62] In a further attempt to slow down intruders, they created false email accounts and filled them with phony documents. Some of those false emails constituted the hacker dump, along with authentic and phony documents fabricated by the hackers.[63] The deception technique served to craft a situation in which the public would doubt the authenticity of the data.[64] In addition, French authorities tried to contain the fallout from the hack a day before the vote. The electoral commission told the public and the media that the dumped files were probably laced with fake documents and warned that sharing and publishing information on the files' contents could lead to criminal penalties.[65] The government's twenty-four-hour blackout rule for the media also helped to contain the spread of the leaks. Despite the influence campaign, Emmanuel Macron received 65 percent of the vote to decisively win the election over Le Pen.[66]

The National Cybersecurity Agency of France declined to name Russia despite similarities between the hackers of the Macron campaign and Pawn Storm,[67] while Macron's campaign claimed that "hundreds if not thousands of attacks" on its systems "originated from inside Russia or its vicinity."[68] Although public evidence could not definitively prove Russia's involvement, NSA director Michael Rogers suggested to Congress that the agency pinned at least some of the electoral interference on Russia. When Senator McCain asked Rogers, "Have you seen any reduction in Russian behavior?" Rogers answered flatly "No, I do not."[69] Rogers's statement dispelled any doubt that Russian cyber operations had continued to interfere in the electoral process of democratic states, despite the multitude of US government responses to the hacks and leaks in the 2016 presidential election.

Name and Shame

The United States continues to use its "name-and-shame" strategy in an attempt to hold the Russian government and its proxies accountable for their cyber operations.[70] Russia has been amused by the attention but not deterred in its undesired actions. After public proclamations in October 2016 that Russia had interfered in the US presidential election, the Kremlin simply called the allegations "nonsense."[71] Foreign Minister Sergei Lavrov went on to say it was flattering but a baseless accusation, without "a single fact, a single proof."[72] Despite paltry attempts by the US administration to change the Russians' behavior, they have continued their destabilizing cyber operations in the United States, in Europe, and particularly in Ukraine. In February 2018, the United States tried the name-and-shame strategy once again in publicly blaming the Russian military for unleashing the NotPetya destructive wiper worm that spread across the world.[73] The White House press secretary, Sarah Huckabee Sanders, issued a terse statement that NotPetya was "a reckless and indiscriminate cyber-attack that will be met with international consequences,"[74] although she did not announce what those "international consequences" would consist of. The use of instruments of national power have been insufficient to convince Russian leaders that their cyber operations are not worth the cost.

Economic Sanctions

In April 2015, President Obama gave the country "a new tool to combat the most significant cyber threats to our national security, foreign policy, or economy."[75] He signed an executive order that "authorizes the Secretary of the

Treasury, in consultation with the Attorney General and the Secretary of State, to impose sanctions on those individuals and entities that he determines to be responsible for or complicit in malicious cyber-enabled activities."[76] The order would block the property and interests in property and suspend the entry into the United States of responsible persons.[77] Michael Daniel, the cybersecurity coordinator, said, "this will enable us to have a new way of both deterring and imposing costs on malicious cyber actors."[78] Specifically, the executive order allowed the United States to level sanctions against individuals rather than just their governments or organizations. The threat to impose sanctions on Chinese businesses and individuals before the US-China cyber deal would have marked the first use of the order.[79] Instead, the in-place sanctions tool gave Obama a way to supposedly tell Russia after the election hack "that we mean business."[80] In the summer of 2017, President Donald Trump signed a bill imposing further authority to impose new sanctions on Russia.[81]

In March 2018, the United States issued treasury sanctions on Russian individuals and entities for the NotPetya attack and other malicious cyberattacks.[82] The sanctions targeted cyber actors operating on behalf of the Russian government, including the GRU. The sanctions cite the GRU as "directly responsible for the NotPetya cyber-attack in 2017."[83] The sanctions also designated three entities as involved in interference in the 2016 US elections, specifically the Internet Research Agency, Concord Management and Consulting, Concord Catering, and thirteen individuals. Treasury Secretary Steven Mnuchin touted that the "administration is confronting and countering malign Russian cyber activity, including their attempted interference in U.S. elections, destructive cyber-attacks, and intrusions targeting critical infrastructure."[84] The next month, the Treasury Department's Office of Foreign Assets Control designated seven Russian oligarchs, twelve companies they own or control, and seventeen senior Russian government officials, partly for their role in malicious cyber activities. The assets subject to US jurisdiction of the designated individuals and entities were frozen, and US persons were prohibited from dealing with them.[85]

In August 2018, the assistant secretary of the treasury, Marshall Billingslea, testified that the impact of the oligarch designation "was felt within a single day."[86] On April 9, 2018, the combined net worth of Russia's wealthiest twenty-seven people fell by an estimated $16 billion, the Russia Index of stocks fell the most in four years, and the ruble weakened by 3.2 percent.[87] However, the sanctions designations seemed little different from those imposed on Russia by the United States and the EU following its annexation of Crimea in 2014. Yet this time the markets for Russian banks and corporations turned against them, for the United States had made clear that foreign persons were also covered by the designations if they "knowingly facilitate significant transactions, including deceptive or structured transactions, for or on behalf of any person subject to US sanctions."[88] Nonetheless, Billingslea pointed out in testimony that "the size of the Russian economy and its deep integration into the global economy and financial system present a unique challenge."[89] This deep integration is seen in the Trump administration's notification to Congress in December 2018 of its intent to lift sanctions on two of the Russian firms, including Rusal, the second-largest producer and supplier of aluminum in the world.[90]

In the notification, Andrea M. Gacki, the director of the Office of Foreign Assets Control, states that the designation of Rusal "was felt immediately in global aluminum markets. The price of aluminum soared . . . and Rusal subsidiaries in the United States, Ireland, Sweden, Jamaica, Guinea, and elsewhere faced imminent closure."[91] Gacki did say that Rusal had made "significant restructuring and corporate governance changes" and that influential oligarch Oleg V. Deripaska, now severed from control of Rusal, would remain on the sanctions list and his property blocked as required under law. Nonetheless, the move watered down the most impactful targeted sanctions actions ever imposed on Moscow.[92] The Treasury Department decision drew criticism from Democrats that the Trump administration was sending the "wrong signal to Moscow about its conduct toward its neighbors and the United States."[93] The Democratic-controlled House symbolically voted against the relief, while the Republican-controlled Senate voted to proceed.[94] The Trump administration signal only bolsters President Putin's belief that other nations are wrong to regard Russia as a threat, and that mistaken concept can end if they see that the economic sanctions the West has put on Russia do not serve their interests.[95] Putin emphasized that the methods of pressure used by other countries "are ineffective, counterproductive and harmful to all."[96] Although the Department of the Treasury designations had an immediate financial impact, the West's sanctions have morphed into a years-long war of attrition Putin can win.

An array of sanctions by the EU, the United States, Canada, Australia, and others over Ukraine and the downing there of Malaysia Airlines flight MH-17A have hurt the Russian currency and constrained flows of capital. The exchange rate of the ruble depreciated 50 percent against the US dollar from 2014 to 2016, which reduced imports of goods.[97] Likewise, foreign bank lending and gross debt decreased some $210 billion from 2013 to 2017 along with declines in inward foreign direct investment.[98] The Russian GDP contracted from 2014 to 2016, but growth resumed in 2017 and, buoyed by rising oil prices, grew modestly by 1.8 percent in 2018.[99] President Putin has responded to economic pressure by prioritizing stability over growth and stockpiling recent budget surpluses of billions of dollars into the National Welfare Fund and the Central Bank. With low unemployment and inflation under control, it is far from certain that tough economic measures will "provoke a crisis severe enough to have a serious impact on Russian politics."[100]

If anything, the political system is the reason why sanctions are not stopping Russian aggression. President Putin gives elites access to rents and appeals to personal popularity to keep his position at the head of the system.[101] The elites might be unhappy with the penalties but do not contest Putin's foreign policy. The price for challenges could include withdrawal of state support for their companies or corruption investigations. Although some sanctions have meant to split the elites from the Kremlin, instead they have pushed them closer to the Russian government for loans to pay off Western creditors.[102] Furthermore, as noted by Ruslan Pukhov, at the Moscow-based Centre for Analysis of Strategies and Technologies, "it is the general public opinion in Russia that even if Moscow were to capitulate on all key foreign policy fronts, there would be no tangible easing of U.S. sanctions."[103] Therefore, the Russian public appears determined to endure a long-term confrontation until the West grows weary and normalization occurs without relinquishing key holdings, such as Crimea.

Legal Indictments

The Department of Justice issues indictments to charge individuals, regardless of state affiliation, for violations of criminal code. Indictments are meant to impose costs for undesired behavior through incarceration. In July 2018, the grand jury for the District of Columbia charged the GRU for conspiracy to commit an offense against the United States. Specifically, the GRU had multiple units engaged in large-scale cyber operations to interfere with the 2016 US presidential election. In total, eleven GRU officers knowingly and intentionally conspired to gain unauthorized access (to hack) into the computers of US persons involved in the election, steal documents, and stage releases.[104] The grand jury had also charged the IRA in February 2018 for conspiracy to defraud the United States. Specifically, the IRA had multiple individuals working in various capacities to carry out interference operations targeting the United States. The thirteen defendants knowingly and intentionally conspired to create false US personas, steal real US identities, and operate divisive social media pages and groups for the purposes of interfering in the 2016 US presidential election.[105] Both indictments were the result of Special Counsel Robert Mueller's investigation into Russian interference in the 2016 presidential election.

The reaction to Russian indictments for meddling in the 2016 US election was swift and stunning on both sides of the world. In the United States, House Speaker Paul Ryan said, "These Russians engaged in a sinister and systematic attack on our political system,"[106] while Republican senator Ben Sasse stated, "Mueller just put Moscow on notice."[107] However, Russian businessman Yevgeny Prigozhin, on the first indictment list, said, "The Americans are very emotional people, they see what they want to see."[108] President Putin just smirked and brushed off a copy of the July indictment during an interview with Fox

News Channel host Chris Wallace. Putin even laughed as Wallace attempted to explain the contents of the indictment. The Russian president denied all allegations and stated that "Russia, as a state, has never interfered with the internal affairs of the United States, let alone its elections."[109] It is obvious that Russia would never cooperate with the United States to bring the GRU and IRA defendants to justice. In fact, when Alexsey Belan, one of the FBI's most wanted criminals, was indicted for leading a devastating cyber hack of Yahoo, Russia, instead of responding to requests for law enforcement cooperation, signed him up as an intelligence asset.[110] Russia has also obstructed efforts at prosecution. In recent years, Moscow convinced a Cypriot court to return a hacker wanted by the United States for hacking an American Fortune 100 company and argued in Greece to bring home a hacker indicted by the United States for a $4 billion bitcoin exchange scheme.[111]

It is true that Russian actors have been successfully indicted and extradited to the United States for cyber crimes. Roman Seleznev, the son of a member of Russia's parliament, was apprehended in 2014 on vacation in the Maldives.[112] He was convicted on thirty-eight counts by a Seattle jury in 2017 and sentenced to twenty-seven years in prison.[113] The chances are miniscule that GRU and IRA defendants would wander outside of Russia, especially to locations that have a mutual legal assistance treaty with the United States. Nonetheless, the United States appears intent on pressing forward with more frequent use of indictments against state-sponsored hackers, especially those penetrating critical infrastructure.[114] Yet the risk of retribution in kind does exist. Jake Williams, who worked in the elite hacking unit Tailored Access Operations at the NSA, has "expressed concern that prosecuting foreign hackers could put him and others at risk of arrest overseas."[115] Ever since the Shadow Brokers called out and doxed ex-NSA hackers (published private information about them on the Internet), including him, Williams has refused to take jobs overseas. Robert Lee, who worked at Cyber Command, has stated, "It's a horrible and dangerous precedent" for the US government to charge other government's hackers.[116] Dave Aitel, a former NSA member, explained that it is more than likely Russia "will indict somebody just to be a tit for tat kind of operation" and "we do not have the answer for what happens when they do that."[117]

Coercive Diplomacy

Patrick Morgan has stated that deterrence is "one aspect of what is called coercive diplomacy in which a government uses force or threats to get what it wants."[118] The mechanisms of economic sanctions and legal indictments serve as part of a coercive diplomacy toolkit. For example, the US-China cyber deal came after weeks of intense US negotiations and maneuvers with senior

Chinese officials in both Beijing and Washington. The United States had issued indictments a year earlier against five Chinese hackers affiliated with a military unit for a cyber campaign against American businesses, including US Steel and Westinghouse Electric.[119] Just a few weeks before the visit to Washington by President Xi, the Obama administration developed a package of potential sanctions against Chinese companies and individuals who benefit from the cyber-enabled theft of American trade secrets by the government.[120] US officials decided they would confront China during the state visit before further action. While recognizing the two countries have bolstered cooperation in many areas, President Obama "would make clear that China must change its practices in other, more sensitive areas, particularly state-sponsored, cyber-enabled economic espionage."[121]

In a direct comparison to President Obama, President Trump insisted at a cabinet meeting that "there has never been a president as tough on Russia as I have been."[122] He proceeded to outline sanctions and other ways, including closure of diplomatic properties, that he has used to punish Russia.[123] Trump had even approved the supply of Javelin antitank missiles to Ukraine to counter Russian aggression, which Obama had not.[124] Yet despite a tough stance, Trump faced criticism for failing to publicly confront Russian president Putin at a joint press conference after their summit meeting in Helsinki in July 2018. In response to a press question about whether Trump believes that Russia meddled in the US presidential election, he stated, "My people came to me, Dan Coats came to me and some others, they said they think it's Russia. I have President Putin: he just said it's not Russia. I will say this: I don't see any reason why it would be."[125] This remarkable statement was made after holding a two-hour one-on-one meeting with Putin, which happened only days after the aforementioned indictment of Russians for hacking the Democratic Party campaign computers. Senate Foreign Relations Committee chairman Bob Corker said that "the president's comments made us look as a nation more like a pushover."[126]

The imperative in coercive diplomacy is to maintain pressure on the opponent. Lawrence Freedman once said deterrence "is a sub-set of the study of coercion, which can also include threats designed to compel action from others."[127] President Trump did not compel a change in behavior in his stunning answer at Helsinki. House Speaker Paul Ryan was quick to remark that "the president must appreciate that Russia is not our ally."[128] The next day, Trump recanted in saying he misspoke by saying "'would' instead of 'wouldn't' . . . sort of a double negative."[129] That really did not matter, as Trump had emboldened the Russian president by stating that "Putin was extremely strong and powerful in his denial [of election interference] today."[130] It was no surprise that Russian's political and media establishment heralded the summit as a victory for Putin. Famed opinion columnist Thomas Friedman stated that Trump missed that the point of the meeting was not to develop an extraordinary relationship but to deter a "Russia that has been increasingly reckless and destabilizing."[131] On the contrary, Trump seemed to believe his relationship with Putin makes a difference, by answering no to the reporter's blunt question, "Is Russia still targeting the U.S., Mr. President?"[132]

Less than a year later, it was Helsinki all over again. In May 2019, President Trump spoke with President Putin by phone about the end of Special Counsel Mueller's investigation. Two weeks previously, Mueller had asserted on the very first page of his report that "the Russian government interfered in the 2016 presidential election in sweeping and systematic fashion."[133] Yet it appears that Trump did not bother to condemn Putin or complain about the interference. The only account given to reporters was "We discussed it. He actually sort of smiled when he said something to the effect that it started off as a mountain and it ended up being a mouse," according to Trump, "But he knew that, because he knew there was no collusion whatsoever."[134] When asked by a reporter "Did you tell him not to meddle in the next election?" Trump answered, "We didn't discuss that."[135] House Intelligence Committee chairman Adam Schiff was quick to criticize Trump: "Once again, he betrays our national security and for what? Nothing more than his own vanity and delusion."[136] If nothing more, the phone call was another missed opportunity to apply coercive diplomacy.

Military Action

One of three cyber missions for the Department of Defense is to "defend the nation against cyberattacks of significant consequence."[137] In early 2018, the Pentagon quietly empowered US Cyber Command to "take a far more aggressive approach to defending the nation against cyberattacks."[138] According to military and intelligence officials, when the Pentagon elevated the command's status to a unified combatant command, it opened the door for raids on foreign networks.[139] This new authority enabled the latest command vision for US Cyber Command to "pursue attackers across networks and systems" and "contest dangerous adversary activity before it impairs our national power."[140] Pushing "defenses forward" extends the command's reach to "expose adversaries' weaknesses, learn their intentions and capabilities, and counter attacks close to their origins."[141] However, operating forward in adversary networks also raises the risk of state-on-state conflict if discovered. In addition, taking action against an adversary "often requires surreptitiously operating in the networks of an ally, like Germany—a problem that often gave the Obama administration pause."[142] These types of complicating factors in the use of offensive operations were tempered by the Obama administration through deliberate, often slow, approval decisions made by an extensive interagency process.

The Trump administration dismantled this interagency process, starting with the elimination of the position of White House cyber coordinator, who had led a team of senior directors who worked with agencies to develop a unified strategy for cyber issues, such as digital deterrence.[143] The task was instead assigned to two National Security Council senior directors. Michael Daniel, who served as the cyber coordinator under President Obama, believes the change communicated the wrong signal, stating, "If anything, our enemies are only going to do more, not less."[144] Next, the White House rescinded a classified Obama-era memorandum, known as Presidential Policy Directive (PPD) 20, that articulated when the government could deploy cyber weapons against its adversaries.[145] The old rules were replaced by classified guidance, titled National Security Presidential Memorandum 13, which is intended to give the DOD more flexibility to launch offensive operations without first vetting decisions through an elaborate interagency process. John Bolton, then Trump's national security adviser, proclaimed, "Our hands are not tied as they were in the Obama administration."[146] Under the previous rules, cyber operations that resulted in "significant consequences" required presidential approval.[147]

In addition, a new provision in the National Defense Authorization Act cleared the way for military action in cyberspace that does not rise to acts of war, categorizing them as "traditional military activity."[148] US Cyber Command wasted no time in employing its new authority. Days before the 2018 midterm elections, it targeted Russian trolls to try to deter them from spreading disinformation. Using emails, pop-ups, texts, and direct messages, the command told them that "American operatives have identified them and are tracking their work."[149] Officials said the Russians were not directly threatened but should know they could be indicted or targeted with sanctions. These warnings to prevent Russian information warfare appeared limited, most likely to keep the Kremlin from escalating cyber operations in response. The full range of offensive selections span cyber operations that "manipulate, deny, disrupt, degrade, or destroy targeted computers, information systems or networks."[150] Therefore, the risk of escalation from increased US action in foreign networks through retaliatory strikes against American energy, banks, or dams is considerable. Regarding a forward-defense approach, Jason Healy, at Columbia University, has said, "Clearly, what we have been doing so far isn't working. But you want to think through the consequences carefully."[151] For instance, Dave Weinstein, a cybersecurity policy fellow at New America, pointed out that if US Cyber Command launched malware, "would the Kremlin stop hacking American politicians and remove their implants in American critical infrastructure? Or would the code be reverse-engineered and used against American interests?"[152] Fear of the latter is just one factor that engenders a cautious approach to fully engaging Russia in cyberspace.

Conclusion

Lt. Gen. Vincent Stewart, deputy commander of US Cyber Command, said during a conference keynote presentation in November 2018 that "adversaries have discovered that they can't compete with the U.S. kinetically, meaning they would lose a battle with missiles or tanks, but they can successfully engage below the level of conflict through cyber."[153] Likewise, Adm. Michael Rogers, the former commander of US Cyber Command, agreed in Senate testimony in February 2018 that many cyberattacks occur "outside the context of armed conflict, but cumulatively accrue strategic gains to our adversaries."[154] He argued the United States must "persistently engage and contest cyber attacks, in order to reset adversary expectations about our behavior and commitment."[155] General Stewart described this approach as persistent engagement, which does not allow adversaries to move against the United States in cyberspace without facing consequences. Stewart reiterated, "We're going to impose cost on their behavior and make sure that we are going to shape norms and behavior in this space."[156]

The 2018 DOD Cyber Strategy states the department's "focus will be on the States that can pose strategic threats to US prosperity and security, particularly China and Russia."[157] The DOD will "defend forward to disrupt or halt malicious cyber activity at its source, including activity that falls below the level of armed conflict," as a primary way to compete and deter in cyberspace.[158] Furthermore, as part of strategic competition in cyberspace, the DOD "seeks to preempt, defeat, or deter malicious cyber activity targeting U.S. critical infrastructure that could cause a significant cyber incident."[159] Professors Brandon Valeriano and Benjamin Jensen contend that the US Cyber Command approach "increasingly sees preemption as the only viable path to security."[160] The command vision infers that US cyber operations will compete more effectively beneath the threshold of armed conflict to "improve the security and stability of cyberspace."[161] Yet Valeriano and Jensen argue that "an offensively postured cyber policy is dangerous, counterproductive, and undermines norms in cyberspace." They argue for the United States to adopt "a defensive posture consisting of limited cyber operations aimed at restraining rivals and avoiding escalation." This posture should "focus on protective measures to make U.S. systems less vulnerable," using defensive hardening and deception techniques, like what the French used to confuse Russian hackers inside the Macron campaign network.[162]

Furthermore, Peter Cooper, a senior fellow at the Atlantic Council, points out that "deterrence using a single domain is rarely effective," primarily due to the difficulty in signaling capabilities in the cyber domain.[163] Instead, Cooper opines that "effective deterrence requires a whole-of-government approach ideally with cooperation from other countries."[164] The United States continues to employ the whole-of-government approach in a name-and-shame attempt to deter Russian cyber operations. Every instrument of national power (economic sanctions, coercive diplomacy, law enforcement, and military action) has been used in some fashion against Russia. Yet, since the initial US response to interference in the 2016 presidential election, Russia has conducted a series of cyber operations to penetrate or damage critical infrastructure and influence or disrupt democratic societies. Even the latest warnings by US Cyber Command to Russian operatives did not prevent disinformation on social media during the 2018 US midterm elections.[165] Obviously the Russian operatives did not fear potential sanctions or indictments. While the United States has gotten better at attributing the source of cyber operations, its responses have failed to keep pace.[166] The latest Department of Defense Cyber Strategy communicates resolve through use of forward-defense capability, in an attempt to rebuild eroded credibility. However, the United States has failed so far to reintroduce the belief in Russia that malicious cyber operations will not be tolerated. Instead, Russia continues to conduct cyber operations without fear of reprisal.[167]

Notes

1. Andrew Blake, "Foreign Hackers Don't Fear Retaliation, Trump's Nominee for NSA Director Warns," *Washington Times*, March 2, 2018.
2. Blake.
3. Steve Turnham, "NSA Nominee Says Russian Adversaries Do Not Fear Us,'" ABC News, March 1, 2018.
4. Aaron Hughes, Statement before the House of Representatives Committee on Oversight and Government Reform, Information Technology and National Security Subcommittee, July 13, 2016, 2.
5. Donald Trump, *National Cyber Strategy of the United States of America* (Washington, DC: White House, September 2018), 21.
6. Trump, 21.
7. Trump, 21.
8. Scott Jasper, "U.S. Strategic Cyber Deterrence Options" (PhD thesis, University of Reading, August 2017), 152–59.
9. Thomas Schelling, *Arms and Influence* (New Haven, CT: Yale University Press, 1966), 71.
10. DOD, *Deterrence Operations Joint Operating Concept*, version 2.0 (Offutt Air Force Base, NE: US Strategic Command, December 2006), 8.
11. DOD, 8.
12. Jasper, *Strategic Cyber Deterrence*, 60.
13. Joint Chiefs of Staff, *Joint Operations*, Joint Publication 3-0 (January 2017), xxii.
14. Peter Roberts and Andrew Hardie, *The Validity of Deterrence in the Twenty-First Century*, occasional paper (London: Royal United Services Institute, August 2015), 5–9.
15. Jasper, *Strategic Cyber Deterrence*, 61.
16. Lawrence Freedman, *Deterrence* (Cambridge: Polity Press, 2004), 6.

17. Patrick M. Morgan, *Deterrence Now* (Cambridge: Cambridge University Press, 2003), 1.

18. Joint Chiefs of Staff, *Joint Operation Planning*, Joint Publication 5-0 (August 11, 2011), E-2.

19. Glenn H. Snyder, *Deterrence and Defense: Toward a Theory of National Security* (Princeton, NJ: Princeton University Press, 1961), 11.

20. Patrick M. Morgan, "Taking the Long View of Deterrence," *Journal of Strategic Studies* 28, no. 5 (October 2005): 751–52.

21. Robert Jervis, "Deterrence and Perception," *International Security* 7, no. 3 (Winter 1982/83): 3.

22. Jervis, 4.

23. Michael Mandelbaum, "It's the Deterrence, Stupid," *American Interest*, July 30, 2015.

24. Roberts and Hardie, "Validity of Deterrence," 26.

25. Keren Yarhi-Milo, "In the Eye of the Beholder," *International Security* 38, no. 1 (Summer 2013): 9.

26. Thomas Schelling, *The Strategy of Conflict* (Cambridge, MA: Harvard University Press, 1960), 15.

27. Freedman, *Deterrence*, 116.

28. Aaron F. Brantly, "The Cyber Deterrence Problem," *10th International Conference on Cyber Conflict* (Tallinn: NATO CCD COE Publications, 2018), 31.

29. Kamal T. Jabbour and E. Paul Ratazzi, "Deterrence in Cyberspace," *Thinking about Deterrence* (Montgomery, AL: Air University Press, 2013), 42–43.

30. Dorothy E. Denning, "Rethinking the Cyber Domain and Deterrence," *Joint Force Quarterly*, no. 77 (Second Quarter, 2015): 8–12.

31. Brad D. Williams, "Meet the Scholar Challenging the Cyber Deterrence Paradigm," Fifth Domain, July 19, 2017.

32. Martin C. Libicki, "Expectations of Cyber Deterrence," *Strategic Studies Quarterly* (Winter 2018): 54.

33. Dmitri Alperovitch, "Bears in the Midst: Intrusion into the Democratic National Committee," CrowdStrike (blog), June 15, 2016.

34. Carol Morello, "State Department Shuts Down Its E-mail System amid Concerns about Hacking," *Washington Post*, November 17, 2014.

35. Evan Perez and Shimon Prokupecz, "How the U.S. Thinks Russians Hacked the White House," CNN, April 8, 2015.

36. David Sanger, "Why Hackers Aren't Afraid of Us," *New York Times*, June 16, 2018.

37. Shane Harris, "Obama to Putin: Stop Hacking Me," Daily Beast, April 8, 2015.

38. Sanger, "Why Hackers Aren't Afraid of Us."

39. Director of National Intelligence, "Joint DHS and ODNI Election Security Statement," press release, October 7, 2016, 1.

40. Director of National Intelligence.

41. Ellen Nakashima, "U.S. Government Officially Accuses Russia of Hacking Campaign to Interfere with Elections," *Washington Post*, October 7, 2016.

42. "Obama Says US Needs to Respond to Russian Cyberattacks—'And We Will,'" Fox News, December 15, 2016.

43. David E. Sanger, "Obama Confronts Complexity of Using a Mighty Cyberarsenal against Russia," *New York Times*, December 17, 2016.

44. Sanger.

45. Michael Isikoff and David Corn, *Russian Roulette: The Inside Story of Putin's War on America and the Election of Donald Trump* (New York: Hachette, 2018).

46. David E. Sanger and Nicole Perlroth, "What Options Does the U.S. Have after Accusing Russia of Hacks?," *New York Times*, October 8, 2016.

47. Adam Segal, "After Attributing a Cyberattack to Russia, the Most Likely Response Is Non Cyber," Net Politics, October 10, 2016.

48. White House, Office of the Press Secretary, "Statement by the President on Actions in Response to Russian Malicious Cyber Activity and Harassment," December 29, 2016.

49. White House, Office of the Press Secretary, "Actions in Response to Russian Malicious Cyber Activity and Harassment," fact sheet, December 29, 2016.

50. Greg Miller, Ellen Nakashima, and Adam Entous, "Obama's Secret Struggle to Punish Russia for Putin's Election Assault," *Washington Post*, June 23, 2017.

51. Carol E. Lee and Paul Sonne, "Obama Sanctions Russia, Expels 35," *Wall Street Journal*, December 30, 2016.

52. Miller, Nakashima, and Entous, "Obama's Secret Struggle."

53. White House, "Statement by the President."

54. James Marson, "Putin Says He Won't Retaliate," *Wall Street Journal*, December 31, 2016.

55. United States v. Michael T. Flynn, US District Court, District of Columbia, criminal complaint, December 1, 2017, 2.

56. Paul Sonne, "U.S. Warned France That Russia Was Meddling in Election, NSA Director Says," *Wall Street Journal*, May 9, 2017.

57. Laura Galante and Shaun Ee, "Defining Russian Election Interference: An Analysis of Select 2014 to 2018 Cyber Enabled Incidents," issue brief, Atlantic Council, September 2018, 11.

58. Matthew Dalton, William Horobin, and Sam Schechner, "Emmanuel Macron Campaign Says Victim of 'Massive Hacking,'" *Wall Street Journal*, May 6, 2017.

59. Adam Nossiter, David E. Sanger, and Nicole Perlroth, "Hackers Came, but the French Were Prepared," *New York Times*, May 10, 2017.

60. Alina Polyakova and Spencer P. Boyer, "The Future of Political Warfare: Russia, the West, and the Coming Age of Global Digital Competition," Brookings Institution, Robert Bosch Foundation Transatlantic Initiative, March 2018, 5–6.

61. Erik Brattberg and Tim Maurer, "Russian Election Interference: Europe's Counter to Fake News and Cyber Attacks," Carnegie Endowment for International Peace, May 23, 2018, 6.

62. Christopher Dickey, "Fighting Back against Putin's Hackers," Daily Beast, April 25, 2017.

63. Nossiter, Sanger, and Perlroth, "Hackers Came."

64. Teri Robinson, "Macron's Campaign Proactive after Hack, Mitigated Damage," *SC Magazine*, May 8, 2017.

65. Matthew Dalton and Alan Cullison, "France Rushes to Limit Impact of Macron Campaign Hack," *Wall Street Journal*, May 6, 2017.

66. Yasmeen Serhan, "Macron's Win: The Center Holds Firm in France," *The Atlantic*, May 7, 2017.

67. Brattberg and Maurer, "Russian Election Interference," 7.

68. Michel Rose and Eric Auchard, "Macron Campaign Confirms Phishing Attempts, Says No Data Stolen," Reuters, April 26, 2017.

69. Andy Greenberg, "The NSA Confirms It: Russia Hacked French Election 'Infrastructure,'" *Wired*, May 9, 2017.

70. FBI, "State-Sponsored Cyber Theft: Nine Iranians Charged in Massive Hacking Campaign on Behalf of Iran Government," March 23, 2018.

71. Dmitry Solovyov, "Moscow Says U.S. Cyber Attack Claims Fan 'Anti-Russian Hysteria,'" Reuters, October 8, 2016.

72. Nicole Gaouette and Elise Labott, "Russia, US Move Past Cold War to Unpredictable Confrontation," CNN, October 12, 2016.
73. Sean Gallagher, "In Terse Statement, White House Blames Russia for NotPetya Worm," Ars Technica, Tech-Policy (blog), February 15, 2018.
74. Gallagher.
75. Michael Daniel, "Our Latest Tool to Combat Cyber Attacks: What You Need to Know," White House, April 1, 2015.
76. Daniel.
77. White House, Office of the Press Secretary, "Blocking the Property of Certain Persons Engaging in Significant Malicious Cyber-Enabled Activities," executive order, April 1, 2015.
78. Aaron Boyd, "Obama: Cyberattacks Continue to Be National Emergency," *Federal Times*, March 30, 2016.
79. Ellen Nakashima, "U.S. Won't Impose Sanctions on Chinese Companies before Xi Visit," *Washington Post*, September 14, 2015.
80. Ellen Nakashima, "Hacked U.S. Companies Have More Options, Departing Cybersecurity Official Says," *Washington Post*, March 2, 2016.
81. Abby Phillip, "Trump Signs 'Seriously Flawed' Bill Imposing New Sanctions on Russia," *Washington Post*, August 2, 2017.
82. Department of the Treasury, "Treasury Sanctions Russian Cyber Actors for Interference with the 2016 U.S. Elections and Malicious Cyber-Attacks," press release, March 15, 2018.
83. Department of the Treasury.
84. Department of the Treasury.
85. Department of the Treasury, "Treasury Designates Russian Oligarchs, Officials, and Entities in Response to Worldwide Malign Activity," press release, April 6, 2018.
86. Marshall Billingslea, Statement before the US Senate Committee on Foreign Relations, August 21, 2018, 2.
87. Alexander Sazonov, Devon Pendleton, and Jack Witzig, "Russia's Richest Lose $16 Billion over Latest U.S. Sanctions," Bloomberg News, April 9, 2018.
88. Tom Keatinge, "This Time Sanctions on Russia Are Having the Desired Effect," *Financial Times*, April 13, 2018.
89. Marshall Billingslea, Statement before Committee, 3.
90. Donna Borak, "Treasury Plans to Lift Sanctions on Russian Aluminum Giant Rusal," CNN Business, December 19, 2018.
91. Department of the Treasury, Letter to the Honorable Mitch McConnell, Majority Leader of the US Senate, December 19, 2018.
92. Polina Devitt, "Aluminum Plunges, Rusal Shares Soar as U.S. to Lift Sanctions," Reuters, December 19, 2018.
93. Kenneth P. Vogel, "Trump Administration to Lift Sanctions on Russian Oligarch's Companies," *New York Times*, December 19, 2018.
94. Patricia Zengerle, "U.S. House Backs Sanctions on Russia's Rusal in Symbolic Vote," Reuters, January 17, 2019.
95. Nataliya Vasilyeva and Jim Heintz, "Putin Says Russian Military Not Building Long-Term in Syria," Associated Press, June 7, 2018.
96. Vasilyeva and Heintz.
97. Iikka Korhonen, Heli Simola, and Laura Solanko, *Sanctions, Counter-sanctions and Russia: Effects on Economy, Trade and Finance*, Policy Brief 2018 no. 4 (Helsinki: Bank of Finland, Institute for Economies in Transition, May 30, 2018), 11.

98. Korhonen, Simola, and Solanko, 19–21.

99. Anna Andrianova and Ilya Arkhipov, "Russian Economy Feels Impact of U.S. Sanctions," *The Columbian*, August 23, 2018.

100. Anton Troianovski, "Putin Manages to Defang Sanctions, but at Long-Term Cost," *Washington Post*, August 23, 2018.

101. Thomas Wonder, "Why Russian Domestic Politics Make U.S. Sanctions Less Effective," War on the Rocks, December 7, 2018.

102. Thomas Grove and Alan Cullison, "U.S. Sanctions Tighten Putin's Circle, Extend Kremlin's Reach," *Wall Street Journal*, September 11, 2019.

103. Ruslan Pukhov, "Putin: A Leader Made for the Russian Federation," *Defense News*, December 10, 2018, 27.

104. US District Court, criminal indictment, United States of America v. Viktor Borisovich Netyksho et al., received July 13, 2018, 1–2.

105. US District Court, criminal indictment, United States of America v. Internet Research Agency LLC et al., filed February 16, 2018, 1–2.

106. "Reactions to Russian Indictments in 2016 U.S. Election, Meddling Probe," Reuters, February 16, 2018.

107. "Reactions to Russian Indictments."

108. "Reactions to Russian Indictments."

109. David Choi, "Fox News' Chris Wallace Tried to Hand Vladimir Putin a Copy of Mueller's Latest Indictment," Fox News, July 17, 2018.

110. John P. Carlin, "Putin Is Running a Destructive Cybercrime Syndicate out of Russia," *New York Times*, July 16, 2018.

111. Carlin.

112. Kate O'Keefe and Jacob Gershman, "Russian Convicted in Hacking Case," *Wall Street Journal*, August 26, 2016.

113. Kelly Sheridan, "Inside the Investigation and Trial of Roman Seleznev," Dark Reading, July 27, 2017.

114. Rebecca Smith, "U.S. Officials Push New Penalties for Hackers of Electrical Grid," *Wall Street Journal*, August 5, 2018.

115. Luca D'Urbino, "America's Government Is Putting Foreign Cyber-Spies in the Dock," *The Economist*, September 13, 2018.

116. Lorenzo Franceschi-Bicchierai, "Ex-NSA Hackers Worry China and Russia Will Try to Arrest Them," Motherboard, December 1, 2017.

117. Franceschi-Bicchierai.

118. Patrick M. Morgan, *International Security: Problems and Solutions* (Washington, DC: CQ Press, 2006), 77.

119. US District Court, criminal indictment no. 14-118, filed May 1, 2014, 1–48.

120. Ellen Nakashima, "U.S. Developing Sanctions against China over Cyberthefts," *Washington Post*, August 30, 2015.

121. Damian Paletta, "Obama to Press Chinese President Xi Jimping on Cyberattacks, Human Rights, Advisor Says," *Wall Street Journal*, September 21, 2015.

122. Dave Boyer, "Trump Says He's Been Tougher on Russia than Any Other President," *Washington Times*, July 18, 2018.

123. Jen Kerns, "President Trump Is Tougher on Russia in 18 Months than Obama in Eight Years," *The Hill*, July 16, 2018.

124. Peter J. Marzalik and Aric Toler, "Lethal Weapons to Ukraine: A Primer," Atlantic Council, January 26, 2018.

125. Chris Cillizza, "The 21 Most Disturbing Lines from Donald Trump's Press Conference with Vladimir Putin," CNN, July 17, 2018.

126. Matthew Nussbaum, "Trump Publicly Sides with Putin on Election Interference," *Politico*, July 16, 2018.

127. Lawrence Freedman, "Deterrence: A Reply," *Journal of Strategic Studies* 28, no. 5 (October 2005): 789–90.

128. Lauren Fox, "Top Republications in Congress Break with Trump over Putin Comments," CNN, July 16, 2018.

129. Brooke Singman, "Trump Says He Misspoke on Russian Meddling during Press Conference, Accepts US Intel Findings," Fox News, July 17, 2018.

130. Sophie Tatum, "Putin Denies Election Attack but Justifies DNC Hack Because 'It Is True,'" CNN, July 16, 2018.

131. Thomas L. Friedman, "Trump and Putin vs. America," *New York Times*, July 16, 2018.

132. Meg Wagner and Brian Ries, "President Trump Today," CNN, July 19, 2018.

133. Robert S. Mueller III, *Report on the Investigation into Russian Interference in the 2016 Presidential Election*, vol. 1 (Washington, DC: Department of Justice, 2019), 1.

134. Anne Gearan, John Wagner, and Anton Troianovski, "Trump Says He Talked to Putin about 'Russian Hoax' but Not about Ongoing Election Interference," *Washington Post*, May 3, 2019.

135. David A. Graham, "Trump's Surreal Phone Call with Vladimir Putin," *The Atlantic*, May 3, 2019.

136. Jessica Kwong, "Adam Schiff Says Donald Trump 'Betrays Our National Security' after President Discussed 'Russian Hoax' with Putin," *Newsweek*, May 3, 2019.

137. Ash Carter, "The DOD Cyber Strategy," DOD, April 2015, 3.

138. David E. Sanger, "Pentagon Puts Cyberwarriors on the Offensive, Increasing the Risk of Conflict," *New York Times*, June 18, 2018.

139. Katie Lange, "Cybercom Becomes DoD's 10th Unified Command," DoD Live, May 3, 2018.

140. Michael Rogers, "Achieve and Maintain Cyberspace Superiority: Command Vision for U.S. Cyber Command," US Cyber Command, March 2018, 6.

141. Rogers, 6.

142. Sanger, "Pentagon Puts Cyberwarriors on the Offensive."

143. Eric Geller, "White House Eliminates Top Cyber Adviser Post," *Politico*, May 15, 2018.

144. Brian Barrett, "White House Cuts Critical Cybersecurity Role as Threats Loom," *Wired*, May 15, 2018.

145. Dustin Volz, "Trump, Seeking to Relax Rules on U.S. Cyberattacks, Reverses Obama Directive," *Wall Street Journal*, August 15, 2018.

146. Dustin Volz, "Cyberattack Rules Reversed," *Wall Street Journal*, September 21, 2018.

147. Justin Lynch, "Trump Has Scrapped a 2012 Policy on When to Attack in Cyberspace," Fifth Domain, August 16, 2018.

148. Ellen Nakashima, "U.S. Cyber Force Credited with Helping Stop Russia from Undermining Midterms," *Washington Post*, February 14, 2019.

149. Julian E. Barnes, "U.S. Begins First Cyber Operation against Russia Aimed at Protecting Elections," *New York Times*, October 23, 2018.

150. Tom Uren, Bart Hogeveen, and Fergus Hanson, "Defining Offensive Cyber Capabilities," Australian Strategic Policy Institute, September 24, 2018.

151. Sanger, "Pentagon Puts Cyberwarriors on the Offensive."

152. Dave Weinstein, "America Goes on the Cyberoffensive," *Wall Street Journal*, August 29, 2018.

153. Mark Pomerleau, "Is the Defense Department's Entire Vision of Cybersecurity Wrong?," Fifth Domain, November 14, 2018.

154. Michael S. Rogers, Statement before the United States Senate Committee on Armed Services, February 27, 2018, 13.

155. Rogers, 13.

156. Pomerleau, "Defense Department's Vision of Cybersecurity."

157. DOD, "Summary: Department of Defense Cyber Strategy," 1, https://media.defense.gov/2018/Sep/18/2002041658/-1/-1/1/CYBER_STRATEGY_SUMMARY_FINAL.PDF.

158. DOD, 1.

159. DOD, 1.

160. Brandon Valeriano and Benjamin Jensen, *The Myth of the Cyber Offense: The Case for Restraint*, Policy Analysis no. 862 (Washington, DC: Cato Institute, January 15, 2019), 3.

161. Rogers, "Achieve and Maintain Cyberspace Superiority," 6.

162. Valeriano and Jensen, "Myth of the Cyber Offense," 1.

163. Justin Lynch, "Trump Administration Scraps a 2012 Policy on When to Attack in Cyberspace," C4ISR Networks, October 2018, 27.

164. Lynch, 27.

165. Dustin Volz, "No Major Vote Interference Detected," *Wall Street Journal*, November 7, 2018.

166. Sanger, "Why Hackers Aren't Afraid of Us."

167. Kevin Poulsen, "Russian DNC Hackers Launch Fresh Wave of Cyberattacks on U.S.," Daily Beast, January 31, 2019.

PART III
Defensive Solutions

CHAPTER 7

Current Security Strategies

The objective of the deterrence strategy outlined in the 2018 National Cyber Strategy of the United States appears to be imposition of "consequences for irresponsible behavior that harms the United States and our partners."[1] In theory, adversaries are deterred by the threat of retaliation. The question is whether the new US strategy that intends to "punish those who use cyber tools for malicious purposes" is the best way to change their decision-making calculus. Reliance on offensive strategies "that impose swift, costly, and transparent consequences" through cyber and noncyber means is fraught with fears of escalation or retribution. An alternative approach is to focus on instilling a belief in an adversary that the intended action cannot succeed. In theory, adversaries are deterred by denial of benefit. The adoption of a defensive form of cost imposition through cybersecurity strategies has the potential to make the adversary believe that any attack will be futile. The adversary encounters multiple layers of defense that prevent intrusion and detect evasion before exfiltration or other damage is done. However, whether current security strategies can change the perceptions of the Russian actors that cyber operations will not succeed is doubtful given their technical success to date.

The strategy of deterrence by denial is an alternative way to change the decision-making calculus of the adversary by "signaling, or proving, that an attack will fail."[2] Cybersecurity strategies start with ways to manage risks to systems and operations. They use various risk frameworks that structure the selection and implementation of security controls. In a defense-in-depth strategy, an array of security controls and associated solutions are judiciously allocated and deployed to block, detect, and interrupt the adversary at each phase of the cyber kill chain, a series of sequential steps to achieve the objective of the cyber operation. Ideally, security controls are enriched by shared cyber-threat intelligence. This chapter will examine the structures of cybersecurity risk-management frameworks and the advantages of defense-in-depth strategies to improve the security of networks and systems. It will then analyze Russian cyber operations for espionage against US critical infrastructure in the energy sector since at least March 2016. The chapter will finish with an analysis of suggested security measures to prevent similar types of attacks and deny benefit from irresponsible behavior in cyberspace.

Risk Management

Risk is defined as "a measure of the extent to which an entity is threatened by a potential circumstance or event, and typically is a function of: (i) the adverse impact, or magnitude of harm, that would arise if the circumstance or event occurs; and (ii) the likelihood of occurrence."[3] The World Economic Forum identified data fraud and theft and cyberattacks as the fourth and fifth top global risks in terms of likelihood in its 2019 annual report, behind extreme weather, climate change, and natural disasters. A large majority of respondents to their survey "expected increased risks in 2019 of cyber attacks leading to theft of money and data (82%) and disruption of operations (80%)."[4] For evidence that cyberattacks pose risk to critical infrastructure, the report specifically called out a US government statement that hackers had gained access to the control rooms of American utility companies, the case study in this chapter. Likewise, a 2018 study performed by the Ponemon Institute "found that 60% of organizations had suffered two or more business-disrupting cyber events—defined as cyber attacks causing data breaches of significant disruption and downtime to business operations, plant and operational equipment—in the last 24 months."[5] This period includes the previously illuminated NotPetya ransomware attack on Ukraine attributed to Russia, mentioned in the World Economic Forum 2018 report as a notable example of the rising financial impact of cybersecurity breaches. The data points of the Ponemon study reveal that the approaches and tools used by organizations fail to provide the focus and visibility necessary to manage, measure, and reduce cyber risks. The latter are properly termed information system–related security risks, which arise from "the loss of confidentiality, integrity, or availability of information or information systems and reflect the potential adverse impacts to organizational operations, assets, individuals, other organizations and the nations."[6]

The approach taken by the Department of Defense to reduce information system–related security risks is to "implement a multi-tiered cybersecurity risk management process to protect U.S. interests, DoD operational capabilities, and DoD individuals, organizations, and assets . . . as described in the National Institute of Standards and Technology (NIST) Special Publication (SP) 800-39 and Committee on National Security Systems (CNSS) Policy (CNSSP) 22."[7] The second reference document proclaims that the comprehensive process of risk management "requires organizations to frame risk, assess risk, respond to risk once determined, and monitor risk on an ongoing basis."[8] CNSSP 22 expands policy for risk management beyond individuals, organizations, and assets to organizational operations (i.e., mission, functions, and reputation). NIST SP 800-39 describes the four components of the risk-management process. The first, frame risk, establishes a risk context by describing the parameters for which to make risk-based decisions. In order to establish a realistic and credible risk frame, an organization has to identify risk assumptions (on threats, vulnerabilities, consequences or impact, and likelihood of occurrence), risk constraints (on alternatives), risk tolerance (acceptable levels of risk, types of risk, and degree of risk uncertainty), and priorities and trade-offs (in mission or business functions, time frames, and other factors).[9]

The second component of risk assessment moves from assumptions to identification of threats to organizations—vulnerabilities both internal and external of organizations, consequences to organizations if threats exploit vulnerabilities, and the likelihood that this harm will occur. The third component responds to risk. It provides a consistent, organization-wide response by developing alternative courses of action, evaluating them, determining which are appropriate, and implementing them. The types of risk responses that can be implemented are accepting, avoiding, mitigating, sharing, or transferring risk. The final component of monitoring risk serves to verify that response measures are implemented, determine that they are effective, and identify impact of changes to information systems.[10] The risk-management process is employed at multitiered levels, specifically at tier 1, the organizational level; at tier 2, the mission/business process level; and at tier 3, the information system level. The primary means to address the risk frame at the tier 3 level is the Risk Management Framework (RMF), described in NIST SP 800-37.[11]

Risk Management Framework

The RMF provides a "disciplined and structured process for managing security and privacy risk."[12] Its use is mandatory in the United States for the federal government, including the DOD, but can be applied to other fields, such as business, industry, and academia. The RMF addresses these risks from two perspectives: information system and common controls. For the first, an authorization is issued to "operate or use" the system, accepting the security and privacy risks. For the second, an authorization is issued for a specific set of controls to be used in designated organizational systems. The term *controls* encompasses both privacy and security controls. Privacy controls are the "administrative, technical, or physical safeguards employed within an agency to ensure compliance with applicable privacy requirements and manage privacy risks."[13] Safeguards may include "security features, management constraints, personnel security, and security of physical structures, areas, and devices."[14] Whereas security controls are "the safeguards or countermeasures prescribed for an information system or an organization to protect the confidentiality, integrity, and availability of the system and its information."[15] Security controls are meant to be policy and technology neutral, regardless of operational environments, communities of interest, or mission or business functions. Their use encourages organizations to focus on security capabilities or policies for the protection of systems and/or information.

The RMF consists of seven essential steps (see fig. 7.1). The first step, prepare, establishes a context and priorities for managing risk.[16] The second, categorize, identifies the potential impact (low, moderate, or high) resulting from loss of confidentiality, integrity, or availability of a system and/or associated information if a security breach occurs. The third, select, chooses an initial set of controls for the system to reduce risk to an acceptable level based on the assessment of risk. The fourth step, implement, installs the controls in accordance with system- and software-engineering methodologies, security-engineering principles, and secure-coding techniques.[17] The fifth, assess, evaluates if the controls are properly implemented and operate as envisioned. The sixth, authorize, reviews vulnerabilities found in the control assessment and determines if risk is acceptable. The final step, monitor, determines the impact of changes in system configuration and the operating environment. While the sequential order of the steps is important, divergence can occur in iterative cycles. For instance, the control assessment step can identify need for remediation actions in the form of new controls. In addition, the steps might have to be revisited if changes occur in risk.[18]

Each step in the RMF has a clear purpose statement, a distinct set of outcomes, and a set of tasks that are necessary to achieve those outcomes. Just like security controls, the RMF is designed to be technology neutral. Therefore, the methodology "can be applied to any type of information system without modification" since all "systems process, store or transmit some type of information."[19] This means various types of systems, such as cloud-based, industrial control, weapons, cyber-physical, Internet of things (IoT), and mobile, do not necessarily require a different risk-management process—just a particular selection of controls and implementation details.

Cybersecurity Framework

The NIST Framework for Improving Critical Infrastructure Cybersecurity (hereafter, the Cybersecurity Framework) can also be used to identify, align, and deconflict the selection of controls or enhance the execution of RMF tasks. The intent of the Cybersecurity Framework is to provide "a prioritized, flexible, repeatable, performance-based, and cost-effective approach, including information security measures and controls that may be voluntarily adopted by owners and operators of critical infrastructure to help them identify, assess and manage cyber risk."[20] Critical infrastructure is defined in the USA PATRIOT Act of 2001 as "systems and assets, whether physical or virtual, so vital to the United States that the incapacity or destruction of such systems and assets

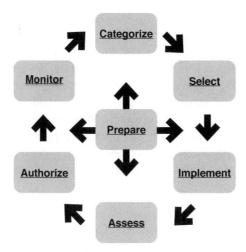

Figure 7.1. Risk-Management Framework Steps

Source: NIST, "Risk Management Framework for Information Systems and Organizations," NIST Special Publication 800-37, Revision 2, December 2018, 9.

would have a debilitating impact on security, national economic security, national public health or safety, or any combination of those matters."[21]

The Cybersecurity Framework consists of a core set of cybersecurity activities, desired outcomes, and informative references that are common across critical infrastructure sectors. The core consists of five concurrent and continuous functions: identify, protect, detect, respond, and recover.[22] It offers voluntary consensus standards and industry best practices to achieve outcomes under the functions. The Cybersecurity Framework suggests using a profile to represent the outcomes, which can help to identify ways to improve the cybersecurity posture by comparing a "current" profile (the "as is" state) with a "target" profile (the "to be" state).[23] The comparison determines gaps in controls. After a cost-benefit analysis of available resources, an organization can implement new controls to address the gaps. While the Cybersecurity Framework was developed for critical infrastructure, it can be used by organizations in any sector of the economy or society, regardless of their focus or size. Moreover, it can be used by organizations in countries outside the United States because it references globally recognized standards for cybersecurity.

As early as 2015, leading corporations such as Intel attested that the Cybersecurity Framework had enhanced their ability "to set security priorities, develop budgets and deploy security solutions."[24] Former Homeland Security deputy secretary Alejandro Mayorkas urged global experts at the 2016 Billington International Cybersecurity Summit to use it in their countries.[25] In

May 2017, President Trump signed an executive order that required the heads of federal agencies to use the Cybersecurity Framework.[26] In April 2018, NIST released version 1.1 of the Cybersecurity Framework, which added new sections on self-assessing cybersecurity risk and buying decisions while expanding verbiage related to cyber supply-chain risk management. Federal agencies, private companies, and other organizations that have adopted the Cybersecurity Framework can also use the tasks of the RMF for control implementation, assessment, and monitoring as well as authorizing their systems. For example, RMF Task P-4, on organizationally tailored control baselines and cybersecurity framework profiles, aligns closely with the Cybersecurity Framework profile construct.

Defense-in-Depth Strategies

While cybersecurity frameworks for risk management enable the prioritized selection, implementation, and evaluation of security and privacy controls, defense-in-depth strategies guide their allocation and placement. The term *defense-in-depth* means an "information security strategy integrating people, technology, and operations capabilities to establish variable barriers across multiple layers and missions of the organization."[27] In this manner, organizations "strategically allocate security safeguards (procedural, technical, or both) in the security architecture so that adversaries must overcome multiple safeguards to achieve their objective."[28] The need to defeat multiple safeguards increases the workload of the adversary. A study by the Ponemon Institute revealed that "organizations with strong defenses take adversaries more than double the time to plan and execute attacks."[29] A layered approach minimizes the adverse impact of a cyberattack. If properly employed, defense-in-depth solutions turn networks and systems into unattractive targets. The strategy frustrates hackers and raises their cost-benefit calculations, encouraging their perception that cyber operations are a pointless endeavor.

The security firm Symantec recommends that businesses employ defense-in-depth strategies. Its annual reports emphasize the use of "multiple, overlapping, and mutually supportive defensive systems to guard against single-point failures in any specific technology or protection method."[30] Defense-in-depth strategies likewise apply to military organizations. The US Navy attests that the employment of a defense-in-depth strategy "leveraging multiple security countermeasures will help protect the integrity of USN platforms and IT assets in the enterprise."[31] Furthermore, navy instructions dictate that all navy IT must be safeguarded at all times in a defense-in-depth strategy. While many private and public organizations employ defense-in-depth measures within their IT infrastructures, in the past the owners and operators of critical infrastructure did not see a need to do so to protect industrial control systems

(ICS).[32] However, with the convergence of IT and ICS architectures, high-profile cyber incidents have highlighted the potential risk to ICS. Therefore, the DHS recommends in its document "Improving Industrial Control Systems Cybersecurity with Defense-in-Depth Strategies" an approach that "uses specific countermeasures implemented in layers to create an aggregated, risk-based security posture."[33] NIST also proclaims that the placement of security controls "is an important activity requiring thoughtful analysis."[34] A strategic defense-in-depth approach for security deployment requires an understanding of security challenges, seen in the cyber kill chain, and tailored countermeasures, such as the Center for Internet Security (CIS) controls.

Cyber Kill Chain

In 2011, Lockheed Martin researchers adapted the military concept of a kill chain, a series of targeting and engagement steps for conducting a kinetic attack, to define the stages of a cyber intrusion. Their model is based on the premise that intruders attempt to infiltrate and exploit networks and systems in "a sequential, incremental and progressive way."[35] The seven stages of the Lockheed Martin intrusion kill chain model are reconnaissance, weaponization, delivery, exploitation, installation, command and control, and actions on objectives. Each stage of the end-to-end process describes tools and techniques used by attackers to proceed to the next stage.[36] The popular and simplified model is structured so that a break in any link of the chain will interrupt the entire process. To paraphrase the specific stages described by Lockheed Martin,

Intrusion Kill Chain
1. Reconnaissance: Research, identification, and selection of the target by collecting email addresses, social relationships, and useful information on specific technologies such as systems, applications, and services.
2. Weaponization: Identification of the attack vector—for example, the coupling of a remote access trojan with an exploit into a deliverable payload (e.g., a weaponized document) or a customized tool.
3. Delivery: Transmission of the weapon to the target environment—for instance, via email, USB stick, or mobile device.
4. Exploitation: Of application or operating system vulnerability or an operating system feature, in order to trigger and execute intruder code.
5. Installation: Of backdoor malware on the asset to maintain persistence.
6. Command and Control: Beacon outbound to a command-and-control server for remote manipulation of target system by the attacker.

7. Action on Objectives: Intruders accomplish their goal inside the target environment—for example, destruction, manipulation, or exfiltration.[37]

Other security firms modified the kill chain concept over the next few years to understand advanced cyber-threat actor tactics and techniques. The seven stages of the Websense cyberattack kill chain model are reconnaissance, lure, redirect, exploit kit, dropper file, call home, and data theft.[38] The primary difference in this version is its emphasis on innocuous-looking lures that can fool users into clicking links to compromised websites containing exploit kits. Dell Corporation breaks the anatomy of a cyberattack into only four basic stages: "reconnaissance (finding vulnerabilities), intrusion (actual penetration of the network), malware insertion (secretly leaving code behind), and cleanup (covering tracks)."[39] Dell moves beyond the Lockheed Martin intention of strictly intrusion to include denial-of-service attacks. The security firm Cybereason claims the six stages of the attack lifecycle are external reconnaissance, breach, command and control, spread, lateral movement, and damage.[40] The latter models attest to the fact that hacks are being executed in a different way. While the different phases of a cyberattack have not changed dramatically, the stages contain more options. For instance, the delivery phase has evolved from sending phishing emails to redirecting users to fake Web pages (which look exactly like the real thing and seek to steal login credentials).[41] However, in any version or option, the idea is the same for the defender: you need to understand the enemy before you can defeat them.

Center for Internet Security Controls

The cyber kill chain concept illuminates opportunities across multiple phases to limit the damage associated with attacks. Defenders can take advantage of the opportunities at each phase to interrupt the attack process with security controls. In order to think like the attacker, defenders need access to security controls that are based on knowledge of actual attacks. The CIS controls were created by a community of security experts who have firsthand experience determining which safeguards are effective against cyberattacks. These security experts represent a wide range of sectors, including retail, manufacturing, health care, education, government, and defense. Version 7 of the CIS controls is heralded as "a prioritized set of actions that collectively form a defense-in-depth set of best practices that mitigate the most common attacks against systems and networks."[42] The CIS controls address the questions, What are the most critical areas we need to address? and How should an enterprise take the first step to mature their risk-management program?[43]

The CIS controls suggest twenty sets of technical measures that are designed to prevent, detect, respond, and mitigate damage from the most common to the most advanced attacks. The original focus on blocking the compromise of systems in the critical security controls developed by the SANS Institute has evolved in the CIS controls to detecting already compromised computers and preventing follow-on actions by attackers. The five critical tenets of an effective cyber defense posture reflected in the CIS controls are the following:

1. Offense informs defense: Use practical defenses that have shown to stop known real-world attacks.
2. Prioritization: Invest first in controls that give the greatest risk reduction against the most dangerous cyber-threat actors.
3. Measurements and metrics: Establish common metrics to measure security measure effectiveness.
4. Continuous diagnostics and mitigation: Test and validate current security measures to prioritize next steps.
5. Automation: Automate defenses to achieve reliable and continuous measurements of adherence and metrics.[44]

The twenty CIS controls are grouped under the categories of basic, foundational, and organizational. A relatively small number of well-vetted controls outlined in a fifty-five-page document offers a more condensed approach than the defender selection of numerous controls found in the nearly five hundred pages of NIST Special Publication 800-53.

The CIS controls serve as an informative reference in the NIST Cybersecurity Framework, where they are mapped to the five core functions. They can also be mapped to the cyber kill chain. Opportunities exist to layer controls at each phase to minimize impact. For example, at the reconnaissance phase, the use of a log analytical tool for aggregation, correlation, and real-time analysis of security events in "CIS Control 6: Maintenance, Monitoring and Analysis of Audit Logs" could spot reconnaissance activity.[45] At the exploitation phase, the conduct of regular external and internal penetration tests in "CIS Control 20: Penetration Tests and Red Team Exercises" could determine the existence of vulnerabilities for remediation.[46] In addition, at the latter actions on objectives phase, the monitor and block of unauthorized network traffic in "CIS Control 13: Data Protection" could prevent the unauthorized transfer of sensitive information.[47] The inclusion of shared cyber-threat intelligence across attack vectors will further enhance the ability of security controls to prevent and detect attacks.

Shared Cyber-Threat Intelligence

A study by the Ponemon Institute revealed that 39 percent of attacks can be thwarted by cyber-threat intelligence sharing.[48] Threat intelligence is defined as "threat information that has been aggregated, transformed, analyzed, interpreted, or enriched to provide the necessary context for decision-making processes."[49] Threat information is "any information related to a threat that might help an organization protect itself against a threat or detect the activities of an actor."[50] The major types of threat information include indicators; tactics, techniques, and procedures (TTPs); security alerts; threat-intelligence reports; and security tool configurations. Indicators are system artifacts or observables. Indicators of attack represent the series of actions required to execute the cyber kill chain, such as persistence or lateral movement, whereas indicators of compromise are electronic evidence, such as an MD5 hash (an encoded string of letters or numbers), a command-and-control domain, or a hard-coded IP address.[51] TTPs are the behavior of an actor, described in a hierarchy of detail, from the highest level for tactic, to more detailed for technique in the context of a tactic, and to highly detailed for procedure in the context of a technique. Security alerts often provide details on threats, vulnerabilities, and incidents, while commercial threat-intelligence reports frequently reveal actor strategies and motivations, tactics and methods, and campaigns.

Cyber-threat intelligence helps an organization identify, assess, monitor, and respond to cyber threats. Choices for organizations to ingest threat intelligence include threat data feeds (intelligent machine-readable indicators such as malicious C2 domains for botnet servers and URLs hosting or distributing malware), threat-mitigation solutions (automated security-architecture integrations), threat-intelligence services (augmented security operations with outside analysts to monitor for threats and/or subscribe to periodic industry-specific reports), or threat-intelligence platforms.[52] A commercial threat-management platform will look for artifacts or observables on deployed sensors and aggregate, normalize, enrich, analyze, and prioritize the data to create actionable threat intelligence that is relevant to the specific company.[53] In a survey of IT security practitioners in North America and the United Kingdom by the Ponemon Institute, 84 percent of respondents rated the value of threat intelligence as essential to a strong security posture.[54] Attesting to the importance of threat intelligence in how to respond to threats, 63 percent of the respondents said that threat intelligence drives decision-making within their organizations' security operations center. In addition, 62 percent of respondents say their organizations share threat intelligence. They share it with trusted security vendors, trusted peer groups (through a platform or email list), their industry (through community sharing groups such as information sharing and analysis centers [ISACs] and information sharing and analysis organizations [ISAOs]), the government (through programs such as automated indicator sharing [AIS] and cyber information sharing and collaboration program [CISCP]), or publicly through threat bulletins, feeds, or other mechanisms.[55] Besides the virtues of outbound sharing, habitual sharing relations also facilitate the ingesting of relevant threat intelligence.

Attackers often reuse tactics and tools to target organizations in the same industry sector or the same type of critical infrastructure. Collaboration between organizations with the same type of systems and information helps to reduce risk. The prevailing paradigm is that the detection of a cyberattack by one organization can become the prevention of a cyberattack by another organization. Sharing cyber-threat intelligence allows an organization to benefit from the collective knowledge, experience, and capabilities of its peers. An organization can use communal resources to make "threat-informed decisions regarding defensive capabilities, threat detection techniques, and mitigation strategies."[56] More specifically, an organization can use shared cyber-threat intelligence to update "security controls for continuous monitoring with new indicators and configurations to detect the latest attacks and compromises."[57] For example, at the exploitation phase of the cyber kill chain, the usage of threat intelligence in existing security technologies, such as security information and event management (SIEM), firewalls, and intrusion prevention systems can provide additional prevention and detection opportunities.[58] Threat intelligence can identify security gaps and disruptive measures throughout each phase of the cyber kill chain.[59] Organizations should map indicators to the relevant stage of the chain and prioritize action on those further down the chain because they correspond to more damaging events.[60]

Kill Chain Analysis

The US-CERT routinely uses the cyber kill chain model to analyze, discuss, and dissect malicious cyber activity. The technical alert titled "Russian Government Cyber Activity Targeting Energy and Other Critical Infrastructure Sectors" (TA18-074A) provided a high-level overview using the model. The Department of the Treasury announced that since at least March 2016, Russian government cyber actors have "targeted U.S. government entities and multiple U.S. critical infrastructure sectors, including the energy, nuclear, commercial facilities, water, aviation, and critical manufacturing sectors."[61] The technical alert provided details on indicators of compromise and tactics, techniques, and procedures and characterized the activity as a "multi-stage intrusion campaign" where Russian actors "staged malware, conducted spear phishing, and gained remote access into energy sector networks. After obtaining access, the [actors] conducted network reconnaissance, moved laterally, and collected information pertaining to Industrial Control Systems (ICS)."[62] The Russian espionage campaign demonstrated proficient use of legitimate functions, batch scripts, and administrative and public tools to gain access to and potential control of operational systems for utilities while staying below the level of armed conflict.

US Energy Sector Attacks

Technical alert TA18-074A noted that a report by the security vendor Symantec, "Dragonfly: Western Energy Sector Targeted by Sophisticated Attack Group," provided additional information on the ongoing campaign.[63] The Symantec report heralded a new wave of cyberattacks on the energy sector in Europe and North America powered by the Dragonfly group, also known as Energetic Bear.[64] The group had been active since at least 2011 but went silent for almost two years after exposure by Symantec and other security researchers in 2014. Early targets of the group were energy grid operators, electricity-generation firms, petroleum pipeline operators, and energy industrial equipment providers.[65] Targets in the new wave were also energy facilities. While the first campaign appeared to be more of a reconnaissance phase, the second, labeled Dragonfly 2.0, seems to have destructive purposes.[66] Both campaigns used the same attack vectors: malicious emails, watering hole attacks, and supply-chain compromise. The first compromised ICS equipment suppliers, and the second compromised the corporate networks of suppliers who have special access to update software, run diagnostics on equipment, and perform other services.[67] Once inside the vendor networks, they leveraged access to pivot to the utilities.[68] TA18-074A outlines the specific steps taken in the cyber kill chain in Dragonfly 2.0. To paraphrase,

1. Reconnaissance: The threat actors deliberately selected staging targets that held habitual relationships with intended targets. They found information on network and organizational design and control-system capabilities on publicly accessible sites.

2. Weaponization: The threat actors used email attachments to leverage legitimate Microsoft Office functions for retrieving a document from a remote server using the SMB protocol, which sent the user's credential hash to be cracked. They also developed watering holes to reach intended targets, including trade publications and websites related to process control, ICS, or critical infrastructure. They modified the website content to accomplish similar techniques for credential harvesting.

3. Delivery: The threat actors used a second spear-phishing technique that contained a generic PDF (Portable Document Format) document that did not have any active code. Instead, the document had a shortened URL that, if clicked, took users to a fake website that deceived the user into entering his or her email address and password.

4. Exploitation: For staging targets, the threat actors used unusual successive redirects of links to get to the website, which mimicked a login page containing bogus input fields for an email address and password. For intended targets, the threat actors emailed a malicious .docx file that captured user credentials by attempting to retrieve a file over a C2 server, which provided a hash of the password.

5. Installation: The threat actors used compromised credentials to enter networks that did not require multifactor authentication. Then they used scripts to create local administrator accounts, disable the host-based firewall, open a port for remote access, and gained elevated privileges inside the administrator's group.

6. Command and Control: The threat actors used Web shells to establish channels on the intended target's email and Web servers.

7. Action on Objectives: Once on the intended targets, the threat actors used privileged credentials, batch scripts, and Windows tools to access workstations.[69]

The Dragonfly 2.0 campaign used what are commonly called "living off the land" tools, such as administration tools Powershell, PsExec, and Bitsadmin.[70] They also used publicly available tools, such as Mimikatz, CrackMapExec, Angry IP, SecretsDump, and Hydra, available on the Github website.[71] Energetic Bear also used cyber deception tactics, specifically inserting code strings into the malware written in French in addition to Russian.[72] This deliberate attempt at misdirection was amplified by attempts at misattribution through use of the proxy name to divert or take the blame.

The Russian cyber actors in Dragonfly 2.0 sought continual access to operational systems at energy-generation facilities that could be used for disruptive purposes in the future. They retrieved files pertaining to ICS and SCADA systems, for which they copied profile and configuration information for accessing them.[73] The incursions represent a dramatic escalation. Eric Chien, technical director at Symantec, summed up the concern in stating, "Before, we were talking about them being one step away, and what we see now is that they are potentially in those networks and are zero steps away."[74] Federal officials confirmed in July 2018 that Russian hackers working for Dragonfly 2.0 "got to the point where they could have thrown switches and disrupted power flows" at American electric utilities.[75] From a legal standpoint, the unsettling scenario of massive blackouts could equate to the use of force, but until blackouts occur with demonstrated severe effects, international law would probably not determine the existence of an armed attack. After all, even after gaining access to control systems, the Russian hackers did nothing to manipulate the system.[76] At best there would be a ruling on the respect for sovereignty, in the case of the emplacement of malware.[77] That qualification, with proven attribution to Russian government cyber actors, could lead to a determination of an internationally wrongful act and justify countermeasures.

Suggested Strategy Shortfalls

A variety of interconnected ways exist to manage risk (the RMF and the Cybersecurity Framework) and secure systems (the NIST SP800-53 and CIS controls) in a defense-in-depth strategy. In February 2019, NIST posted an info graphic on its website on the impacts and outcomes of the Cybersecurity Framework over the five years since its inception. The Cybersecurity Framework has been downloaded over five hundred thousand times, and over ten thousand people have participated in webcasts promoting it. In addition, half a dozen success stories were posted attesting to its value. For example, the chief information and security officer (CISO) for the University of Chicago Biological Sciences Division stated, "We found that the Cybersecurity Framework was well aligned with our main objective, which was to establish a common language for communicating cybersecurity risks across the Division."[78] The use of the Cybersecurity Framework to communicate and organize is certainly one virtue, along with its use to set policies aligned with controls and to map technical capability aligned to subcategories. That said, the challenge in evaluating the effectiveness of formal ways to manage risk, such as by the Cybersecurity Framework, is the unknown extent or scope of voluntary implementation. Ideally organizations will compare their target state to their current state and, based on a risk assessment, will implement appropriate controls to close gaps in security. The issue is their determination of risk tolerance that might hamper the fielding of sufficient controls tied to the 108 subcategories.

Instead of using only formal ways to manage risks, organizations can choose to implement best practices, such as those offered by Symantec. Its 2017 annual report outlined best practices by categories of threats, such as targeted, email, Web, and ransomware attacks and by types of devices, such as IoT, mobile, and cloud.[79] Another option is for organizations to monitor and respond to the myriad of incident reports and technical alerts that provide best practices and threat intelligence. For instance, the technical alert titled "Russian Government Cyber Activity Targeting Energy and Other Critical Infrastructure Sectors" (TA18-074A) provided a list of twenty-eight general best practices to protect against similar activity. It advised sector organizations to "establish least-privilege controls," "monitor VPN logs for abnormal activity (e.g., off-hour logins, unauthorized IP address logins, and multiple concurrent logins)," and "deploy web and email filters on the network . . . to scan for known bad domain names, sources and addresses [and] block these before receiving and downloading messages."[80] In essence, these particular suggestions are addressed in common security controls ("CIS Control 4: Controlled Use of

Privileges," "CIS Control 6: Monitor Logs," and "CIS Control 7: Email and Web Browser Protections").[81] TA18-074 also provided indicators of compromise, network signatures, and host-based rules for administrators to use to detect malicious activity associated with threat actor TTPs. In addition, TA18-074 recommended that sector organizations create and participate in information-sharing programs. A recent report by the Lexington Institute concurred that sharing threat data decreases cyber risk to the point where without informa-tion sharing, "it is almost impossible to detect systemic attacks early enough to contain them."[82] However, despite legislation designed to protect organiza-tions, some might be hesitant to share due to privacy and liability concerns.[83]

The US Industrial Control Systems Cyber Emergency Response Team (ICS-CERT) provided similar best-practice suggestions in the aftermath of the 2015 cyberattack against Ukrainian critical infrastructure in IR-ALERT-H-16-056-01, which also recommended use of practices in the document "Improving Industrial Control Systems Cybersecurity with Defense-in-Depth Strategies." Despite the mitigation recommendation in the incident report that "asset owners take defensive measures by leveraging best practices to minimize the risk from similar malicious cyber activity," it is uncertain whether the vic-tim utilities in the Dragonfly 2.0 campaign heeded this advice, given at least two years before successful intrusions.[84] For whatever risk frameworks, best practices, and threat-sharing mechanisms that were in place, the Russians were not denied the benefit of their attack. To make matters worse, sophisticated cyber adversaries such as the Russians present evolving attack vectors and in-genious techniques for defenders to counter, and in many cases they conduct multiprong attacks. For instance, Russian actors spread the NotPetya malware via "drive-by exploit kits, e-mails with malicious attachments, embedded URI links, and compromised software update services (i.e. MeDoc accounting soft-ware update) to gain initial access to the host."[85]

The Russians used the latter tactic of infecting software updates in the original Dragonfly campaign, where they gained access to the networks of three different ICS equipment providers and inserted malware into software bundles available for download on their websites.[86] These types of intrusion tactics put the Russians inside target networks at stage 5 of the cyber kill chain model. In NotPetya, the Russians exploited the Windows SMB vulnerability with EternalBlue and EternalRomance (leaked NSA tools) for lateral move-ment, even though the patch had been issued in March 2017, four months prior to NotPetya. This technique inside the network highlights the lack of ba-sic security controls in victim organizations (see "CIS Control 3: Continuous Vulnerability Management").[87] Furthermore, whatever controls were in place on victim systems did not detect other propagation methods that used legiti-mate Windows administration tools. That failure resulted in wholesale damage in organizations. The US-CERT did release a technical alert (TA17-181A) for

NotPetya, with malware analysis, network signatures, and recommended steps for prevention, but for those organizations initially infected, such as Maersk and Merck, that was four days too late.[88] Given the difficulties in mitigating risk, organizations can choose an alternative course of action for risk response: to transfer risk responsibility or liability to another organization, normally through cyber insurance.

Many public- and private-sector organizations are purchasing cyber insurance to help manage the costs related to breaches, including 38 percent of US states.[89] Likewise, the majority of the twenty-five most-populous US cities have cyber insurance, after the ransomware attack on Atlanta in 2018 that cost more than $20 million served as a warning.[90] Cyber insurance products generally tend to reimburse the policy holder for the costs of retrieving or repairing data, software, and hardware, paying compensation for data-privacy loss, conducting forensic investigations, obtaining legal advice, and repairing reputational damage,[91] although the concept of risk transfer generally does not apply to federal agencies, including the DOD, which operate under different liability constraints.[92] Nonetheless, payouts from cyber insurance are not certain. Zurich American Insurance rejected a claim for $100 million by snack-food maker Mondelez related to the NotPetya ransomware attack. The NotPetya virus resulted in the shutdown of seventeen hundred servers and twenty-four thousand laptops at the company, which halted factory production. Zurich based its rejection on an exclusion clause in the policy against loses caused by "hostile or warlike action in time of peace or war by any government or sovereign power."[93] Likewise, insurers have cited the war exemption in denying claims by Merck after NotPetya hit its pharmaceutical research, sales, and manufacturing operations.[94]

Conclusion

Organizations threaten to be overwhelmed by the complexity of today's cyber threats.[95] The security firm Trend Micro revealed a 16 percent rise in reported breaches in the United States from the second half of 2017 to the first six months of 2018. Detections of cryptocurrency mining on unsuspecting computers rose 141 percent, and while ransomware slowed down in terms of volume growth to 3 percent, it was still detected by Trend Micro tools 380,000 times in the first half of 2018.[96] As the likelihood of occurrence of a cyber incident increases, so do information system–related security risks. The risks are most prevalent for small and medium enterprises that cannot afford to implement risk frameworks or layers of security controls. In the Dragonfly 2.0 campaign, the initial victims were trusted third-party suppliers, many of which were small companies without big cybersecurity budgets. The hackers went after hundreds of contractors and subcontractors, such as All-Ways Excavating USA, a fifteen-person company in Oregon that works with utilities.[97] The Russian hackers used the vendor's credentials to gain direct access to the "supposedly secure, air-gapped, or isolated" utility networks.[98]

Despite DHS recommendations for utilities to improve ICS cybersecurity through a layered, multitiered strategy, Energetic Bear breached two dozen or more utilities in the giant and long campaign. Apparently any security controls and associated tools for detection that were installed in the suggested defense-in-depth security architecture failed to detect advanced Russian activity inside the utility networks before threat actors reached the point where damage could have been done.[99] The prevailing industry view for a comprehensive data-protection strategy is to implement "security measures and multilayered technologies" to defeat the most common threats.[100] Implementation of the first six basic CIS controls has been advertised to stop 85 percent of cyberattacks. In addition, there is a recognized need for sharing threats and vulnerabilities, especially for protection of ICS after exposure of Dragonfly 2.0.[101] While defense-in-depth tools such as firewalls and email gateways, intrusion-detection and intrusion-prevention software, and data-loss prevention are powerful, they have proven to be inadequate for organizations that hope to thwart advanced threat groups.[102]

Russian hacking groups demonstrate increasing technical complexity in their intrusion methods and evasion capabilities. Hackers working for the Russian government have used office printers and voice-over-IP phones with default passwords to penetrate targeted computer networks.[103] They have also used well-known libraries, such as OpenSSL (a cryptographic library for applications that secure communications over networks), to try to hide code in plain sight.[104] Technical alert TA18-074A exposed the use by Energetic Bear of innovative tactics (such as Microsoft Office function exploitation) and techniques (such as batch scripts). The Russians are prolific, skilled, and the fastest of state-sponsored actors. An analysis of data by the security firm CrowdStrike on more than thirty thousand hacking incidents found that Russian hackers move from "the initial breach to exploring other computers and devices connected to the compromised network [referred to as breakout] in just 18 minutes."[105] Far behind in hours, not even in minutes, from compromise to lateral movement across a network are, in descending order, North Korea, China, and Iran. Speed matters, for the faster the attacker moves, the harder it is for the defender to counter. Unfortunately, current security strategies do not work against a resourceful and nimble state adversary who is not convinced its attacks will fail. The sum of the actions, operations, and tools of Russian threat actors requires an entirely different approach—one that is proactive, adaptable, and, most important, resilient.

Notes

1. Donald Trump, *National Cyber Strategy of the United States of America* (Washington, DC: White House, September 2018), 21.

2. Peter Roberts and Andrew Hardie, "The Validity of Deterrence in the Twenty-First Century," occasional paper, Royal United Services Institute, August 2015" 20.

3. Office of Management and Budget, "Managing Information as a Strategic Resource," Circular A-130, July 2016, 35.

4. World Economic Forum, *The Global Risks Report 2019*, 14th ed. (Geneva: World Economic Forum, January 15, 2019), 16.

5. Help Net Security, "Most Organizations Suffered a Business-Disrupting Cyber Event," December 14, 2018.

6. National Institute of Standards and Technology (NIST), *Glossary of Key Information Security Terms*, Draft NISTIR 7298, Revision 3, September 2018.

7. DOD, *Cybersecurity*, DOD Instruction 8500.01 (Washington, DC: March 14, 2014), 2.

8. Committee on National Security Systems, "Policy on Information Assurance Risk Management for National Security Systems," CNSSP no. 22, January 2012, 3.

9. NIST, "Managing Information Security Risk," NIST Special Publication 800-39, March 2011, 6.

10. NIST, 7.

11. NIST, "Risk Management Framework for Information Systems and Organizations," NIST Special Publication 800-37, December 2018, 8.

12. DOD, *Risk Management (RMF) for DoD Information Technology (IT)*, DOD Instruction 8510.01, July 28, 2017, 2.

13. Office of Management and Budget, "Managing Information," 34.

14. NIST, "Security and Privacy Controls for Federal Information Systems and Organizations," NIST Special Publication 800-53, revision 5, August 2017; NIST, *Glossary of Key Information Security Terms*.

15. NIST, "Security and Privacy Controls," 303.

16. NIST, "Risk Management Framework," 8–9.

17. DOD, *Risk Management*, 31.

18. NIST, "Risk Management Framework," 9–10.

19. NIST, xi.

20. Cybersecurity Enhancement Act of 2014 (S.1353), public law 113-274, December 18, 2014.

21. USA PATRIOT Act of 2001 (H.R. 3162), public law 107-56, October 26, 2001.

22. NIST, "Framework for Improving Critical Infrastructure Cybersecurity," version 1.1, April 16, 2018, 3.

23. NIST, 4.

24. Intel Corporation, "The Cybersecurity Framework in Action: An Intel Use Case," solution brief, 2015, 1–9.

25. Greg Otto, "U.S. Officials: World Needs to Follow Our Lead on Cyber Norms," Fedscoop, April 5, 2016.

26. White House, Office of the Press Secretary, "Strengthening the Cybersecurity of Federal Networks and Critical Infrastructure," executive order, May 11, 2017.

27. NIST, *Glossary of Key Information Security Terms*.

28. NIST, "Security and Privacy Controls," 168.

29. Ponemon Institute, "Flipping the Economics of Attacks," research report, January 2016, 3.

30. Symantec, "Internet Security Threat Report," vol. 22, April 2017, 22.

31. Office of the Chief of Naval Operations, *U.S. Navy Cybersecurity Program*, OPNAVINST 5239.1D, N2N6 (Washington, DC: Department of the Navy, July 18, 2018), 9.

32. ICS-CERT, "Recommended Practice: Improving Industrial Control System Cybersecurity with Defense-in-Depth Strategies," DHS, September 2016, iii.

33. ICS-CERT, iii.

34. NIST, "Security and Privacy Controls," 168.

35. Muhammad Salman Khan, Sana Siddiqui, and Ken Ferens, "A Cognitive and Concurrent Cyber Kill Chain Model," in *Computer and Network Security Essentials*, ed. Kevin Daimi (New York: Springer, 2018), 585.

36. Markus Maybaum, "Technical Methods, Techniques, Tools and Effects of Cyber Operations," in *Peacetime Regime for State Activities in Cyberspace*, ed. Katharina Ziolkowski (Tallinn: NATO Cooperative Cyber Defence Centre of Excellence, 2013), 103–31.

37. Eric M. Hutchins, Michael J. Cloppert, and Rohan M. Amin, "Intelligence-Driven Computer Network Defense Informed by Analysis of Adversary Campaigns and Intrusion Kill Chains," Lockheed Martin, March 2011, 4.

38. Websense, "The Seven Stages of Advanced Threats," white paper, 2013, 2–3.

39. Dell, "Anatomy of a Cyber-Attack," white paper, 2013, 2.

40. Cybereason, "Six Stages of an Attack," security presentation, 2015, 2.

41. Julia Sowells, "The Different Phases of a Cyber Attack," Hacker Combat, May 14, 2018.

42. CIS, *CIS Controls*, version 7, Center for Internet Security, March 19, 2018, 1.

43. CIS, 1.

44. CIS, 2.

45. NTT Security, "Global Threat Intelligence Report: Practical Application of Security Controls to the Cyber Kill Chain," 2016, 25.

46. NTT Security, 35.

47. NTT Security, 45.

48. Karin Shopen, "3 Ways to Counter Multi-Vector Attacks," Palo Alto Networks, Cybersecurity (blog), February 8, 2016.

49. NIST, *Glossary of Key Information Security Terms*.

50. NIST.

51. CrowdStrike, "Indicators of Attack versus Indicators of Compromise," white paper, 2015, 3.

52. LookingGlass, "Technical Threat Indicators," data sheet, 2018; LookingGlass, "Threat Intelligence-as-a-Service," data sheet, 2018; LookingGlass, "Strategic Intelligence Subscription Service," data sheet, 2018.

53. "Operationalizing Threat Intelligence for Dynamic Defense," in Gartner, *Addressing the Cyber Kill Chain: Full Gartner Research Report and LookingGlass Perspectives* (LookingGlass Cyber Solution, 2016), 4, https://www.gartner.com/imagesrv/media -products/pdf/lookingglass/lookingglass-1-34D62N3.pdf.

54. Ponemon Institute, "The Value of Threat Intelligence: The Second Annual Study of North American and United Kingdom Companies," research report, September 2017, 2.

55. Ponemon Institute, 7.

56. NIST, "Guide to Cyber Threat Information Sharing," NIST Special Publication 800-150, October 2016, iii.

57. NIST, 3.

58. Gartner, *Addressing the Cyber Kill Chain*, 11.

59. NTT Security, "Global Threat Intelligence Report: The Role of the Cyber Kill Chain in Threat Intelligence," 2016, 53.

60. Lockheed Martin, "Seven Ways to Apply the Cyber Kill Chain with a Threat Intelligence Platform," white paper, 2015, 5.

61. Department of the Treasury, "Treasury Sanctions Russian Cyber Actors."
62. US-CERT, "Russian Government Cyber Activity Targeting Energy and Other Critical Infrastructure Sectors," alert TA18-074A, March 15, 2018.
63. US-CERT.
64. Pierluigi Paganini, "Dragonfly 2.0: The Sophisticated Attack Group Is Back with Destructive Purposes," Security Affairs, September 7, 2017.
65. Symantec, "Dragonfly: Western Energy Companies under Sabotage Threat," Security Response (blog), June 30, 2014.
66. Symantec.
67. Rebecca Smith, "Russian Hackers Reach U.S. Utility Control Rooms, Homeland Security Officials Say," Wall Street Journal, July 23, 2018.
68. National Cybersecurity and Communications Integration Center, "Russian Activity against Critical Infrastructure," awareness briefing, July 25, 2018.
69. US-CERT, "Russian Government Cyber Activity."
70. Symantec, "Dragonfly."
71. National Cybersecurity and Communications Integration Center, "Russian Activity."
72. Symantec, "Dragonfly."
73. A screenshot of a configuration diagram that the threat actors accessed can be found at https://www.us-cert.gov/ncas/alerts/TA18-074A.
74. Dan Goodin, "Hackers Lie in Wait after Penetrating US and Europe Power Grid Networks," Ars Technica, September 6, 2017.
75. Smith, "Russian Hackers."
76. Philip Bump, "Why Russian Hackers Aren't Poised to Plunge the United States into Darkness," Washington Post, March 16, 2018.
77. Michael N. Schmitt, "'Below the Threshold' Cyber Operations: The Countermeasures Response Option and International Law," Virginia Journal of International Law 54, no. 3 (2014): 704–5.
78. NIST, "Cybersecurity Framework Success Stories," February 28, 2019.
79. Symantec, "Internet Security Threat Report," 22, 31, 36, 62, 67, 72, 74.
80. US-CERT, "Russian Government Cyber Activity."
81. CIS, "CIS Controls," 13, 18, 21.
82. Constance Douris, "Cyber Threat Data Sharing Needs Refinement," Future of the Power Grid Series, Lexington Institute, August 2017, 3.
83. Travis Farral, "The Definitive Guide to Sharing Threat Intelligence," white paper, Anomali, 2017, 2–3.
84. US ICS CERT, "Cyber-Attack against Ukrainian Critical Infrastructure," alert IR-ALERT-H-16-056-01, February 25, 2016.
85. Kadri Kutt, "NotPetya and WannaCry Call for a Joint Response from International Community," NATO Cooperative Cyber Defense Centre of Excellence, June 30, 2017.
86. Symantec, "Dragonfly," 7.
87. CIS, "CIS Controls," 11.
88. US-CERT, "Petya Ransomware."
89. Stephanie Kanowitz, "Can You Afford Not to Have Cyber Insurance?," GCN 37, no. 4 (September 2018): 40.
90. Scott Calvert and Jon Kamp, "More U.S. Cities Brace for 'Inevitable' Hackers," Wall Street Journal, September 4, 2018.
91. Kevin Jones, "Insurance vs Cyber Attacks: A Conundrum for SMEs," Hacker Combat, December 20, 2018.
92. NIST, "Managing Information Security Risk," 43.

93. Cormac Bracken, "Calling Virus 'Act of War,' Insurer Refuses to Pay Ransomware Claim," Toolbox Tech (blog), January 22, 2019.

94. Adam Satariano and Nicole Perlroth, "Big Companies Thought Insurance Covered a Cyberattack. They May Be Wrong," *New York Times*, April 15, 2019.

95. T. J. Alldridge, "Four Ways Layered Security Will Improve Your Detection and Response," Trend Micro, Business (blog), November 12, 2018.

96. "2018 Midyear Security Roundup: Unseen Threats, Imminent Losses," Trend Micro, August 28, 2018, 9–14.

97. Rebecca Smith and Rob Barry, "America's Electric Grid Has a Vulnerable Back Door—and Russia Walked through It," *Wall Street Journal*, January 10, 2019.

98. Smith, "Russian Hackers."

99. ICST-CERT, "Recommended Practice," 2–6.

100. "2018 Midyear Security Roundup," Trend Micro, 18.

101. Smith, "Russian Hackers."

102. LookingGlass, "The Power of a Tailored Threat Model," white paper, 2018.

103. Dan Goodwin, "Microsoft Catches Russian State Hackers Using IoT Devices to Breach Networks," Ars Technica, August 5, 2019.

104. Robert Lemos, "Fancy Bear Dons Plain Clothes to Try to Defeat Machine Learning," *Dark Reading*, August 28, 2019.

105. Lee Matthews, "Russia's State-Sponsored Hackers Are the World's Fastest," *Forbes*, February 20, 2019.

CHAPTER 8

Automated Cyber Defense

The objective for the protection of information networks in the 2018 National Cyber Strategy of the United States is to "manage cybersecurity risks to increase the security and resilience of the Nation's information and information systems."[1] The new National Cyber Strategy recognizes that "public and private entities have struggled to secure their systems as adversaries increase the frequency and sophistication of their malicious cyber activities."[2] While the term *security* means the capability to prevent an attack, the term *resilience* infers the capability to withstand an attack if it penetrates defenses and continue operations. Former secretary of homeland security Kirstjen Nielsen recognized in a 2018 speech at a US Chamber of Commerce event that resilience, not preventing an attack or breach, should guide organizational decision-making.[3] Part of the reason for her statement is that today governmental and private entities face huge challenges in protecting their systems from advanced threat actors that have an asymmetric advantage in the cyber domain. Russia especially has capitalized on innovative techniques and tools, some stolen and released or widely available to the public, to increase the speed, scale, and sophistication of their cyber operations.

Attackers use tools to automate the cyber kill chain process by leveraging modern polymorphic malware to outpace human-centered cyber defense in both the rapidity with which it accomplishes its mission and the speed at which it changes form, often compressing early stages to penetrate and exploit systems with ease. For instance, the majority of ransomware applications finish the encryption process in less than a minute—far too quickly to be countered by manual intervention alone. In the NotPetya ransomware attack, it took only forty-five seconds to infect the network of a large Ukrainian bank.[4] Once attackers have a foothold within the infrastructure, they adeptly evade defenses inside the network to achieve their objectives. Meanwhile, massive numbers of uncorrelated and unprioritized alerts from layered independent components, each generating their own unique set of alerts, overwhelm network security operations. Staff are unable to respond to breaches of and movement inside systems in anywhere near real time. A different approach is needed, one that can operate effectively at network scale and attack tempo against sophisticated techniques. This approach requires a new architecture that fuses endpoint solutions with network- and cloud-based capabilities, such as centralized threat intelligence gathering and distribution. Automation of the correlation and prioritization process solves the volume of alerts and the velocity and complexity of threats. This chapter starts with a theoretical review of resilience and how complex tactics and techniques challenge the battle for resilience. It then describes investments in automation and endpoint security that reduce the time required to detect and respond to advanced persistent threat actors operating seamlessly inside the network. The chapter finishes with an analysis of the 2017 Bad Rabbit ransomware attack and the utility of automated cyber defenses that act at the speed, scale, and sophistication of emerging attacks.

Resilience Theories

A 2018 survey by the security firm Attivo Networks highlighted that "the battle to keep cyber hackers from successfully compromising networks is not working."[5] Respondents said prevention solutions are ineffective, mostly due to targeted attacks and credential theft, which are renowned for bypassing prevention controls. Therefore, a quarter of the respondents reported that "they are spending more on detection than prevention security controls."[6] Meanwhile, the security firm FireEye reported that median dwell time (the number of days that an attacker is present in a victim network from first evidence of compromise to detection) was at seventy-eight days in 2018.[7] Although FireEye signaled an improvement in detecting breaches, both survey results cumulatively reinforce the notion that the battle is inside the network. This finding affirms the need for resilience, which in regard to critical infrastructure means "the ability to prepare for and adapt to changing conditions and withstand and recover rapidly from disruptions. Resilience includes the ability to withstand and recover from deliberate attacks, accidents, or naturally occurring threats or incidents."[8] Information system resilience is more specifically defined by NIST as "the ability of an information system to continue to operate while under attack, even if in a degraded or debilitated state, and to rapidly recover operational capabilities for essential functions after a successful attack."[9]

The concept of resilience is normally viewed in the context of low-chance, high-impact events such as natural disasters, terrorist attacks, pandemics, and critical infrastructure failures. For instance, scholars Louise Comfort, Arjen Boin, and Chris Demchak study societal capacity to deal with these emerging contingencies,[10] whereas, in the context of digital events, P. W. Singer and Allan Friedman, at the Brookings Institution, illuminate the need to build resilience against shocks (such as losing Internet access) that impact on things such as politics and economics. They think about resilience in terms of systems and organizations that are prepared for attacks and can maintain some functionality while under attack.[11] Researchers Alexander Kott and Igor Linkov define *cyber resilience* as "the ability of the system to prepare, absorb, recover, and adapt to adverse effects, especially those associated with cyber attacks."[12] They use the term to describe the features and components (sensing, hardware, and software) of the system that collectively contribute to sustaining system operations. This view is in line with the perspectives of the IT Sector Resiliency Working Group. Its common definition of *cyber resilience* is "the capacity of an enterprise to maintain its core purpose and integrity in the face of cyberattacks. A cyber resilient enterprise is one that can prevent, detect, contain and recover from a plethora of serious threats against data, applications and IT infrastructure."[13] Industry and governmental security experts in the IT sector have agreed that the goals of cyber resilience require "the ability to withstand cyberattacks and the ability to prevent degradation to mission or business effectiveness."[14] The system must be robust enough in redundancy and protection that it remains up and running, no matter what. Therefore, one aspect of cyber resilience is to reduce the time between an event and recovery, which limits the operational impact. That means, in effect, reducing the response time through specific technical solutions that are able to withstand cyberattacks. The technical solutions are intelligent enough and real-time enough to catch the threat actor someplace along the kill chain before he or she gets to the phase of final action on objectives. In this manner, the specific industry perspective on cyber resilience is that it manages the inevitable penetration of defensive perimeters. The federal perspective recognizes that complex attacks or previously unknown "zero-day" attacks continually outpace cybersecurity solutions. Therefore, the acknowledgment of resilience in national strategy demonstrates the federal government's commitment to improving overall cyber resilience.

The Department of Homeland Security's 2018 Cybersecurity Strategy reflects that commitment in expressing its vision: "By 2023, the Department of Homeland Security will have improved national cybersecurity risk management by increasing security and resilience across government networks and critical infrastructure."[15] A 2018 public-private report sponsored by the DHS illustrates an important distinction: "A key point that differentiates cyber resiliency from cybersecurity is that cyber resiliency continues to function even after the adversary has penetrated the security perimeter of a network and has compromised cyber assets. Even at the later stages of the cyber kill chain, cyber resiliency can help to prevent the adversary gathering intelligence on, exfiltrating data from, or taking control of mission-essential systems."[16] NIST draft Special Publication (SP) 800-160, volume 2, describes many functions that cyber resiliency can serve after the compromise, also assuming an advanced adversary will compromise or breach the system or organization since there will always be "weaknesses and flaws in the systems, the operational environments, and supply chains."[17] It also assumes an advanced adversary will maintain a presence in the system or organization. The special publication ascertains that "cyber resiliency is oriented toward capabilities and harms to systems containing cyber resources."[18] Accordingly, an objective of the DHS Cybersecurity Strategy is to "develop and pilot emerging capabilities, tools, and practices to more effectively detect and mitigate evolving threats and vulnerabilities in a timely fashion and ensure that our cybersecurity approaches are flexible and dynamic enough to counter determined and creative adversaries."[19] These emerging capabilities, tools, and practices for cyber resilience can ideally support the 2017 US National Security Strategy contention that a "more resilient critical infrastructure will strengthen deterrence by creating doubt in our adversaries that they can achieve their objectives."[20] Said otherwise, as a factor in effective deterrence, cyber resilience can change the perception of the adversary by denying the benefit of an attack.[21] NIST SP 800-160, volume 2, recognizes there are four abilities necessary for cyber resiliency: to anticipate, withstand, recover, and adapt to adverse conditions, stresses, attacks, or compromises on systems. To *anticipate* is to maintain a state of informed preparedness for adversity. To *withstand* means to maintain operations without performance degradation during an attack. To *recover* is defined as to rebound or restore from an adverse event to full functionalities. To *adapt* is to modify functions or capabilities for changes in the technical, operational, or threat environments. This chapter will focus primarily on the capabilities, tools, and practices to withstand without having the need to recover.[22]

Tactics and Techniques

Winning the battle of resilience inside the network starts with a thorough understanding of how the adversary operates. While the cyber kill chain originated by Lockheed Martin is a popular model, a security professional at the 2016 Black Hat convention in Las Vegas astutely pointed out that it does not focus enough on what happens after the adversary successfully breaks into the network, which he or she inevitably does.[23] Most of the steps relate solely to intrusion, which was the focus of cybersecurity when the model was created.[24] Therefore, an alternative is to focus on which tactics and techniques are likely used after successful intrusion. That means, for instance, during the execution of reconnaissance across the network, adding the subsequent steps of privilege escalation and lateral movement because, after obtaining a beachhead within a system, an attacker scans for accessible servers, services, and vulnerabilities to extend his or her footprint by obtaining additional credentials and compromising additional workstations.[25] Threat-actor strategies today target every link in the entire length of the attack chain, while defenders have traditionally focused on only a handful of attack components.[26] In 2018, the cybersecurity industry started to adopt the Mitre Corporation's ATT&CK framework to better classify the tactics and techniques used by the attacker from initial access to exfiltration. The eleven discrete tactics in the Mitre ATT&CK framework are described as follows:

1. Initial Access: Represents the vectors adversaries use to gain an initial foothold within a network.
2. Execution: Results in execution of adversary-controlled code on a local or remote system.
3. Persistence: Any access, action, or configuration change to a system that gives an adversary a continual presence on that system.
4. Privilege Escalation: Allows an adversary to obtain a higher level of permissions on a system or network.
5. Defense Evasion: Used to evade detection or avoid other defenses.
6. Credential Access: Results in access to or control over system, domain, or service credentials.
7. Discovery: Allows the adversary to gain knowledge about the system and internal network.
8. Lateral Movement: Enables an adversary to access and control remote systems on a target network.
9. Collection: Used to identify and gather information, such as sensitive files, from a target network.
10. Exfiltration: Results or aids in the adversary removing files and information from a target network.
11. Command and Control: Represents how adversaries communicate with systems under their control.[27]

Each tactic contains a set of discrete techniques. For example, under the Lateral Movement tactic, the ATT&CK framework describes seventeen techniques, such as Pass the Hash (bypass standard authentication), Remote Desktop Protocol (remote login to desktop via graphic user interface), and Windows.

The traditional Lockheed Martin kill chain amply describes the steps leading to initial intrusion, such as target selection, information gathering, weakness identification, capability development, payload delivery, exploitation, and installation. The Mitre ATT&CK framework expands on the remaining steps after intrusion that are necessary to achieve actor objectives. It provides a common taxonomy to describe tactics and techniques used inside the network, which is updated continuously online at the Mitre website. The taxonomy is vendor agnostic, although many vendors use the taxonomy in their reports on advanced persistent threat groups. For instance, the vendor will use a heat map to display the group's most common techniques.[28] By connecting the identified techniques in an attack sequence, the defender can emulate the adversary. The subsequent installation of security controls to block the specific techniques can theoretically impose costs by forcing the adversary to shift to new techniques, although a patient attacker will just go back to the drawing board, adding new and innovative weapons to his or her cyber arsenal while probing for a less defended point of entry.

The speed at which the attacker can break out in the ATT&CK framework matters, for it represents the time limit for defenders to respond, contain, and remediate an intrusion before it spreads widely across their network. The concept of breakout time is defined as "the window of time from when an adversary first compromises an endpoint machine, to when they begin moving laterally across your network."[29] Defenders cannot waste a second when dealing with the Russian government–affiliated actors, who break out in under twenty minutes. They are almost eight times as fast as the closest state-sponsored actors, from North Korea.[30] The Russians appear determined to accomplish their mission as rapidly as possible before being detected and thwarted. Yet speed is only one benchmark to evaluate the operational capabilities of major threat actors, and for the Russians sophistication and scale are just as important.

Part of the challenge for defenders is that after initial intrusion, the Russians and other advanced threat actors employ sophisticated techniques, such as "living off the land" tradecraft, leveraging applications already present on the target system. This concept involves use of regular, legitimate tools such as Microsoft PowerShell to exploit user systems. PowerShell can be used to run scripts for command functions or to inject malware into a system's memory. In 2018, Symantec reported that it blocked 115,000 malicious PowerShell scripts every month, a 1,000 percent increase over the previous year.[31] CrowdStrike also observed in 2018 a substantial use of scripting techniques to hide or obscure attacker behavior.[32] Scripts are highly prevalent in the Mitre ATT&CK framework in the discovery, persistence, and lateral movement tactics and are used profusely in Russian cyber operations.

In the Dragonfly 2.0 campaign, after Russian government cyber actors gained access to victim networks with compromised credentials, they used scripts to create local administrator accounts disguised as legitimate backup accounts. The script "enu.cmd" created an administrator account, disabled the host-based firewall, and opened a port for Remote Desktop Protocol (RDP) access. The script then attempted to add the newly created account to the administrators group to gain elevated privileges. Next, the threat actors created multiple accounts for specific purposes, such as to conduct reconnaissance, to remotely access intended targets, and to delete logs and cover tracks. In one case during an authenticated RDP session with an impersonated email administration account, they used a PowerShell script to create another account within the target network. The Russians also used batch scripts to run the legitimate PsExec tool to collect screenshots of systems across the network.[33]

An aspect of scale in these types of tactics is the choice and often simultaneous use of multiple techniques. For instance, in the discovery tactic, almost every technique (eighteen of twenty) is color coded as nearly or mostly prevalent in the CrowdStrike OverWatch ATT&CK Heat Map.[34]

New Investments

The Defense Science Board in 2016 recommended that the DOD leverage emerging technologies to increase resilience. Prominent in its recommendations for new areas of investment were increasing automation for cyber defense and improving endpoint security. The 2018 DOD Cyber Strategy echoed the need to leverage automation and data analysis to improve the effectiveness of cyber defense capabilities.[35] In January 2019, the DOD chief information officer, Dana Deasy, testified that for the DOD, current security operations are "a largely manual and very labor-intensive process."[36] Deasy recognized in congressional testimony the need for increased investments in data protection. He concluded that the DOD "must automate IT SECOPS [security operations] to protect mission critical systems."[37] That goal requires a plan and architecture for an increasingly automated cyber environment that capitalizes on highly contextual event logging from both the network infrastructure and emerging endpoint security technologies.

Security Operations Automation

Security operations personnel are being overloaded with event data, especially false positive alerts (errors in evaluations) from SIEM systems. Individual analysts are forced to deal with fifty to one hundred alerts a day, which causes "alert fatigue." A survey by the Cloud Security Alliance found that more than a third of analysts regularly ignore alerts due to the number of false positives.[38] This is partly because it is a tedious process for an analyst to manually verify the authenticity of alerts to determine whether they are malicious or benign and whether the event is related to a skillful threat actor (such as a nation-state) or is a generic, nontargeted attack from an unsophisticated attacker and then to prioritize them appropriately.[39] Furthermore, the deceptive and evasive qualities of the tactics and techniques seen in the Mitre ATT&CK framework have moved beyond a human's ability to recognize and respond manually to the threat. "In a world where security breaches continue to get more sophisticated and more damaging," Joel Dolisy, chief information officer at SolarWinds, says, "automating network security can help to quickly pinpoint a breach, identify the root cause and often help to resolve the issue quicker than manually checking every endpoint and connection."[40]

Automation of security responses improves the "ability to react to many easily identifiable threats that fit into well-defined patterns."[41] In cases where the impact is high and confidence is high, declared security policy should dictate that controls automatically terminate or block suspicious traffic.[42] In other cases, "automation allows experts to focus on where they are required," according to Allan Thomson, chief technology officer at LookingGlass, "which is understanding the more advanced threats and leveraging threat intelligence to respond to those advanced threats in a more meaningful manner."[43] In addition, automation of the correlation and prioritization process can provide increased awareness and visibility on the rapidly changing profiles of the more advanced threats. That results in more suitable response and remediation decisions. Those actions can also be automated, such as to revise user authorization privileges, place systems into protected zones, or redirect network flows. Once operators are replaced with automated processes, networks become more responsive to attacks.

Automation of security operations has become more popular for multiple reasons. First, the complexity of today's modern cyberattacks are no match for human security teams. Automation platforms facilitate a more streamlined and effective defense against advanced persistent threats. They serve as an ever-vigilant force that stands ready around the clock to detect and address potential breaches. When an alert is generated, it is either automatically assessed and remediated electronically or escalated for human attention.[44] Second, the velocity at which attacks transpire is driving the need for automation. The Microsoft Global Incident Response and Recovery team has seen "attackers move from an initial endpoint infection via a phishing email, to full domain control within 24 hours."[45] Automation helps security teams reduce the amount of time it takes to address and resolve successful attacks. The limitation of damage depends on how quick attackers can be identified and stopped. Third, the sheer volume of attacks and alerts triaged daily continues to grow and overwhelm security operations teams. Ideally automation would reduce the number of alerts that require manual interpolation to a manageable level. Finally, the automation of security tasks frees up scarce manpower resources. There are simply not enough skilled security professionals to meet the need. A 2017 report sponsored by the Herjavec Group predicts there will be 3.5 million cybersecurity job openings across the globe by 2021.[46]

Endpoint Detection and Response

In 2013, the endpoint detection and response (EDR) market was born through the realization that it was impossible to prevent 100 percent of attacks.[47] This led to the development of capabilities to discover aspects of technical operations occurring on the endpoint. This information could then be analyzed for suspicious and malicious behavior. Security operations centers adopted EDR solutions as a way to investigate activity that had not been prevented by perimeter defenses. EDR provides visibility into what is happening on endpoints. The types of endpoints that are most at risk are, in descending order, laptops, servers, desktops, cloud-based servers, and mobile devices (tablets, notebooks/iPads, and smartphones).[48] In theory, EDR protects against malware, fileless attacks, misuse of legitimate applications, and abuse of stolen user credentials. It is designed to not just track the tactics and techniques that an attacker uses but also their path of activity. Once an EDR agent is installed, it uses advanced algorithms to analyze the behavior of users in real time. Sensors collect process, connection, file, driver, auto-run, system, machine, and user information. EDR compares that information to previous or normal dataset patterns and alerts on signs of behavior that are out of the ordinary.[49]

In a typical endpoint response scenario, the alert on an unusual behavior from a detection source is sent to the security operations center. An analyst can then scan the endpoint to search for any unusual processes, connections, or other artifacts. If the alert is not a false positive, the analyst would quarantine the endpoint to prevent the spread of the attack. In a 2018 survey by the SANS Institute, 61 percent of respondents said they were able to detect a threat in under twenty-four hours, whereas the time to respond was the same or longer, with 62 percent reporting response took up to twenty-four hours and another 19 percent saying it took two to seven days to remediate a single endpoint. Automated threat intelligence that can feed directly into detection and response systems should reduce these intervals. With threat actor breakouts across networks occurring in minutes or, at most, hours, these lengthy windows provide the advantage to the attacker. Next-generation tools promise to bring the automation needed to model normal behavior and document unexpected behavior. The SANS survey concludes that "organizations must augment their abilities to more proactively defend their systems and detect threats earlier in the cyber kill chain."[50] Organizations have taken notice and allocated extra budget to endpoint security. In a recent survey by Forrester, 41 percent of security technology decision-makers in all industries said their organization will increase spending on endpoint security by more than 5 percent in 2019.[51] Moreover, the survey finds that the challenge of ineffective antivirus technologies has led decision-makers to consider integrated suites with automated threat prevention, detection, and response.

Procurement of an endpoint security platform should be motived by the fact that 64 percent of respondents in a 2018 survey sponsored by the security firm Barkly revealed their company experienced at least one successful attack on their endpoints. A checklist of critical capabilities to look for in a next-generation security solution at all stages of maturity could help in buying decisions.[52] For organizations that are just starting to embrace endpoint security, at a minimum they need the capability to prevent fileless and other emerging attacks based on behavior patterns. Once the organization has established the resource with documented processes and a trained security team, they can look for integrated threat intelligence and Mitre ATT&CK enrichment. Next, as the organization grows in maturity, they can create customized prevention policies, which can enable automated decisions. The ultimate goal is the capability for automated processes based on increased integration with the security stack. SANS has created evaluation criteria that can be used to determine how well products protect against and detect modern attacks. For instance, for an evaluation of how well products detect and prevent malicious processes, a false positive rate can be used to determine a product's ability to recognize patterns and kill those processes that are executing malicious behaviors, such as binaries or scripts.[53]

Evolving attack tactics and techniques have fueled the growth of the commercial endpoint security market. In 2018, the Mitre Corporation conducted an evaluation of the technical capability of selected vendors to detect adversary behavior along the ATT&CK framework. Mitre chose to emulate APT3 for its initial evaluation because there is substantial analysis of the group's post-exploit behavior that "relies on harvesting credentials, issuing on-keyboard commands, and using programs already trusted by the operating system ('living off the land')."[54] The Mitre evaluation results describe how product users could detect specific ATT&CK techniques. The evaluation does not make a direct comparison between vendors but does help organizations make decisions about which vendor products meet their needs.

Carbon Black, CrowdStrike, and Cybereason were among the vendors that volunteered for the Mitre ATT&CK framework evaluation. CB Defense by Carbon Black uses predictive modeling that purportedly identifies known and unknown threats, including malware, fileless attacks, and ransomware with minimal false positives.[55] CB Defense is advertised to reveal threat activity in real time. It visualizes every stage of the attack to uncover the root causes in minutes and enable administrators to immediately triage alerts by isolating endpoints, blacklisting applications, or terminating processes. Falcon Insight by CrowdStrike is marketed to deliver complete endpoint visibility across an organization. It maps alerts to the Mitre ATT&CK framework, allowing understanding of complex detections at a glance, shortening time to triage alerts, and accelerating remediation. Complex context of an attack is provided by integrated threat intelligence. Falcon Insights acts against adversaries in real time, with response actions that enable containment and investigation.[56] The Cybereason Detection and Response Platform is advertised to automatically defeat malicious activity and provide end-to-end context of an attack campaign. It uses a hunting engine with a range of detection models to identify known and unknown attack elements and techniques. An interface tells a visual attack story and incorporates a remediator to kill processes and quarantine files and a blocker to stop process execution and network communication.[57] The evolution of EDR products is timely. The Russians continue to find ways to penetrate perimeter defenses and move quickly across networks, as indicated by the Bad Rabbit attack against Ukraine only four months after its NotPetya campaign. The Russians used a clever watering hole attack for intrusion and a modified NSA tool for propagation.

Quasi Ransomware

The Bad Rabbit pseudo ransomware campaign in October 2017 disrupted electronic payments at the Kiev metro system and caused flight delays at Odessa airport in a massive dispersal in the country. Bad Rabbit appeared to be a variant of NotPetya, also self-propagating and capable of spreading across corporate networks. The goal of Bad Rabbit seemed to be the same as NotPetya: to cause as much disruption as possible in Ukraine and those associated with it. Although the Singapore-based cybersecurity firm Group-IB said in a blog post that "the attack at a first glance appears to be financially motivated," researchers said the impetus for Bad Rabbit may have been "as a cover-up or smokescreen, or for both disruption and extortion."[58] The Ukrainian state police would probably agree with the smokescreen theory, since their chief, Serhiy Demedyuk, stated, "During these attacks, we repeatedly detected more powerful, quiet attacks that were aimed at obtaining financial and confidential information."[59] Regardless of the goal or motive, the Russians had once again displayed unique capability in the speed, scale, and sophistication of their cyber operations.

Bad Rabbit Campaign

In October 2017, a new ransomware outbreak occurred in several European countries, in particular Ukraine, Bulgaria, Turkey, and Germany, plus Russia, Japan, and the United States. The ransomware demanded a payment of 0.05 bitcoin, worth at the time about $275, from its victims.[60] The outbreak spread to visitors of infected Russian-language media websites who fell for a masqueraded update to Adobe Systems Flash multimedia product. Once the fake Flash installer was downloaded, the ransomware spread within victim's networks.[61] Malware researchers at Group-IB claimed that "it is highly likely that the same group of hackers was behind [the] BadRabbit [*sic*] ransomware attack . . . and the epidemic of the NotPetya virus."[62] It concluded that Bad Rabbit was "compiled from NotPetya source code as another project with several additions."[63] Other similarities between the two viruses include the same hashing algorithm and the same domains. One significant addition to Bad Rabbit was the ability to collect cash with a mechanism in place to give those who paid a key.[64]

While most victims did not pay, the security firm Rapid7 heard of a couple of instances in which those who paid received the key. The Security Service of Ukraine (SBU) laid blame on APT28, or Fancy Bear, associated with the GRU, for launching the massive, coordinated attack that disrupted business operations for hundreds of organizations located in Ukraine and Russia.[65] The SBU based its claim on the scale of the infrastructure (more than fifty compromised websites), the qualifications of the developers, and the lack of mercenary motives for the attack.

Russian hackers used the same watering hole tactic with drive-by downloads seen in the Dragonfly 2.0 campaign. Specifically, there after victims visited specific URLs, a file named "install_flash_player.exe" was observed on their computers, followed shortly by the Trojan.Karagany.B backdoor.[66] In the Bad Rabbit campaign, the user was presented with a pop-up for the fake Flash update on the compromised website. Infection was dependent on user interaction because the user had to click "install" to initiate the download of the fake Flash dropper along the path "flash_install.php" or "index.php".[67] Once the ransomware infected a machine, it scanned the network for adjacent IP addresses. It then used the legitimate open-source Mimikatz password-cracking tool to extract login credentials, like in NotPetya.[68] Next, Bad Rabbit dropped copies of itself into the compromised network and executed the copies with the legitimate WMIC tool. Bad Rabbit did not use EternalBlue but did use a modified version of the other exploit named EternalRomance, employed in the NotPetya campaign. This particular tool also used the SMB protocol vulnerability for malware distribution, although since EternalRomance had been modified, security experts could not immediately identify it.[69] After ciphering data on a victim's hard drive with the legitimate program DiskCryptor, also used in NotPetya, the malware altered the master book record, rebooted the computer, and displayed the ransom demand on a red-on-black screen.[70]

The Bad Rabbit campaign slowly died down in about a week. The attacker's server went off-line, and many of the infected websites hosting the script for the malicious Flash download fixed the issue.[71] Enough public awareness and researcher discovery of methods to defeat the ransomware helped to confine the infection to the original target region and prevent widespread infection in the United States.[72] A Cybereason researcher developed a so-called vaccine for the ransomware. The procedures were fairly simple and essentially removed or disabled "inheritable permissions" from computers.[73] In addition, Kaspersky Lab researchers found a way to recover files without paying the ransom, having learned that Bad Rabbit does not delete shadow copies and that if the shadow copies were enabled prior to infection, they could be restored by means of the standard Windows mechanism.[74] After the campaign terminated, the damage and culprit seemed to be forgotten by the international community. Unlike after the previous pseudo ransomware campaign, where the UK Foreign

Office minister of state proclaimed, "The UK government judges that the Russian Government, specifically the Russian military, was responsible for the destructive NotPetya cyber-attack of June 2017," no Western government publicly laid blame on Russia for Bad Rabbit. However, with technical attribution having been made to the same authors, this statement by the minister would seem to apply: "We call upon Russia to be the responsible member of the international community it claims to be rather than secretly trying to undermine it."[75]

Security Operating Platform

Gus Hunt, the managing director and cyber strategy lead for Accenture Federal Services, states that reaching cyber resilience means organizations must think differently about how they build and implement their systems. He admits that while "a security-driven focus has had beneficial effects, the cyber-threat landscape is moving at a far greater velocity, with a far larger threat landscape, and is growing more complex than federal agencies—or any other organization—can keep pace with."[76] Hunt reiterates the proverbial belief of security professionals that the issue is "not whether our defenses will be breached but when they will be."[77] This is why organizations need to shift from a reactive to a more proactive stance. The objective is a platform that can correlate indicators of compromise from many sensors, handle attacks autonomously by infrastructure, prioritize events triggered by known adversaries, and determine the bad actors' progress along the kill chain. Ideally it would reduce the number of alerts that require manual interpolation to a manageable level and correlate information across attack vectors, enabling operators to react at network scale and attack tempo against sophisticated techniques. This shift in approach requires an integrated security operating platform with automated threat prevention, detection, and response.

The Security Operating Platform offered by Palo Alto Networks has been chosen for detailed examination because its capabilities are installed at the Naval Postgraduate School, where the author of this book teaches and conducts research. The platform contains the Traps endpoint protection device, which focuses on recognizing behaviors (i.e., heuristics), such as methodologies used by an attacker to attempt to exploit the endpoint during intrusion. This endpoint solution monitors for distinctive markers associated with malware applications, such as new, unique processes or unusual network flows. For instance, the Child Process Protection Module evaluates the command line execution of a child or parent process (the latter a main process that creates subprocesses to perform certain operations) as criteria for blocking or allowing a process to run. This means the module would block PowerShell when it attempts to run a script from a specific path not in accordance with default rule settings. During the Bad Rabbit attack, the Traps device would have blocked several execution processes. In the malware installation phase, the DLL File Protection Module would block the injected dynamic link library (DLL) payload (containing embedded ransomware) from starting the encryption process and lateral movement. The DLL module examines the DLL file if it is loaded by a process configured in the DLL files security policy, such as the Windows System loading process rundll32.exe used by Bad Rabbit and the DLL file itself if it is not in the DLL whitelist. Traps would analyze file-execution behavior and if deemed malicious would block the file, preventing the need to take the endpoint off-line and later recover it. In addition, it would send a sample of the suspect software to its cloud-based sandboxing and threat-analysis service known as Wildfire for in-depth analysis. Once the sample was confirmed as malware, new signatures recognizing the malware payload would be created and distributed within minutes to all corporate next-generation firewalls installed around the world, the networking component of the security platform. This would disable the ability for Bad Rabbit to install the fake Flash dropper on the endpoint.

The Security Operating Platform protects the endpoint, pushes unknown files back up to the cloud for detonation, and then reinforces the network firewall with newly generated signatures, turning previously unknown threats into known threats, closing zero-day vulnerabilities in minutes. An implementation use case for automated cyber defense can provide a practical description of this type of secure automation functionality. Therefore, a use case was constructed with the Naval Postgraduate School to demonstrate the technical feasibility of the Palo Alto Networks commercial capabilities in a difficult scenario, such as the use of evasive techniques in WannaCry, NotPetya, and Bad Rabbit. This troubling trend is reflected in a recent CrowdStrike report that the majority of attacks it investigated in 2017 leveraged Windows features, such as PowerShell or WMIC, with fileless memory-only malware and compromised credentials to gain access, persist, and spread laterally throughout targeted networks.[78] The Traps tool defeats fileless or attached payload-free attacks by concentrating on exploit techniques rather than relying on signatures. Multiple protection methods are supported, including blocking memory-corruption techniques such as heap spraying, which attempts to inject malicious code into memory for eventual execution, and blocking malicious processes from accessing such injected malicious code, thereby preventing attacks without impacting legitimate processes, allowing continued operations. Traps also watches for and stops unusual network activity, such as downloading credential-gathering tools. Additionally, the next-generation firewall limits legitimate applications (such as Secure Shell [SSH] and WMI) to known, authenticated, and approved

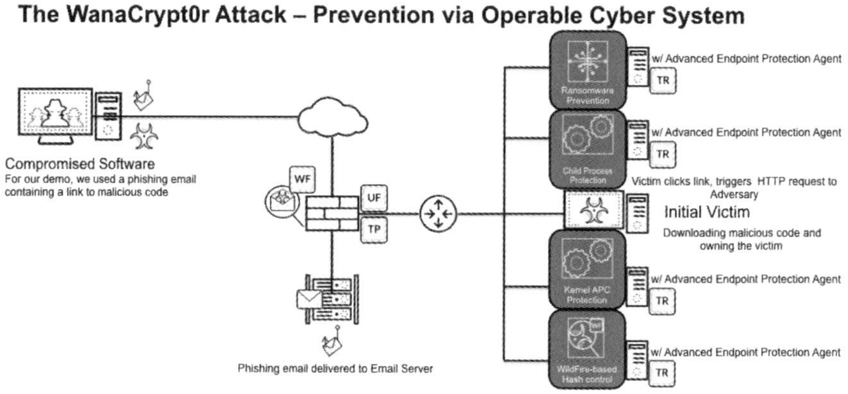

The WanaCrypt0r Attack – Prevention via Operable Cyber System

Figure 8.1. Automated Cyber-Defense Demonstration

Source: Palo Alto Networks, Corporate Communications Team.

users and their systems, prevents the submission of credentials to external systems (such as is typical in a phishing attack at the initial compromise stage), and requires multifactor authentication to internal systems by application (to prevent the use of any credentials that do happen to be stolen from being used to access additional systems).

To illustrate that commercial capabilities can successfully work together in this manner, a demonstration of the use case for automated breach detection and mitigation was given at the Integrated Cyber event at Johns Hopkins University in April 2018.[79] The demo employed the Circadence virtual cyber range to depict platform results against live WannaCry ransomware. The Traps endpoint protection device modules proved capable of blocking several execution processes (see fig. 8.1). For example, in the installation phase, it stopped the injected DLL (containing embedded ransomware) from creating the process to launch the encryption process. The demo also automated threat intelligence from firewall and endpoint log and tag correlations to prioritize events in a Splunk SIEM display. The proof-of-concept demonstration showed that automated threat prevention, detection, and response solutions in an integrated cyber-defense architecture are capable of defeating an adaptive attacker before damage is done, while continuing to operate.

Conclusion

The term *cybersecurity* infers a defense-in-depth architecture consisting of technologies, people, and processes, designed to protect information and information systems. The challenge today is that advanced threat actors appear capable of compromising nearly any organization. A 2018 survey by Accenture Security found on average that organizations are experiencing two to three security breaches a month.[80] Organizations have no choice but to assume they will suffer a breach. Rather than relying solely on security strategies, they should also employ resilience strategies to respond quickly to threats in order to minimize damage and continue to operate. This does not imply that identification of and protection against the threat through preventive security controls, such as firewalls and malware prevention, is not an important aspect of a comprehensive cyber-resilience strategy—just that it is essential to have robust detection mechanisms to constantly monitor networks.[81] The Accenture survey also found that security teams are finding breaches faster—in half the cases under a week. Although a vast improvement over the previous year, this detection rate still allows threat actors plenty of time to extract or cause damage to high-value assets. Worse is the other half of the cases, which take up to a month or longer to detect or are detected not at all. If an organization lacks the necessary solutions to detect the breach in the first place, the threat actor can wreak havoc indefinitely. The only way to proactively achieve cyber resilience is to have the necessary detection and response capabilities in place prior to breach.[82]

The Russians in particular capitalize on security gaps, acting at speed across networks, at scale in vectors and targets, and with sophistication to evade detection and avoid remediation. Endpoint protection solutions offer a way to process and analyze structured and unstructured security-relevant data. Their use in automated cyber defenses accelerates not only the detection process but also response actions to contain and remediate the threat. A quick response will limit damage and prevent the need to recover. For the IT team, recovering from a disruption can be a complex and time-consuming process, especially bringing a data center back online, restoring any lost data, replacing inaccessible devices, and reconfiguring applications.[83] Nearly half of global power and utilities chief operating officers feel cyberattacks are imminent, and not all are well prepared to manage such an event.[84] One reason is that many organizations use more than twenty-five different discrete or point security tools to manage, investigate, and respond to security threats.[85] Having a variety of systems and products is a burden to security operations center personnel, and as a result nearly half (49 percent) of legitimate alerts are not remediated.[86] A tightly integrated security operating platform with automated threat prevention, detection, and response solutions is essential for a single, unified view of the threat environment.

Notes

1. Donald Trump, *National Cyber Strategy of the United States of America* (Washington, DC: White House, September 2018), 6.

2. Trump, 6.
3. Derek B. Johnson, "With Elections Over, CISA Focus Shifts to Risk Management Center," FCW, November 17, 2018.
4. Andy Greenberg, "The Untold Story of NotPetya, the Most Devastating Cyberattack in History," *Wired*, August 22, 2018.
5. Help Net Security, "Most Concerning Security Controls for Cyberattackers? Deception and IDS," December 14, 2018.
6. Help Net Security.
7. FireEye, "M-Trends 2019," special report, March 2019, 6.
8. White House, Office of the Press Secretary, "Critical Infrastructure Security and Resilience," PPD-21 (February 12, 2013).
9. NIST, "Guide for Conducting Risk Assessments," NIST Special Publication 800-30, revision 1, September 2012, B-6.
10. Louise K. Comfort, Arjen Boin, and Chris C. Demchak, *Designing Resilience: Preparing for Extreme Events* (Pittsburgh: University of Pittsburgh Press, September 2010).
11. P. W. Singer and Allan Friedman, "Rethink Security: What Is Resilience and Why Is It Important?," in *Cybersecurity and Cyberwar* (New York: Oxford University Press, 2014), 169–73.
12. Alexander Kott and Linkov, *Cyber Resilience of Systems and Networks (Risks, Systems and Decisions)*, 1st ed. (New York: Springer, May 31, 2018), 2.
13. DHS, "Cyber Resilience White Paper: An Information Technology Sector Perspective," March 2017, 2.
14. DHS, 2.
15. DHS, "Cybersecurity Strategy," May 15, 2018, cover.
16. DHS, "Cyber Resilience and Response: Public-Private Analytic Exchange Program," 2018, 9.
17. NIST, "Cyber Resiliency Considerations for the Engineering of Trustworthy Secure Systems," Draft NIST Special Publication 800-160, vol. 2, March 2018, 9.
18. NIST, 11.
19. DHS, "Cybersecurity Strategy," 10.
20. Trump, "National Security Strategy," 13.
21. Ash Carter, "The DOD Cyber Strategy," Department of Defense, April 2015, 11.
22. DHS, "Cyber Resilience and Response," 5.
23. Tim Greene, "Why the 'Cyber Kill Chain' Needs an Upgrade," Network World, August 8, 2016.
24. Giora Engel, "Deconstructing the Cyber Kill Chain," Dark Reading, November 18, 2014.
25. LightCyber, "Behavioral Attack Detection," white paper, November 2015, 5–7.
26. Anthony Giandomenico, "Understanding the Attack Chain," CSO Online, December 3, 2018.
27. Mitre Corporation, "Enterprise Tactics," ATT&CK website, assessed March 9, 2019.
28. Freddy Dezeure and Rich Struse, "ATT&CK in Practice: A Primer to Improve Your Cyber Defense," RSA Conference, San Francisco, March 2019.
29. CrowdStrike, "2019 Global Threat Report: Adversary Tradecraft and the Importance of Speed," March 2019, 2.
30. CrowdStrike, 15.
31. Symantec, "Internet Security Threat Report," vol. 24, February 2019, 17.
32. CrowdStrike, "2019 Global Threat Report," 19.
33. US-CERT, "Russian Government Cyber Activity."
34. US-CERT, 21.

35. DOD, "Summary: Department of Defense Cyber Strategy," 4.
36. Dana Deasy, "DOD Cybersecurity Policies and Architecture," statement before the United States Senate Armed Services Subcommittee on Cybersecurity, January 29, 2019, 10.
37. Deasy, 11.
38. Recorded Future, "Best Practices for Applying Threat Intelligence," white paper, July 2017, 7.
39. Cybereason, "The Seven Struggles of Detection and Response," white paper, 2015.
40. John Edwards and Eve Keiser, "Automating Security," *C4ISR and Networks*, October 2016, 16.
41. Edwards and Keiser, 16.
42. John Kindervag and Stephanie Balaouras, "Rules of Engagement: A Call to Action to Automate Breach Response," Forrester Research, Inc., December 2, 2014, 8.
43. Edwards and Keiser, 16.
44. Gabby Nizri, "The Rise of SOC Automation," Ayehu (blog), February 27, 2017.
45. Jonathan Trull, "Top 5 Best Practices to Automate Security Operations," Microsoft Security, August 3, 2017.
46. Steve Morgan, "Cybersecurity Jobs Report," Cybersecurity Ventures, 2017, 2.
47. Gartner, "The Evolution of Endpoint Protection," research paper, 2018, 3, https://www.gartner.com/imagesrv/media-products/pdf/symantec/symantec-1-4SNI36O.pdf?es_p=6816496.
48. Lee Neely, "Endpoint Protection and Response: A SANS Survey," SANS Analyst Program, June 2018, 6.
49. Infogressive, "The Complete Guide to Endpoint Detection and Response," blog post, 2019.
50. Neely, "Endpoint Protection and Response," 12.
51. Chris Sherman and Salvatore Schiano, "The State of Endpoint Security, 2019," security report, January 22, 2019, 5, https://services.forrester.com/report/The+State+Of+Endpoint+Security+2019/-/E-RES141772.
52. Carbon Black, "How Does Your Security Stack Up?," white paper, 2019.
53. Barbara Filkins, "Essential Requirements for Cloud-Based Endpoint Security," white paper, SANS, September 2018, 10.
54. Mitre ATT&CK Evaluations website, accessed July 8, 2019.
55. Carbon Black, "CB Defense on the PSC," fact sheet, 2019, 2.
56. CrowdStrike, "Falcon Endpoint Detection and Response," product sheet, 2019, 2.
57. Cybereason, "Cybereason Detection and Response Platform," fact sheet, 2018, 2–3.
58. Mathew Schwartz, "BadRabbit Attack Appeared to Be Months in Planning," Bank Info Security (blog), October 26, 2017.
59. Pavel Polityuk, "Ukraine Hit by Stealthier Phishing Attacks during BadRabbit Strike," Reuters, November 2, 2017.
60. Robert McMillian, "New Ransomware Outbreak Spreads through U.S., Russia and Ukraine," *Wall Street Journal*, October 24, 2017.
61. James Rogers, "Bad Rabbit Ransomware: Should You Be Scared?," Fox News, October 25, 2017.
62. Doug Olenick, "Group IB Shows Even Tighter Ties between BadRabbit and NotPetya," *SC Magazine*, October 26, 2017.
63. Olenick.
64. Doug Olenick, "BadRabbit Ransomware Moves to the U.S., Links to Petya/NotPetya Being Debated," *SC Magazine*, October 25, 2017.

65. Olenick.
66. Symantec, "Dragonfly: Western Energy Companies under Sabotage Threat," Security Response (blog), June 30, 2014.
67. Radware, "Bad Rabbit," ERT threat alert, October 30, 2017.
68. John Leyden, "BadRabbit Encrypts Russian Media, Ukraine Transport Hub PCs," The Register, October 24, 2017.
69. Wagas, "EternalRomance NSA Exploit a Key Play in Bad Rabbit Ransomware Mayhem," Hack Read (blog), October 27, 2017.
70. Wagas.
71. Selena Larson, "New Ransomware Attack Hits Russia and Spreads around the Globe," CNN Tech, October 25, 2017.
72. James Rogers, "BadRabbit Ransomware."
73. Lital Asher-Dotan, "Cybereason Researcher Discovers Vaccine for Bad Rabbit Ransomware," Cybereason (blog), October 25, 2017.
74. Pierluigi Paganini, "Documents Encrypted by Bad Rabbit Ransomware Could Be Recovered without Paying Ransom," Security Affairs, October 28, 2017.
75. National Cyber Security Centre, "Russian Military 'Almost Certainly' Responsible for Destructive 2017 Cyber Attack," February 15, 2018.
76. Gus Hunt, "A Shift from Cybersecurity to Cyber Resilience: 6 Steps," Dark Reading, December 5, 2018.
77. Hunt.
78. Sean Gallagher, "'Malware-Free' Attacks Mount in Big Breaches, CrowdStrike Finds," Ars Technica, December 6, 2017.
79. Scott Jasper, "Implementing Automated Cyber Defense," *United States Cybersecurity Magazine* 6, no. 18 (Winter 2018): 22–25.
80. Accenture Security, "Gaining Ground on the Cyber Attacker: 2018 State of Cyber Resilience," executive summary, 2018, 7.
81. IT Governance, "An Introduction to Implementing Cyber Resilience," green paper, January 2019, 5.
82. Symantec, "The Cyber Resilience Blueprint: A New Perspective on Security," white paper, 2014, 5.
83. Citrix, "Guidelines for Maintaining Business Continuity for Your Organization," white paper, 2014, 3.
84. Julia Sowells, "48 Percent of Utility CEOs Feel Cyberattacks Are Imminent," Hacker Combat, November 15, 2018.
85. ESG Research, "Cybersecurity Operations Challenges and Strategies," research report, 2018.
86. Cisco, "2018 Annual Cybersecurity Report."

CHAPTER 9

Technical Offset Strategy

The 2017 US National Security Strategy claims that the United States and its allies and partners are engaged in a long-term strategic competition with Russia.[1] In August 2018, the assistant secretary of state for European and Eurasian affairs, A. Wess Mitchell, testified before Congress that "past U.S. policies have neither sufficiently grasped the scope of this emerging trend nor adequately equipped our nation to succeed in it."[2] According to Secretary Mitchell, Russia is a serious competitor that is "building up the material and ideological wherewithal to contest U.S. primacy and leadership in the 21st Century."[3] Furthermore, the Kremlin's ability to conduct a range of coercive and subversive activities that stay below the threshold of armed conflict will contribute to "persistent economic, political and security competition," according to the National Intelligence Council.[4] The extension of this competition through cyber operations erodes military advantages, threatens infrastructure, and reduces economic prosperity. A key aspect of the latest DOD Cyber Strategy is to "strengthen the security and resilience of networks and systems that contribute to current and future U.S. military advantages."[5] Given the speed, scale, and sophistication of Russian cyber operations that challenge security and resilience, a technical offset strategy is necessary to achieve that objective.

NATO secretary-general Jens Stoltenberg says, "There is no indication that Russia intends to change its behavior."[6] Stoltenberg states, "We have witnessed an increasingly dangerous and unacceptable pattern of behavior from Russia: its military buildup and aggressive actions from the north of Europe to the Middle East [and] its use of hybrid tactics including cyberattacks, disinformation and interference with the democratic processes of other countries. It also continues to undermine Ukraine's sovereignty and territorial integrity."[7] This chapter will present a closing case in the Russians' pattern of provocative behavior against Ukraine to illustrate their continued employment of cyber operations and disinformation in conjunction with military actions. It will explain how Russia manipulates a lack of clarity in international norms to conduct cyber operations without concern and will describe the promise of technical offsets to compete with Russian military advances. The chapter will finish with how use of data-correlation technologies in an integrated security operating platform can regain advantage over Russian cyber operations.

Continued Confrontation

On November 25, 2018, the FSB intercepted three Ukrainian naval vessels traveling from Odessa, their main naval base, to the port of Mariupol.[8] The journey required the boat group to pass from the Black Sea through the Kerch Strait into the Sea of Azov. The previous day, the voyage commander was notified by Russian authorities that navigation was closed to foreign ships in the Kerch Strait area. The contingent requested approval for passage on the morning of the incident but was ordered to halt by Russian maritime control services.[9] The vessels supposedly refused to comply and attempted to pass through the strait. Russia patrol ships sought to block their passage, and in a series of close maneuvers one ship rammed and damaged the hull of the Ukrainian tugboat in the boat group. Russia then blocked the Kerch Strait by placing a huge tanker lengthwise under the bridge across the Strait, stranding dozens of cargo ships awaiting passage.[10] Russia called in airpower reinforcements consisting of Ka-52 attack helicopters and Su-25 fighters. Late in the day as the standoff continued, the Russian ships unexpectedly opened fire, and one of the Russian attack aircraft launched two unguided missiles against the Ukrainian artillery gunboats, wounding six Ukrainian service members.[11] Russia then seized all three Ukrainian vessels, took captive their crews, and towed the vessels to the Crimean port city of Kerch, then under Russian control. The next day, Russia reopened navigation through the Kerch Strait.

The Russian confrontation in the Black Sea followed a year-long, intensive propaganda campaign spreading disinformation about Western and Ukrainian activity. Russian media first published claims that Kiev was dredging in the Sea of Azov to host a NATO fleet.[12] Then it spread stories that Ukraine had infected the sea with cholera. Next were allegations of a US plan to spark clashes between Ukrainian and Russian forces. Finally, a preposterous report surfaced that Russian special operations forces had prevented the transport by British and Ukrainian secret services of a nuclear bomb intended to blow up the bridge over the Kerch Strait.[13] In addition, before and during the encounter with the Ukrainian vessels, Russian government–affiliated actors conducted cyber operations against Ukrainian government and military targets. The state-backed group Carbanak executed a phishing campaign in late October against entities that would have had information related to Ukrainian naval affairs.[14] Attached to the phishing emails were PDF documents with links to malicious code. The exfiltrated information would have been useful if Russia wanted to engineer a maritime crisis. Then, a week before the confrontation, the Gamaredon Group, a separate actor with ties to the FSB, targeted Ukrainian government agencies using a backdoor named Pterodo. Finally, the day after the imprisonment of the Ukrainian sailors, Carbanak started a second coordinated attack against Ukrainian agencies.[15] The use of cyber operations in the Kerch Strait confrontation follows the continued pattern of timing before Russian offensive operations, going back to Georgia in 2008.

Initially NATO members could not agree on a powerful response to what the Pentagon has characterized as "unlawful and destabilizing actions" in Ukraine. The immediate course of action for the United States was to step up surveillance flights in early December under the Open Skies Treaty "to reaffirm US commitment to Ukraine."[16] Kiev's vice premier for European and Euro-Atlantic integration, Ivanna Klympush-Tsintsadze, condemned the "shortsightedness" of some European capitals over the depth of Russia's ambitions and urged the bloc to impose new sanctions. Part of the reason for the discord on an integrated response was that Russian president Vladimir Putin had abused fractures within European societies, fueled by his political warfare campaign to bolster the ambitions of parties in Europe that have adopted a pro-Kremlin stance, such as the Austrian Freedom Party and the Italian League.[17] Catherine Harris and Mason Clark, at the Institute for the Study of War, write that the lack of a unified NATO response to Moscow's aggression in the Sea of Azov was likely to be perceived by Russia as "an opportunity to escalate against Ukraine and elsewhere in the future."[18]

Vice Premier Klympush-Tsintsadze asserted that Russia was waging "war against the West and against rules and procedures that have been guiding the world order."[19] She called for NATO to further increase its presence in the Black Sea. In January 2019, the USS *Fort McHenry* pulled into the Romanian port Constanta, the first Black Sea visit of a US Navy warship since Russian forces seized the Ukrainian vessels. The commander of the US Sixth Fleet, Vice Adm. Lisa Franchetti, said that by sending the amphibious warship with its embarked Marines into the Black Sea, the US Navy was "signaling to all nations in the area a U.S. commitment to upholding international law in the region."[20] Ukraine claims the Russian ships unlawfully used force in violation of the UN Charter and in doing so "committed an act of aggression as defined in Article 3, paragraph 3 (blockade) and 4 (attack on the sea forces of a state) of the United Nations General Assembly resolution 29/3314 ['Definition of Aggression']."[21] The official Russian position is that the Kerch Strait confrontation occurred because the Ukrainian vessels "illegally entered the country's territorial waters and ignored warnings to stop while maneuvering dangerously."[22] The position fails to take into account that the Ukrainian vessels had to maneuver at high speed to avoid being rammed by the Russian ships.

From a legal point of view, it seems clear the Russian ships violated the UN Convention on the Law of the Sea, the UN Charter, and the Treaty on Cooperation between the Russian Federation and Ukraine on the Use of the

Azov Sea and Kerch Strait (the Azov Sea Treaty), which was ratified by both parliaments in April 2004. The treaty defines the Azov Sea and Kerch Strait as "historically internal waters of the Russian Federation and Ukraine."[23] Under the treaty, "commercial ships and warships under either the Russian flag or the Ukrainian flag shall enjoy freedom of movement in the Azov Sea and Kerch Strait."[24] At the time of the incident, the treaty had not been abandoned by signatory parties.[25] In 2015, Russia adopted rules that required ships passing through the strait to give advance notification to Russian authorities, which the Ukrainian boat group did but not early enough to satisfy Russia's rules. Ukraine has rejected any notion it needed Russian permission for passage, while Russia sees the "situation as a violation of its territorial sovereignty."[26] However, the Ukrainian ships only entered the twelve-mile territorial zone within the Kerch Strait governed by the treaty. According to maritime law, even if a violation of Russian territorial waters did occur, the proper response would have been for the border guards to "escort the violating ships out of the territorial zone, not to fire on them."[27] Thus, on many legal fronts, the incident highlights once more "Russia's lack of concern about violating international norms of behavior," many of which are "part of the international order that it is keen to modify or replace."[28]

Unclear Norms

The Russian interpretation of international law was bolstered by two impediments for consensus in the 2016–17 GGE draft report: the inherent right to self-defense and a reference to international humanitarian law.[29] Previous GGE reports stated that "in particular the Charter of the United Nations, is applicable and is essential to . . . promoting an open, secure, stable, accessible and peaceful ICT environment."[30] This conclusion would include Article 51 of the charter for "the inherent right of individual or collective self-defense."[31] Apparently the issue in GGE deliberations was not the right's existence but the threshold at which it kicked in—namely, an "armed attack which is the condition precedent for exercise of the right of self-defense."[32] Rule 71 of the *Tallinn Manual 2.0* states that "whether a cyber operation constitutes an armed attack depends on its scale and effects."[33] Yet it readily admits "the parameters of the scale and effects criteria remain unsettled beyond the indication they need to be grave."[34]

While the International Group of Experts that wrote the *Tallinn Manual 2.0* offer that "a cyber operation that seriously injures or kills a number of persons or that causes significant damage to, or destruction of, property would satisfy the scale and effects requirement," the terms *seriously* and *significant* are open for broad interpretation.[35] The experts themselves noted that "the law is unclear as to the precise point at which the effects of a cyber operation qualify as an armed attack."[36] Furthermore, in the case of cyber operations that create extensive negative effects, the law is equally unsettled. For instance, a cyber operation that targets essential functions of a state and leads to serious disruption of the functioning or stability of the state could conceivably qualify as an armed attack.[37] An example of abuse of this lack of clarity is the case of Russian cyber operations targeting the Ukrainian energy companies in 2015. The incident did not reach the "scale and effects" threshold to qualify as an armed attack. However, the electric grid could be considered an essential function of the state, raising debate on whether the negative effects led to serious disruption of the stability of the state. In this case, the Russian ability to stay below the threshold of an armed attack, while using the pro-Russian group Sandworm for deception, was critical to maintaining impunity since the threshold of an armed attack is also "the threshold at which a state may lawfully use force in self-defense."[38]

The threshold for determination of the use of force is even more problematic. The position of the United States is that "cyber activities that proximately result in death, injury, or significant destruction would be likely viewed as a use of force."[39] Therefore, the use of force "irrefutably includes acts that cause damage or injury, but not traditional economic or political sanctions."[40] One challenge is the lack of authoritative criteria to "qualify acts falling in the twilight between physically harmful cyber operations and those that are purely economic or political in nature."[41] The exclusion of cyber operations that generate dramatic economic consequences is questionable. Take, for example, the case of Russian-orchestrated DDoS attacks upon Estonia in 2007. Michael Schmitt concluded that "taken together as a single 'cyber operation' the incident arguably reached the use of force threshold in violation of the Charter of the United Nations."[42] He based his assessment on the direct and immediate effects of the DDoS attacks upon governmental services, the economy, and daily life, although the UN Charter itself is not necessarily helpful since it provides no specific criteria by which to determine when an act amounts to a use of force.

Rule 69 of the *Tallinn Manual 2.0* delineates that "a cyber operation constitutes a use of force when its scale and effects are comparable to non-cyber operations rising to the level of a use of force."[43] In order to "identify cyber operations that are analogous to other kinetic or non-kinetic actions that the international community would describe as uses of force," the *Tallinn Manual* offers a number of factors that can influence state use-of-force assessments, specifically severity, immediacy, directness, invasiveness, measurability, military character, state involvement, and presumptive legality.[44] The factors operate in concert. For example, a temporary DDoS operation is unlikely to be classified as a use of force, whereas massive cyber operations that cripple an economy may be categorized as a use of force, which frames debate on Estonia in 2007. The experts found the focus on scale and effects to be an equally useful approach to analyze quantitative and qualitative factors in determining whether a cyber operation amounts to a use of force. Yet under the use of "scale and effects" factors, the challenge is distinguishing between the most grave forms of the use of force (those constituting an armed attack) from other, less grave forms. The *Tallinn Manual* emphasizes "that 'use of force' and 'armed attack' are standards that serve different normative purposes."[45] States facing a use of force not amounting to an armed attack can only use countermeasures. Russia might not have avoided a use-of-force designation for cyber operations against Estonia in 2007. However, Moscow avoided lawful retribution for the cyber operations by manipulating the rules of international law for state responsibility through the use of patriotic hackers.

The second impediment for consensus in the 2016–17 UN GGE draft report was a direct reference to international humanitarian law, also referred to as the law of armed conflict. Rule 80 of the *Tallinn Manual 2.0* delineates that "cyber operations executed in the context of an armed conflict are subject to the law of armed conflict."[46] The International Group of Experts was unanimous in finding "that the law of armed conflict applies to such activities during both international and non-international armed conflicts."[47] This finding applies in the cases of cyber operations that occurred in Georgia in 2008 and have taken place in the Donbass region since 2014. Apparently the issue in GGE deliberations was misguided concern over the reference, which led to "an incorrect legal conclusion: that acknowledging humanitarian law's applicability would somehow justify the cyber operations during such conflicts."[48] This conclusion distorts the humanitarian purpose of the law—for instance, prohibitions on attacking civilians and civilian objects. Instead, Russia has developed its own interpretation of international humanitarian law in the Georgia and Donbass conflicts, where cyber operations against civilian infrastructure are a component of asymmetric and new-generation warfare. The United States is seeking to form a coalition of like-minded states to hold nations accountable for actions that violate norms.[49] Yet a lack of clarity in norms found in recognized treaties and conventions allows Russia to continue cyber operations in either conflict or competition.

Offset Technologies

In November 2014, former secretary of defense Chuck Hagel told the audience at the Reagan National Defense Forum that "Russia's invasion of Ukraine represents one of the most blatant acts of state-on-state aggression on that continent since the end of World War II."[50] He said this invasion was the beginning, not the end, of emerging power challenges to world order. Hagel also noted in his speech that countries like Russia have been investing heavily in military modernization programs to blunt the US military's technological edge, fielding advanced aircraft, submarines, and both longer-range and more accurate missiles. He argued that without unmatched technical superiority, both friends and adversaries could doubt the United States' commitment to enforcing international law and rules of the road. Therefore, an important long-term investment is in the nation's unrivaled capacity for innovation.[51] This is not a new approach, as the United States responded twice before to challenges in Russian primacy with offset strategies. During the Cold War the US military relied on technological superiority to offset the Soviet Union's advantages in time, space, and force size. This edge in technology allowed the adoption of new force postures and operational concepts that compensated for the enormous numerical advantage the Warsaw Pact had in conventional forces.[52]

In the 1950s, the New Look Strategy fielded a formidable nuclear arsenal on the battlefield. A smaller US military, armed with missiles, rockets, and artillery shells tipped with low-yield atomic warheads, deterred Soviet conventional superiority. Then, in the early 1970s, the United States responded to the Warsaw Pact buildup of modernized conventional assault forces arrayed along the inter-German border with an offset strategy based on digital microelectronics and information technology. That offset was found in a new generation of sensors, weapons, and networks that could "look deep and shoot deep."[53] The US deep-strike complex was never tested against the Soviet Union but was demonstrated in Operation Desert Storm in 1991. The guided-munitions battle network routed a capable Iraqi army equipped with Russian and Chinese weapons and trained in Soviet doctrine.[54] Hagel's speech launched a game-changing Third Offset Strategy to regain operational and technological edge, through the Defense Innovation Initiative. The intent is to accelerate innovation in breakthrough technologies and systems that advance the capability of US military power.[55] The need to innovate fast is clear because in an era of rapid technological change, any advantage will not last.[56]

Former deputy secretary of defense Robert Work has said that the focus of ongoing innovation is "really in the commercial sector, biotechnology, nanotechnology, robotics, [and] atomics."[57] A couple key areas that Secretary Work emphasized as worth pursing are "autonomous deep learning machines and systems" and "advanced human-machine teaming."[58] An example of the first category is a "cyber system that can recognize attack, recognize weakness and self-correct its defenses."[59] Although most of the notable examples of proven Third Offset Strategy initiatives are more kinetic, such as the adaptation of the navy's SM-6 surface-to-air missile and the Marine Corps's High Mobility Artillery Rocket System as antiship weapons.[60] These initiatives are designed to boost current conventional capabilities past the ability of near-peer competitors to counter them. The Russians have reacted with indigenous programs of their own, focusing on narrow areas such as artificial intelligence, directed-energy weapons, and hypersonic vehicles.[61] While some Russian technologies are at early stages, hypersonic weapons have rapidly progressed in development or deployment.

Two of the six new so-called invincible weapon systems designed to evade and penetrate US antimissile defenses fall into the hypersonic category. The first is the Avangard hypersonic glide vehicle for strategic missile reentry into the atmosphere. The vehicle has a claimed speed of Mach 27 while maneuvering both horizontally and vertically.[62] The second is the Kinzhal hypersonic missile, with a claimed range of two thousand kilometers. The Kinzhal is most likely a variant of the Iskander missile that can reach speeds of Mach 5 to Mach 10.[63] The first public debut of the Kinzhal was at Moscow's 2018 Victory Day parade, mounted below two MiG-31 fighter jets.[64] At an international policy forum in Sochi, President Putin warned that his new hypersonic missiles give Russia a military edge, boasting that "we have run ahead of the competition" because while others are only planning to start testing such weapons, Russia has already deployed the Kinzhal.[65] That assertion seems to be true. Heather Wilson, then the secretary of the air force, said, "I do not think we should be naïve in what we are facing" from Moscow in "terms of their staggering advances in hypersonics."[66] The United States is just starting to invest in offensive hypersonic strike weapons, followed by unsystematic partial defensive systems.[67] Mike Griffin, the Pentagon undersecretary of research and engineering, readily admits, "We're probably not going to kill hypersonic boost glide missiles," because "by the time you can see it, they are inside our track loop."[68]

The United States may have relinquished dominance in the hypersonic aspect of the air domain. Likewise, in the cyber domain, the Russians have also innovated in their operations past the ability of current security measures to see and kill intruders. Russian actors are constantly adopting and modifying tactics and techniques to penetrate and evade cyber defenses. In response to eroding superiority against asymmetric threats, the Third Offset Strategy is supposed to cultivate, harness, and sustain innovation to "meet new enemies wherever and whenever they arise."[69] Yet a pervasive problem and theme in conference discussions on the strategy is the difficulty in identifying and adapting the wealth of innovation in the commercial sector.[70] In the Third Offset Strategy areas of autonomous deep learning machines and systems and advanced human-machine teaming, there are a wide array of commercial advances in data-correlation technologies already being cultivated, harnessed, and sustained that could regain advantage over Russian cyber operations.

Data-Correlation Technologies

An integrated security operating platform offers automated threat prevention, detection, and response. The first step in prevention is to obtain complete visibility over all applications, users, content, endpoints, and traffic. This equates to the observation and collection of massive amounts of rich data to prevent known and unknown threats. The network firewalls, endpoint devices, and cloud security services in the platform investigate event data, detect any suspicious activity, respond with mitigation actions, and collectively generate log events for fusion and analysis. Log events are ingested into SIEM solutions for log storage and threat correlation and display. The security operating platform is more than a collection of legacy point products. It is a single solution using multiple technologies and techniques that each increase the opportunity to prevent an attack along the cyber kill chain.[71] This capability to defeat an adaptive attacker in seconds rather than days was demonstrated in the previously described use case for automated breach detection and mitigation. The sponsor of the use case, Palo Alto Networks, has since capitalized on the utility of data-correlation technologies by integrating a new Cortex XDR framework and a leading security orchestration, automation, and response (SOAR) solution into their security operating platform. Their approach is intended to prevent the easiest attempts to execute attacks, apply machine learning to detect the most sophisticated attacks, and use orchestration and automation tools to accelerate human-machine investigations. Accordingly, many of the new platform features will be examined to provide examples of the Third Offset Strategy areas of autonomous deep learning machines and systems and advanced human-machine teaming, with conceptual and practical explanations of data-correlation technologies in each area.

Deep-Learning Machines

Advanced attacks often do not incorporate traditional indicators of compromise, such as malware signatures or malicious domains. The best threat prevention can stop 99 percent of known threats, evasive malware, zero-day attacks, and most fileless attacks. Detection of the final 1 percent of the most damaging attacks requires analysis of activity over time and across system layers with machine-learning and behavior analytics. These types of data-correlation technologies learn the unique characteristics of the organization and form a baseline of expected behavior to detect the most sophisticated attacks, including insider threats. Machine learning teaches a machine how to predict an answer or make a decision on its own. The biggest ability of the technology is for the machine to respond to situations that it has not specifically encountered before, replacing arduous human analysis. The machine learns through multiple examples in the form of a dataset and rules or algorithms to apply to that dataset. Two types of machine learning are supervised learning and unsupervised learning. In the first category, the machine is trained using labeled sample data and knows what questions and answers are expected. In unsupervised learning, the machine is trained using unlabeled data, which means it does not know what the data represents and therefore will have to figure out on its own the patterns and structure of the input.[72]

Machine learning is certainly useful for detecting known threats that have been previously seen. However, the real value of machine learning is to detect previously unseen variations of known threats and also unknown threats, such as zero-days.[73] The variations are detected through supervised learning by matching of machine-learned rules or recognition of machine-learned patterns. The unknown threats are detected through unsupervised learning in cases distant from known behavior. Here machine learning models normal behavior by profiling user and device behavior. Next, behavior analytics analyze large volumes of data to detect anomalous or suspicious behavior indicative of attacks. Detection algorithms are used to evaluate past behavior, peer behavior, the type of entity or user, and many other attributes to produce a small number of accurate, actionable alerts. For example, behavior analytics might detect a new peer relationship on the network with hosts that should not be communicating.[74] Machine learning and behavior analytics expose not just targeted attacks but also risky behavior by reckless employees and malicious insiders who abuse trusted credentials and access.[75]

The Cortex XDR Analytics application uses machine learning and behavior analytics to uncover stealthy attacks across the corporate network. It starts by collecting, correlating, and stitching rich data gathered across the security operating platform inside a scalable cloud-based data store. Rich data on the network (IPs, ports, and bytes), user (names, system, and addresses), application (name, protocol, and domain), endpoint (files, process, hash, and registry), and threat intelligence (hashes, IPs, URLs) is combined to provide complete visibility. The Analytics application then provides an analysis of user and device behavior through use of the following specific machine-learning techniques:

- Supervised machine learning: Monitors characteristics of network traffic to classify each device by type and learn which are IT administrators or normal users. Then recognizes deviations from expected behavior based on the type of device or user.
- Unsupervised machine learning: Baselines and models user and device behavior, performs peer group analysis, and clusters devices into relevant groups of behavior. Then detects anomalies from comparisons of past and peer behavior, which indicate malicious activity such as malware behavior, lateral movement, and exfiltration.[76]

The Analytics application tracks more than one thousand dimensions of behavior. Detection algorithms analyze values calculated by machine learning. Stealthy attacks can be found by examining rich data, building behavior profiles, and analyzing these profiles with detection algorithms. For instance, the application would record transfers of amount of data, use of HTTP, HTTP(S) (Hypertext Transfer Protocol [Secure]), or SSH protocols and connections to number of hosts each day. The application then watches for anomalies, such as repeated access to a rarely used site or multiple domain name system (DNS) requests for random-looking domain names, which is indicative of command-and-control activity.

The Cortex XDR Investigation and Response application also employs machine learning and behavior analytics in the Traps endpoint protection sequence for multiple methods of prevention. Traps protects hosts by identifying exploit techniques, not just exploit signatures. When a user attempts to run an executable, the device first queries WildFire threat intelligence with the hash of any Windows, macOS, or Linux executable file or DLL or Office macro to check if the file is known to be malicious or benign. If the file is unknown after the initial hash lookup, local analysis is conducted via machine learning on the endpoint. The endpoint device examines hundreds of file characteristics in real time to determine whether the file should run. Next, for attacks that use multiple legitimate applications and processes, behavioral threat protection is used to identify malicious activity. It detects and acts on malicious flows or chains of events that target multiple operations on endpoints, such as network, process, file, and registry activity. This protection is also ideal for protecting against script-based and fileless attacks. In addition to local analysis, Traps can send unknown files to WildFire for static analysis of characteristics or dynamic analysis in a sandbox to detonate the submission and look for effects and behavior.[77] If WildFire determines a file to be a threat, protection is coordinated with Traps and at the next-generation firewall in the integrated security operating platform. The security firm Gartner has assessed that Traps provides solid exploit prevention and mitigation, while recognizing the use of a stack of nonsignature detection capabilities, such as machine learning.[78]

The security operating platform has also incorporated Israel-based Secdo capabilities into Traps.[79] Secdo's thread-level (sequence of events) approach to data collection and visualization goes beyond traditional endpoint solution methods, which collect only general event data. Secdo uses machine learning to simplify investigations with the following views:

- Root-cause analysis: Automatically identifies the chain of events behind every threat. It visualizes the attack sequence back to the root cause, with details on each element. This view allows an analyst to instantly see which endpoint processes were responsible for alerts without manually correlating events or pivoting between consoles.
- Timeline analysis: Provides actionable detail in a forensic timeline of all attack activity. This view gives informational alerts that identify suspicious behavior.[80]

Once threats are identified, the security team can stop the spread of malware, restrict network activity, and update threat prevention lists, such as bad domains. Using the Remote Terminal response function, the security team can terminate and delete processes in a live environment on any device with precision. This allows users to continue to work without disruption or downtime. The Cortex framework embodies the virtues of deep-learning machines in threat visibility and prevention.

Human-Machine Teaming

A SIEM solution uses a set of frameworks and displays that support monitoring and alerting, to help organizations gain comprehensive visibility into their security posture and respond to attacks.[81] A SIEM ingests and processes large volumes of log data from third-party products to generate initial alerts. The SIEM dashboards can help triage new notable events and assign events to analysts for review.[82] However, today analysts are overly burdened with a manual incident-response process, which is tedious, repetitive, and time consuming. The first step is to investigate the issue to identify the threat, primarily by reviewing logs and activity across the network, including users and devices. This review requires staying abreast of the latest threat intelligence and comparing data against known attack information such as indicators of compromise (virus signatures, malignant IP addresses, hashes of malware files, and URLs linked to command-and-control servers). The next step is to contain the threat by blocking IP addresses, domains, and services or isolating infected users or devices by disabling accounts or preventing devices from accessing the network. The third step is to neutralize the threat by reimaging the affected device, changing passwords, and applying updates. The fourth step is to recover by removing any blocks, enabling accounts, recovering data, and conducting training. The final step is to document the incident, which includes completed tasks and lessons learned. In addition, personnel must set up alerts for future activity and scan across the network with new indicators of compromise. The manual gathering of context on an alert and making of an appropriate decision can take hours or longer.

Fortunately, new data-correlation technologies have emerged to automate and orchestrate the entire incident-response process, from initial event notification to remediation and closure. While the term *security automation* infers the use of information technology in place of manual processes, the term *security orchestration* refers to the use of tools and playbooks designed to streamline the processes.[83] Security actions in both cases, whether execution by automation or coordination by orchestration, are machine-based.[84] Security automation and orchestration decrease an organization's security risk exposure by reducing the amount of uninvestigated and unresolved alerts. They enable threat investigations in seconds and reduce the time for containment and re-mediation, whether the platform is operating with or without a security analyst approving security actions. They also act as a force multiplier for manpower- and skill-constrained security teams that are dealing with an escalating volume of security alerts.[85] A host of SOAR solutions have emerged to automatically gather key information, build decision cases, and execute critical actions to prevent cyber threats.[86] By automating security procedures and workflows in a human-machine teaming arrangement, the SOAR solutions allow analysts to accelerate investigations. For instance, one SOAR customer automated the process to investigate a phishing email that normally took more than ninety minutes to complete manually. The standard procedure was to acknowledge receipt from an employee, look for malicious indicators, and take remediation steps. With automation, the process is now completed in under a minute, free-ing analysts to focus on more complex threats.[87]

Gartner predicts that by 2022, SOAR technologies will be leveraged in 30 percent of organizations that have a security operations center (SOC) team larger than five people.[88] Leading security vendors are acquiring SOAR capa-bilities to add to their portfolio for SOC optimization. Palo Alto Networks has incorporated the Demisto SOAR solution with its security operating platform to deliver immediate threat investigation and response for security teams. Demisto's automated playbooks have proven to "reduce alerts that require hu-man review by as much as 95 percent."[89] Security orchestration playbooks are task-based graphical workflows that help visualize and coordinate processes. In a 2019 survey, close to 50 percent of respondents claimed they are using six or more distinct products for incident response.[90] Using this best-of-breed approach means security products span across vendors, functions, and data standards. Playbooks enable systematization of best practices and automation of the following types of repetitive security actions across the entire stack (neat arrangement) of security products:

- finding indicator reputation from threat-intelligence tools
- opening, editing, and closing support tickets
- sending emails to affected end users
- detonating files in malware analysis tools
- quarantining infected endpoints
- setting the severity levels of incoming alerts
- updating indicator watchlists and blacklists[91]

Demisto utilizes these and other flexible, intuitive drag-and-drop playbooks to drive response actions and investigation queries. The enterprise solution fo-cuses on continuous improvement, using machine learning to power insights on incident ownership, task management, related incidents, and indicator cross-correlation across products and incidents. Since Demisto can ingest alerts across a range of sources (e.g., SIEM, email tools, vulnerability scanners, and the cloud), security teams can visualize common indicators across different incident types. This correlation enables teams to quickly spot whether an indicator is isolated or part of a larger, persistent attack campaign. Demisto also contains a war room–type collaboration platform for analysts to share insights and information. The war room utilizes the concept of "ChatOps," enabling analysts to remotely execute third-party security actions from within Demisto, resulting in minimized context-switching. The war room also automatically documents all tasks, comments, and actions.

Demisto also integrates with Cortex XDR to assimilate incidents and trigger playbooks for enrichment and response.[92] Cross sections of Cortex XDR incident information (such as file or network artifacts) are integrated into playbook tasks or within the war room. Overall, Demisto incident response capabilities "weave in security orchestration and automation for quicker triage, response and coordination in the face of rising attack numbers."[93] This minimizes noise and prevents alert fatigue. The SOAR solution embodies the virtues of human-machine teaming in collaboration, predictability, and repeatability in operations.

Conclusion

In November 2018, Ukrainian president Petro Poroshenko declared that "Russia has been waging a hybrid war against our country for a fifth year. But with an attack on Ukrainian military boats it moved to a new stage of aggression."[94] While the EU, the United Kingdom, France, Poland, Denmark, and Canada all concurred and condemned what they called "Russian aggression," the United States did not take a hard line. President Donald Trump seemed reluctant to blame Russia when asked how he felt about the clash. Trump merely said, "Not good. Not happy about it at all," while adding "we do not like what's happening either way. And hopefully it will get straightened out."[95] Rep. Eliot Engel, on the House Foreign Affairs Committee, said the president sent the wrong message—that NATO is divided and unwilling to react—just as the Russian president was testing its resolve. The president's initial reaction is a far cry from the name-and-shame strategy previously used to hold the Russian government and its proxies accountable for their cyber operations. NATO foreign ministers eventually approved "a series of measures aimed at countering Russia in the Black Sea region," mostly to "provide Georgia and Ukraine with increased maritime cooperation, patrols and port visits,"[96] and Russia eventually released the Ukrainian sailors in a prisoner exchange after more than eight months of detainment and the vessels in very poor condition.[97] Still, the Kerch Strait confrontation, which integrated cyber operations and a disinformation campaign with forceful military actions, signaled the failure of US and European actions to deter Russian aggression.

The Kremlin dared to act in such a brazen way due to the West's feckless response to the annexation of Crimea, the occupation of the Donbass region, and the annexation of Abkhazia and South Ossetia. The Russians had little reason to believe their overt attack in the Kerch Strait, enhanced by covert cyber operations, would prompt a reaction they could not stand, despite obvious violations of an international treaty.[98] But for US lawmakers, Russian cyber operations are a growing concern. Sen. Mark Warner, on the Senate Intelligence Committee, said at the Center for New American Security that "we just aren't waking up" to the Russian "emerging brand of hybrid, cyber warfare."[99] Case evidence clearly indicates that Russia has chosen cyber operations as a method to engage in long-term strategic competition that fractures the rules-based international order.[100] Using a robust "toolkit of asymmetric measures for the 21st Century, including cyberattacks and disinformation campaigns," the Kremlin competes across political, economic, and military arenas.[101] The exploitation of technology and manipulation of information accelerates these contests. Researchers Alina Polyakova and Spencer P. Boyer argue that technological advances in artificial intelligence, automation, and machine learning, combined with big data (large amounts of data), have "set the stage for a new era of sophisticated, inexpensive, and highly impactful political warfare."[102]

In this era the Russians are employing more complex methods and tools to launch and execute cyber operations. Their APT groups engage in persistent campaigns to compromise targets, using modern polymorphic and obfuscated malware, fileless malware, and hijacked legitimate operating system functions to evade traditional defenses. They change the performance of the operating system by leveraging trusted Microsoft applications such as PowerShell.[103] Meanwhile, security teams are stretched thin monitoring numerous products and investigating the rising number of threat alerts. Most organizations do not know if they are compromised and unaware if intruders are living off the land.[104] They struggle to keep pace while Russian actors continue to evolve their tactics. The incorporation of data-correlation technologies into an integrated security operating platform can help defenders overcome the speed, scale, and sophistication of Russian cyber operations. This tightly woven system offers a new approach to detection and response by leveraging machine learning, behavioral analytics, and automated investigations. It is time for the West to turn the tables on the Russians with technological offset advances that deny them any benefit from their cyber operations.

Notes

1. Donald Trump, *National Security Strategy of the United States of America* (Washington, DC: White House, December 2017), 25.
2. A. Wess Mitchell, "U.S. Strategy towards the Russian Federation," statement for Senate Foreign Relations Committee, August 21, 2018, 1.
3. Mitchell, 1.
4. National Intelligence Council, "Global Trends: Paradox of Progress," January 2017, 21.
5. DOD, "Summary: Department of Defense Cyber Strategy," 2018, 1.
6. Jens Stoltenburg, "The Cold War Is Over, but Big Challenges Remain," *Defense News*, December 10, 2018, 10.
7. Stoltenburg, 10.
8. Samuel Chamberlain, "Russian Military Fires on Ukrainian Vessels in Black Sea, Ukraine Says," Fox News, November 25, 2018.
9. "Address of Ukraine's Ambassador to UN Security Council on Kerch Strait Incident," *Kyiv Post*, November 28, 2018.
10. "Russia Uses Cargo Ship to Block Ukrainian Navy Vessels," *World Maritime News*, November 27, 2018.
11. Natalia Zinets, "Ukraine Says Counterintelligence Officer Wounded in Sunday's Russia Clash," Reuters, November 27, 2018.
12. Daniel Boffey, "Russia Paved Way for Ukraine Ship Seizures with Fake News Drive," *The Guardian*, December 10, 2018.
13. Associated Foreign Press, "Russian Infor War Preceded Ukrainian Ship Seizures: EU," *Straits Times*, December 11, 2018.
14. Patrick Tucker, "Russia Launched Cyber Attacks against Ukraine before Ship Seizures, Firm Says," Defense One, December 7, 2018.
15. Tucker.
16. Zachary Cohen and Ryan Browne, "U.S. Military Flexes Muscles in Message to Russia," CNN, December 6, 2018.
17. Alina Polyakova and Spencer P. Boyer, "The Future of Political Warfare: Russia, the West, and the Coming Age of Global Digital Competition," Brookings Institution, Robert Bosch Foundation Transatlantic Initiative, March 2018, 6.
18. Paul D. Shinkman, "Putin Raising Likelihood of War, Ukrainian Navy Chief Says," *U.S. News & World Report*, December 12, 2018.
19. Michael Peel and Roman Olearchyk, "Ukrainian Minister Calls for Fresh Sanctions on Russia," *Financial Times*, December 25, 2018.
20. Ben Werner, "USS *Fort McHenry* Visits Romania while Russian Frigate Watches," United States Naval Institute, Foreign Forces (blog), January 7, 2019.
21. Himanil Raina, "Legal Aspects of the 25th November, 2018 Kerch Strait Incident," issue brief, National Maritime Foundation, December 12, 2018.
22. "Russia and Ukraine Clash over Kerch Strait Explained," *Moscow Times*, November 26, 2018.
23. Vladimir Socor, "Azov Sea, Kerch Strait: Evolution of Their Purported Legal Status," *Eurasia Daily Monitor* 15, no. 169 (December 3, 2018).
24. Socor.
25. Endre Szenasi, "The Kerch Strait Incident: Why the 2003 Treaty Regulating the Azov Sea Rights Has Not Been Terminated by Russia," Academia.edu (blog), December 4, 2018.
26. Dmitry Gorenburg, "The Kerch Strait Skirmish: A Law of the Sea Perspective," Strategic Analysis, December 2018, 3.
27. Gorenburg, 4.

28. Gorenburg, 5.

29. Michael Schmitt and Liis Vihul, "International Cyber Law Politicized: The UN GGE's Failure to Advance Cyber Norms," *Just Security*, June 30, 2017.

30. UN General Assembly, "Group of Governmental Experts," 12.

31. UN, Charter of the United Nations, chapter VII, article 51, October 24, 1945.

32. Michael Schmitt, "Cyberspace and International Law: The Penumbral Mist of Uncertainty," *Harvard Law Review Forum* 126, no. 5 (March 2013): 179.

33. Michael N. Schmitt, ed., *Tallinn Manual 2.0 on the International Law Applicable to Cyber Operations*, 2nd ed. (Cambridge: Cambridge University Press, 2017), 339.

34. Schmitt, 341.

35. Schmitt, 341.

36. Schmitt, 341.

37. Schmitt, 342.

38. Schmitt, 332.

39. Schmitt, 332.

40. Schmitt, "Cyberspace and International Law," 178.

41. Schmitt, 178.

42. Michael N. Schmitt, "Cyber Operations in International Law: The Use of Force, Collective Security, Self-Defense, and Armed Conflicts," *Proceedings of a Workshop on Deterring Cyberattacks: Informing Strategies and Developing Options for U.S. Policy* (Washington, DC: National Academies Press, 2010), 156.

43. Schmitt, *Tallinn Manual 2.0*, 330.

44. Schmitt, 333.

45. Schmitt, 337.

46. Schmitt, 375.

47. Schmitt, 375.

48. Robert McLaughlin and Michael Schmitt, "The Need for Clarity in International Cyber Law," Policy Forum, September 18, 2017.

49. Theresa Hitchens, "US Urges 'Like-Minded' Countries to Collaborate on Cyber Deterrence," Breaking Defense, April 24, 2019.

50. DOD, "Secretary of Defense Speech: Reagan National Defense Forum Keynote," Press Operations, November 15, 2014.

51. DOD.

52. Robert O. Work and Greg Grant, "Beating the Americans at Their Own Game: An Offset Strategy with Chinese Characteristics," Center for New American Security, June 6, 2019, 1.

53. DOD, "Deputy Secretary of Defense Speech: National Defense University Convocation," press release, August 5, 2014.

54. Work and Grant, "Beating the Americans at Their Own Game," 3.

55. Chuck Hagel, "The Defense Innovation Initiative," US secretary of defense memorandum, November 15, 2014, https://news.usni.org/2014/11/19/document-pentagon-innovation-initiative-memo.

56. Otto Kreisher, "Defense Leaders Stress Urgency of Third Offset Strategy," *Seapower*, October 28, 2016.

57. Vago Muradian, "Interview: Bob Work, US Deputy Defense Secretary," *Defense News*, November 26, 2014.

58. Aaron Mehta, "Work Outlines Key Steps in Third Offset Tech Development," C4ISR Networks, December 14, 2015.

59. Richard R. Burgess and Otto Kreisher, "Work: Third Offset Focus Is to Improve U.S. Battle Networks," *Seapower*, December 5, 2016.

60. Sydney J. Freedberg Jr., "Anti-aircraft Missile Sinks Ship: Navy SM-6," Breaking Defense, March 7, 2016; Hope Hodge Seck, "Top Marine Wants to Fire Anti-Ship Missiles
from HIMARS Launcher," Kit Up, December 14, 2016.

61. Vasily Kashin and Michael Raska, "Countering the U.S. Third Offset Strategy: Russian
Perspectives, Responses and Challenges," policy report, S. Rajaratnam School of International Studies, January 2017, 16.

62. Nikolai Novichkov and Robin Hughes, "Russia Announces Flight Test of Avangard
HGV," Jane's International Defence Review, February 2019, 18.

63. Franz-Stefan Gady, "Russia's 5th Generation Stealth Fighter Jet to Be Armed with Hypersonic Missiles," The Diplomat, December 6, 2018.

64. Matthew Bodner, "Russia's Hypersonic Missile Debuts alongside New Military Tech at
Parade," Defense News, May 10, 2018.

65. Vladimir Isachenkov, "Putin: Russia 'Ahead of Competition' with Latest Weapons,"
Stars and Stripes, October 18, 2018.

66. Carol Munoz "Chinese, Russian Hypersonic Weapons Advances a Growing Concern,
Air Force Chief Says," Washington Times, May 16, 2019.

67. Melanie Marlowe, "Hypersonic Threats Need an Offense-Defense Mix," Defense News,
August 5, 2019, 15.

68. Aaron Mehta, "Is the Pentagon Moving Quickly Enough on Hypersonic Defense?,"
Defense News, March 21, 2019.

69. Damon V. Coletta, "Navigating the Third Offset Strategy," Parameters 47, no. 4 (Winter
2017/18): 50.

70. Kathleen Hicks and Andrew Hunter, "Assessing the Third Offset Strategy," project report, Center for Strategic and International Studies, March 2017, 6.

71. Palo Alto Networks, "Security Operating Platform," executive summary, March 2019,
1–5.

72. CrowdStrike, "The Rise of Machine Learning in Cybersecurity," white paper, 2019, 2–4.

73. Cisco, "Annual Cybersecurity Report," 2018, 10.

74. T. K. Keanini, "Machine Learning and Security: Hope or Hype," Brink News, October
21, 2018.

75. Louis Columbus, "Machine Learning Is Helping to Stop Security Breaches with Threat
Analytics," Forbes, June 16, 2019.

76. Palo Alto Networks, "Magnifier," data sheet, 2018, 2.

77. Palo Alto Networks, "Traps Technology Overview," white paper, 2019, 2–4.

78. Gartner, "Magic Quadrant for Endpoint Protection Platforms," industry report, January 24, 2018.

79. Palo Alto Networks, "Closes Acquisition of Secdo," press release, April 24, 2018.

80. Palo Alto Networks, "Cortex XDR," white paper, March 2019, 8.

81. Katelyn Dunn and Matthew Hveben, "Splunk Enterprise Security," Group Test SIEM
and UTM-NGFW, SC Magazine, May 2019, 39.

82. Splunk, "The Six Essential Capabilities of an Analytics-Driven SIEM," white paper,
2018, 3, https://insight.scmagazineuk.com/six-essential-capabilities-of-an-analytics
-driven-siem.

83. Jonathan Trull, "Top 5 Best Practices to Automate Security Operations," Microsoft
Security (blog), August 3, 2017.

84. Splunk, "The SOAR Buyer's Guide," special edition, 2018, 4.

85. Splunk, "Reducing Risk with Security Automation and Orchestration," solution guide,
2018, 1–2, https://www.splunk.com/pdfs/solution-guides/reducing-risk-with-soar
-phantom.pdf.

86. Swimlane, "Security Automation Orchestration," technical data sheet, 2019, 1, https://Swimlane.com.

87. Splunk, "Measuring the ROI of Security Orchestration and Response Platforms," white paper, 2019, 3, https://www.splunk.com/en_us/form/measuring-the-roi-of-security-operations-platforms.html.

88. Gartner, "Market Guide for Security Orchestration, Automation and Response Solutions," industry report, June 27, 2019.

89. Palo Alto Networks, "Announces Intent to Acquire Demisto," press release, February 19, 2019.

90. Demisto, "The State of SOAR Report, 2019," Demisto annual report, 2019, 10.

91. Abhishek Iyer, "Security Orchestration for Dummies," Demisto special edition, 2019, 20–21.

92. Demisto, "Partner Integrations: Demisto and Cortex" (blog), August 22, 2019.

93. Demisto, "Demisto Enterprise for Incident Management," data sheet, 2019, 1–3.

94. Reuters, Agence France Press, "Ukraine Introduces Martial Law Citing Threat of Russian Invasion," *Straits Times*, November 26, 2018.

95. Joe Gould, "US Lawmakers Urge Trump to Arm Ukraine, Break Silence on Russian Blockade," *Defense News*, November 26, 2018.

96. Mathew Lee, "NATO Approves Measures to Counter Russia amid Internal Rifts," *Military Times*, April 4, 2019.

97. Ivan Nechepurenko and Andrew Higgins, "Russia and Ukraine Take the First Step to Stop the War," *New York Times*, September 7, 2019; and Oleg Novikov, "Ukraine Says Russia Returned Ships in Bad Condition," Reuters, November 20, 2019.

98. Adrian Karatnycky, "Ukraine Is Moscow's Guinea Pig," *Wall Street Journal*, November 28, 2018.

99. Tucker, "Russia Launched Cyber Attacks."

100. Curtis M. Scaparrotti, Statement before the United States Senate Committee on Armed Services, March 5, 2019, 3.

101. Polyakova and Boyer, "Future of Political Warfare," 1.

102. Polyakova and Boyer, 1.

103. Kevin Jones, "The Fileless Malware Attacks Are Here to Stay," Hacker Combat, May 10, 2019.

104. Angela Messer and Brad Medairy, "The Future of Cyber Defense . . . Going on the Offensive," *Cyber Defense Review* 3, no. 3 (Fall 2018): 38–39.

Conclusion
A Different Approach

Assistant Secretary A. Wess Mitchell affirmed that US policy toward Russia proceeds from the recognition that US diplomacy "must be backed by military power that is second to none."[1] Accordingly, the United States has reversed years of cuts to its defense budget and worked with NATO allies to increase European defense spending. In response to Russia's aggression in Crimea and Eastern Ukraine, the United States has reassured European allies and partners of its commitment to their security through the European Deterrence Initiative. The EDI has grown steadily since 2014 to reach $6.6 billion for fiscal year 2019, for which funds have increased the US combat presence in Eastern Europe, prepositioned equipment, and improved infrastructure.[2] The United States has demonstrated its military might in exercises and operations, including sending two aircraft battle groups to the Mediterranean Sea in a show of force to Russia.[3] In tandem, the United States has imposed economic costs on the Russian state and its oligarchy to try to stem aggression. According to Russian foreign minister Sergei Lavrov, US policy has resulted in relations at an all-time low. In a 2018 speech to the United Nations, Lavrov accused the United States of engaging in "political blackmail, economic pressure and brute force," all hallmarks of Russian doctrine seen in countries on its periphery.[4] Furthermore, Lavrov repeated the Kremlin's position that it did not interfere in the 2016 US presidential election. Yet Russian interference in democratic elections and other malign activities continue. It is obvious from analysis of actual cyber campaigns and incidents that Moscow holds competitive advantage in the technical complexity and legal ambiguity of its cyber operations.

In 2015, the leaders of the G20 nations "affirmed that international law applies to state conduct in cyberspace."[5] The *Tallinn Manual 2.0* takes an identical stance and attempts to provide guidance for the application of international law to cyber operations. However, the ambiguity in exactly when and how international law applies is an invitation for Russia to launch cyber operations in strategic competition. Case evidence shows how legal ambiguity hampers the right to use countermeasures by cyber means in response. The evidence also reveals how Russia has increased the technical complexity of its cyber operations to bypass current security measures. Unfortunately, a whole-of-government approach using economic, legal, and diplomatic instruments has not prevented undesired Russian behavior in cyberspace. A new strategy for the aggressive use of cyber means has shown early results but with risk of retaliation. Therefore, the concluding considerations highlight the need for a different approach that combines the offensive concept of defend forward with more robust defensive solutions that strengthen the resilience of networks and systems. They finish with the promise of data-correlation technologies in a security operating platform to regain advantage in day-to-day competition.

Legal Ambiguity

Russia sees ambiguity in legal regimes pertaining to the land, maritime, and cyber domains as a way to maintain operational and strategic flexibility. Russia aligned with China, Cuba, and others to reject the 2016–17 GGE draft report "on the basis of reinvigorated concerns about how cyber interacts with a range of legal concepts and schemes."[6] The foremost issue was the extent to which countermeasures can be used in response to unlawful cyber operations. More specifically, "How do we identify when and how a state may respond to a hostile cyber operation with its own cyber capabilities, which would be unlawful but for the fact that its purpose is to induce the attacker to desist?"[7] The case of the 2016 hack and leak of sensitive information from the Democratic National Committee is a prime example of the uncertainty regarding "when and how" a state may respond with countermeasures. The most applicable legal determination for the incident was not an armed attack but unlawful intervention in US internal affairs, which falls into the category of an international wrongful act.

At issue was the matter of whether the influence campaign qualified as coercive intervention, a question on which legal scholars can and do disagree. It was unclear whether "facilitating the release of actual emails—as distinct from, for example, using cyber means to alter election returns—amounts to coercion as a matter of law."[8] Liis Vihul, the managing editor of the *Tallinn Manual*, stated, "It can't possibly be coercive to provide people information on which they'll make a better informed decision."[9] The counterargument posed by Michael Schmitt is that the "breach crossed a line by attempting to manipulate the U.S. political process."[10] Legal ambiguity on whether unlawful intervention occurred in the 2016 US presidential election hobbled how the US administration chose to respond. If the determination was plain and clear under international law, the Barack Obama administration could have used countermeasures in the form of hack-backs to disrupt Russian government and private-cyber activities. Instead, the US administration "condemned the Russian meddling in U.S. elections as 'unacceptable' and stated it 'would not be tolerated' but did not characterize the activity as unlawful."[11]

The US government resorted to the expulsion of diplomats, the closure of compounds, and the imposition of sanctions, which were acts of retorsion (unfriendly acts that do not violate international law). These direct responses were available without needing, as a matter of law, to qualify the Russian influence campaign as an internationally wrongful act.[12] In the case of whether it was interference or intervention in the US presidential election, the Russians aptly selected an area of law for which it is difficult for states to reach consensus on whether they have violated international law and how states can respond accordingly. In the future, Russia will most likely avoid establishing in international forums any clarification on the "when and how" dilemma for responses by legally authorized use of countermeasures. That is not in their best interest, as legal ambiguity keeps nations engaged in disputes and reduces the level of their response to unlawful cyber operations.

Technical Complexity

Current security strategies have not changed the perceptions of Russian actors that cyber operations will not succeed. Instead, they are employing more complex technical means to launch and execute cyber operations. For instance, the objective of the NotPetya attack in June 2017 was to destabilize and debilitate institutions in Ukraine. The mock ransomware succeeded in wiping data at twenty-two banks, four hospitals, six power companies, two airports, ATMs and card payment systems in retailers and transport, and practically every federal agency in the nation.[13] Not only were these victims unprepared for the complexity of the attack but so were global corporations when the worm spread outside national borders. The shipping giant Maersk, based in Copenhagen, had to reinstall software on forty-five thousand personal computers and four thousand servers.[14] Every domain controller was wiped, except for a server in a remote office in Ghana, saved by a blackout that had disconnected it from the network. The worm spread primarily by download of M.E.Doc software, which is used by nearly everyone in Ukraine who files taxes or does business. It took only one download on a single computer in a Maersk finance office in Odessa to infect its entire network. After initial infection, NotPetya leveraged multiple propagation methods to spread across networks and used legitimate Windows administration tools for evasion during lateral movement. It also leveraged the two stolen NSA exploits to infect systems that were not patched for the Microsoft SMB vulnerability.[15] Therefore, if a system was patched or not, NotPetya could spread—which it did in victim networks at lightning speed, infecting a portion of one major Ukrainian transit hub in only sixteen seconds, way too fast for manual incident response by overwhelmed security operations centers.[16]

NotPetya inflicted nine-figure costs at not only Maersk and the aforementioned Merck and Mondelez but also at FedEx subsidiary TNT Express, French construction company Saint-Gobain, and consumer goods manufacturer Reckitt Benckiser.[17] While NotPetya infected critical infrastructure primarily in Europe and Ukraine, Russian cyber actors have also adopted advanced tactics and techniques to penetrate, evade, and deceive cyber defenses for multiple critical infrastructure sectors in the United States since at least March 2016. The cyber actors used typical attack vectors for intrusion such as spear-phishing emails, watering hole domains, and credential gathering, but in ingenious ways. Rather than use email attachments to download malware, they leveraged legitimate Microsoft Office functions to retrieve credential hashes from servers and password-cracking techniques to obtain the password in plaintext. Likewise, they used similar techniques on compromised websites for credential harvesting. A second spear-phishing tactic used a generic PDF document without active code but containing a redirect to a website that prompted the user for email address and password. After accessing victim networks with compromised credentials, the actors used scripts to create local administrator accounts for privilege escalation. For deception, the hard-coded values for the name administrator was in five different languages. The TA18-074A report provides numerous other examples of technical complexity that avoided detection, evident by the actors' ability to collect vital ICS information.

More Aggressive Strategy

The head of NATO, Jens Stoltenberg, warned Russia ahead of European Parliament elections that the Western military alliance is ready to use all means at its disposal to respond to cyberattacks. While not saying what exact steps would be taken, options include "targeted restrictive measures to deter and respond to cyber attacks" adopted by the European Union.[18] In 2016, President Obama gave President Putin a similar warning on hacking at a G20 meeting in Hangzhou, China, just two months before the US presidential election. He directly told the Russian leader "to cut it out, there were going to be serious consequences if he did not."[19] However, in the end, the US presidential election hacking episode highlights how Obama's efforts to deter Russia failed. His administration tried to strengthen cyber defenses (through the Cybersecurity Framework), clarify international law in cyberspace (through international cyber norms), and threaten or enact punishment for hostile cyber operations (through sanctions, expulsions, and closures). The latter were simply dismissed by Putin as a trifling inconvenience.[20] Russia has figured out how to systematically target a democratic but politically divided society that depends on vulnerable electronic technologies. Jim Sciutto at *The Atlantic* succinctly sums up that the essence of the Kremlin's plan is "to attack U.S. interests just below the threshold that would prompt a military response and then, over time, to stretch that threshold further and further."[21] Absent harsher measures, Russia will not let up, for even when the West pushes back, through sanctions or other cost-imposition methods, the regime uses the external pressure as a unifying force at home.[22] Putin at the helm is not really the problem—it is the culture. Remember that Russia is not a democratic state; another strongman will eventually take his place.[23] Unless the United States gets tougher, it could suffer more extreme injuries.[24]

The commander of US Cyber Command, Gen. Paul Nakasone, has said, "We are not going to sit back and take it anymore."[25] His conviction was proven true when evidence emerged of a classified Cyber Command operation named Synthetic Theology to shut down the IRA during the 2018 midterm elections.[26] In addition to earlier stated warnings to Russian operatives, the US military blocked Internet access to the infamous Russian troll farm. The disruption took place while Americans voted and during the election count to prevent the Russians from mounting a disinformation campaign that could cast doubt on the results. This strike represented the first offensive cyber campaign against Russia under new authorities. In a matter of months since signature, the new process under National Security Presidential Memorandum 13 resulted in more operations than in the previous ten years.[27] In addition, the congressional decision to normalize cyber operations has empowered the strategy of persistent engagement. The strategy declares that cyber forces must be in constant contact in cyberspace with strategic competitors.[28] A key pillar of the strategy is the concept to defend forward to see and halt cyber threats at their source before they reach the United States, including those below the level of armed conflict. Defending forward "helps us better protect ourselves," says the director of operations at US Cyber Command, Maj. Gen. Charles Moore, since "when we do this, we can observe enemy techniques and procedures and their tactics as well as potentially uncover any tools or weapons they might be utilizing."[29]

The IRA confirmed it was attacked on the day of the midterm elections but insisted the US operation was a complete failure. The Russian Federal News Agency said the attack knocked out two server hard drives, but that did not stop work entirely,[30] while, on the contrary, US senators from both political parties praised and credited US Cyber Command with averting Russian interference in the midterms.[31] Sen. Mike Rounds stated that without the Cyber Command's efforts, there "would have been some very serious cyber-incursions."[32] Rob Joyce, the senior civilian adviser to General Nakasone, acknowledged that the efforts were successful but also noted that the 2018 DOD Cyber Strategy has not resulted in a change in state behavior. He cites the NotPetya attack attributed to Russia and their hacking and disinformation campaign in the 2016 US presidential election as evidence of a shift from exploitation to disruption in unconstrained operations. In warning that the

United States has to do more than just counter cyberattacks, Joyce said, "We have to impose costs in a visible way to start deterrence."[33] Professor Richard Harknett and researcher Michael Fischerkeller argue that what has emerged in cyberspace is not deterrence but agreed competition, with "a tacit agreement among states that they will actively pursue national interests through cyber operations . . . while carefully avoiding the equivalence of armed attack."[34]

Senior fellow James Miller and adjunct professor Neal Pollard say that the respected scholars miss the mark, asserting, "The U.S. should (and indeed did) describe actions such as . . . Russian cyber-enabled meddling in U.S. elections as neither 'agreed' nor 'competition' but, rather, unacceptable hostile acts for which the U.S. needs (and can achieve) a stronger deterrence posture."[35] The 2018 DOD Cyber Strategy disentangles this argument by stating a line of effort in its strategic approach is to both "compete and deter" in cyberspace.[36] However, it leaves open for interpretation how exactly competition complements deterrence. Instead, the United States now operates continuously to increase options for decision-makers to reduce adversary aggression. General Nakasone explains that in order "to defend critical military and national interests, our forces must operate against our enemies on their virtual territory."[37] Thus, *defend forward* infers an offensive cyber operation. However, every offensive cyber operation poses risk—including discovery of an exploit of a vulnerability used for initial access. If the target responds by patching its network, use of the exploit for future access will be lost. Even worse, the exploit could be repurposed. For instance, the security firm Symantec reported that the Chinese group APT3 obtained and used tools made by the NSA, possibly from artifacts found in its networks.[38]

Although a benefit of discovery, according to the hypothesis of those who support the Cartwright Conjecture (as expressed by Gen. James Cartwright), might be that "adversaries who become aware of U.S. cyber capabilities will in turn restrain their own cyber operations."[39] Recent disclosure of US digital intrusions into Russia's electric power grid serves as a warning, a demonstration, and a foothold to conduct cyber-strikes if a major conflict broke out between Washington and Moscow.[40] Despite the risk of escalation and the loss of future use of capability, disruptive or destructive US cyber operations will probably become more frequent. A prime example is when Iran downed a US surveillance drone in June 2019 during tensions over attacks on oil tankers, President Donald Trump elected to respond in cyberspace after calling off a physical attack over concern about loss of life. The United States launched a digital strike against computer systems and communication networks used by the Islamic Revolutionary Guard Corps.[41] The covert attack wiped out a database used to choose which oil tankers to target and where.[42] Even though officials deemed the cyber-strike to be very effective, the Iranian minister for information and communications technology said it was not successful.[43] Nonetheless,

American companies braced for retaliation by Iran, potentially with destructive wiper attacks that could destroy entire networks.[44] Such a situation dictates that while, in the words of former national security adviser John Bolton, the United States is "now opening the aperture, broadening the areas we're prepared to act in," federal and civilian organizations at risk of nation-state retaliation need to be prepared to withstand cyberattacks.[45]

Concluding Considerations

The United States and NATO seem to ignore the reality that "cooperation for its own sake is of no interest to Moscow."[46] Russia interprets concessions as weakness and an invitation to demand more, rather than to soften a stance. Its violation of international agreements is reinforced by the staunch belief that great nations achieve security through the creation and assertion of power. The destabilization and weakening of others will only make Russia relatively stronger. Hence, for Russia to achieve its aspirations for great power status, it must diminish the status of competitors, which means confronting the West and in particular the United States. This approach includes sowing and stoking discord in US and European societies, consistent with previous practices of subversion used in the Cold War.[47] It also includes exerting systematic political, economic, and military pressure on the buffer states on its periphery, in particular Ukraine, to prevent Euro-Atlantic integration.[48] The intended result of interference is chaos, without any real consequences. Chaos serves Russian interests, as international uncertainty with hedging allies and teetering international institutions provide space for maneuver.[49] The international community has swiftly forgotten and forgiven previous acts of hybrid aggression, for sure in Georgia and Ukraine. President Trump has even pushed to invite Russia back into the G7, despite meeting none of the preconditions for readmission, which include respect for Ukraine's sovereignty.[50] The outcome is to encourage rather than deter Russian military adventurism, fueled by Russian cyber operations. The problem is that this adventurism has become more aggressive and more dangerous—for instance, Russian cyber operations now threaten the security of critical infrastructure, especially the power grids in the United States and Europe.

At a Cyberspace Strategy Symposium convened by US Cyber Command in May 2019, during a debate on the new cyber strategy known as persistent engagement, an unnamed senior US military official said the goal is "imposing cost" since "adversaries, until checked, will keep advancing."[51] It might be true that the United States checked the IRA by reducing its ability to interfere in the 2018 midterm elections. Yet any premise that the tougher cyber doctrine will deter Russian cyber operations remains unproven, and the opposite might just occur when Russia "ups its game." Therefore, the third element of the 2018 DOD Cyber Strategy, "strengthen the security and resilience of networks and systems," becomes even more important.[52] The challenge as shown in the cases is the speed, scale, and sophistication of the Russians' cyber operations. They have mastered many of the tactics and techniques described in the Mitre ATT&CK framework.

A different approach is necessary to not only defend forward but also to withstand attacks. This more aggressive approach intercepts cyber threats and increases cyber resilience if the adversary penetrates the security perimeter. This shift in approach requires technical solutions that are capable of detecting the threat actor somewhere along the cyber kill chain before the action of objectives phase. EDR solutions investigate activity that has not been blocked by security measures. They have proven capability to recognize new, unique processes or unusual network flows. Initial analysis of the execution or connection process and subsequent termination precludes the need to take the endpoint off-line and later recover it. By sending a sample of suspect software to cloud-based threat intelligence, new signatures can be created and distributed to firewalls, protecting other organizations. The ability to react with these components at network scale and attack tempo against sophisticated techniques requires an integrated security operating platform with automated threat prevention, detection, and response. The security operating platform turns unknown threats, even zero-days, into known threats by responding to and processing indicators of compromise in seconds or minutes rather than days or months.

The security operating platform is designed to protect against cyber-threat-actor usage of stolen credentials, fileless malware, scripts, and legitimate applications, typical elements of Russian cyber operations. The most damaging attacks require analysis of activity over time and across system layers. Data-correlation technologies form a baseline of normal behavior and find deviations indicative of malicious activity. Machine learning profiles user and devices behavior. Next, behavior analytics analyzes large volumes of data to detect anomalous behavior. Data-correlation technologies can also assist the security operations team in the investigation of alerts. SOAR solutions replace manual incident-response processes, reducing the time for containment and remediation. They also reduce the number of unresolved alerts, alleviating fatigue in constrained security teams. The future of cybersecurity resides in the integration of emerging data-correlation technologies into the security operating platform. Technical offsets found in autonomous deep-learning machines and advanced human-machine teaming are essential to threat visibility and prevention. The promise of these technologies is to regain the advantage over Russian cyber operations, whether they rise to the level of armed conflict or function as a component of strategic competition.

Notes

1. A. Wess Mitchell, "U.S. Strategy towards the Russian Federation," statement for Senate Foreign Relations Committee, August 21, 2018, 1.
2. Michelle Shevin-Coetzee, "The European Deterrence Initiative," Center for Strategic and Budgetary Assessments, January 2019, 4–5.
3. Mark D. Faram, "Why the US Navy Has 10 Ships, 130 Aircraft and 9,000 Personnel in the Mediterranean," *Navy Times*, April 25, 2019.
4. Farnaz Fassihi and Chris Gordon, "China, Russia Criticize U.S. in U.N. Remarks," *Wall Street Journal*, September 29, 2018.
5. The White House, Office of the Press Secretary, "The 2015 G-20 Summit," fact sheet, November 16, 2015.
6. Robert McLaughlin and Michael Schmitt, "The Need for Clarity in International Cyber Law," Asia and the Pacific Policy Society Policy Forum, September 18, 2017.
7. McLaughlin and Schmitt.
8. Michael N. Schmitt, "Grey Zones in the International Law of Cyberspace," *Yale Journal of International Law Online* 42, no. 2 (2017): 2.
9. Joseph Marks, "There's Cyberwar and Then There's the Big Legal Gray Area," Nextgov, February 9, 2017.
10. Marks.
11. Michael N. Schmitt, "Peacetime Cyber Responses and Wartime Cyber Operations: An Analytical *Vade Mecum*," *Harvard National Security Journal* 8 (2017): 242n5.
12. Schmitt, 258.
13. Andy Greenberg, "The Untold Story of NotPetya, the Most Devastating Cyberattack in History," *Wired*, August 22, 2018.
14. Eduard Kovacs, "Maersk Reinstalled 50,000 Computers after NotPetya Attack," *Security Week*, January 26, 2018.
15. US-CERT, "Petya Ransomware," alert TA17-181A, July 28, 2017.
16. Greenberg, "Untold Story of NotPetya."
17. Jon Henley, "Petya Ransomware Attack Strikes Companies across Europe and US," *The Guardian*, June 27, 2017; John Leyden, "FedEx: TNT NotPetya Infection Blew a $300m Hole in Our Numbers," *The Register*, September 20, 2017.
18. Dmitry Zaks, "NATO Warns Russia of 'Full Range' of Responses to Cyberattack," Agence France Presse, May 23, 2019.
19. Mark Landler and David E. Sanger, "Obama Says He Told Putin: 'Cut It Out' on Hacking," *New York Times*, December 16, 2016.
20. David Fidler, "President Obama's Pursuit of Cyber Deterrence Ends in Failure," Net Politics, January 4, 2017.
21. Jim Sciutto, "Russia Has Americans' Weakness All Figured Out," *The Atlantic*, May 14, 2019.
22. Ian Bond and Igor Yurgens, "Putin's Last Term: Taking the Long View," Centre for European Reform, January 2019, 1.
23. Col. Jaak Tarian, director, NATO Cooperative Cyber Defence Centre of Excellence, closing panel remarks at Cyber Endeavor, Menlo Park, California, June 20, 2019.
24. Stewart Baker, "The U.S. Needs to Think about the Unthinkable on Cybersecurity," *Washington Post*, August 21, 2018.
25. Paul Nakasone, Remarks at the Joint Service Academy Cyber Summit, US Air Force Academy, Colorado Springs, CO, March 15, 2019.
26. Ellen Nakashima, "U.S. Cyber Command Operation Disrupted Internet Access of Russian Troll Factory on Day of 2018 Midterms," *Washington Post*, February 27, 2019.

27. Mark Pomerleau, "New Authorities Mean Lots of New Missions at Cyber Command," Fifth Domain, May 8, 2019.
28. DOD, "Summary: Department of Defense Cyber Strategy," 2018, 4.
29. Pomerleau, "New Authorities."
30. Maxim Shemeipu, "Russian Troll Farm: Yes, the Pentagon Hit Us in Cyber Op. But It Was a Complete Failure," *Daily Beast*, February 28, 2019.
31. Nakashima, "U.S. Cyber Force."
32. Nakashima, "U.S. Cyber Command Operation."
33. Sean Gallagher, "NSA's Top Policy Advisor: It's Time to Start Putting Teeth into Deterrence," Ars Technica, March 4, 2019.
34. Michael P. Fischerkeller and Richard J. Harknett, "Through Persistent Engagement, the U.S. Can Influence 'Agreed Competition,'" Cybersecurity and Deterrence (blog), Lawfare, April 15, 2019.
35. James N. Miller and Neal A. Pollard, "Persistent Engagement, Agreed Competition and Deterrence in Cyberspace," Cybersecurity and Deterrence (blog), Lawfare, April 30, 2019.
36. DOD, "Summary: Department of Defense Cyber Strategy," 2018, 4.
37. Paul M. Nakasone, "A Cyber Force for Persistent Operations," *Joint Force Quarterly* 92 (First Quarter, 2019): 12.
38. Symantec, "Buckeye: Espionage Outfit Used Equation Group Tools Prior to Shadow Brokers Leak," Threat Intelligence (blog), May 6, 2019.
39. Jason Healey, "The Cartwright Conjecture," *Bytes, Bombs, and Spies* (Washington, DC: Brookings Institution Press, 2019), 173–74.
40. David E. Sanger and Nicole Perlroth, "U.S. Escalates Online Attacks on Russia's Power Grid," *New York Times*, June 15, 2019.
41. Tim Starks, "U.S.-Iran Cyber Skirmishes Break Out," *Politico*, June 24, 2019.
42. Julian Barnes, "U.S. Cyberattack Hurt Iran's Ability to Target Oil Tankers, Officials Say," *New York Times*, August 29, 2019.
43. Bozorgmehr Sharafedin, "U.S. Cyber Attacks on Iranian Targets Not Successful, Iran Minister Says," Reuters, June 23, 2019.
44. DHS, "CISA Statement on Iranian Cybersecurity Threats," June 22, 2019.
45. Dustin Volz, "Trump Administration Hasn't Briefed Congress on New Rules for Cyberattacks, Lawmakers Say," *Wall Street Journal*, July 10, 2019.
46. Keir Giles, *Moscow Rules: What Drives Russia to Confront the West* (Washington, DC: Brookings Institution Press, 2019), 22.
47. Giles, 22–23.
48. Volodymyr Horbulin, *The World Hybrid War: Ukrainian Forefront* (Kiev: Ukrainian Institute for the Future, 2017), 27.
49. James Fallows, "Chaos Serves Putin's Interest: A Veteran Diplomat Takes Stock," Defense One, March 11, 2019.
50. Michael Birnbaum and Philip Rucker, "Leaders Mostly Reject Trump's Push to Reverse Russia's 2014 Expulsion," *Washington Post*, August 27, 2019.
51. David Ignatius, "America Is at War in Cyberspace," *Washington Post*, May 31, 2019.
52. DOD, "Summary: Department of Defense Cyber Strategy," 1.

Index

About the Author

Capt. Scott Jasper, USN (Ret.), is a lecturer in the National Security Affairs Department and for the Institute for Security Governance at the Naval Postgraduate School in Monterey, California. He designs and teaches the courses Cyberspace Operations Fundamentals, Defense Capability Development, and Hybrid Warfare. His fourth book, *Strategic Cyber Deterrence: The Active Cyber Defense Option*, was published in 2017. He has published chapters in various handbooks related to cybersecurity and articles in *Strategic Studies Quarterly*, the *International Journal of Intelligence and CounterIntelligence, United States Cybersecurity Magazine, The National Interest, Small Wars Journal, The Diplomat*, and the *Journal of International Peacekeeping*. His PhD was awarded by the University of Reading in the United Kingdom.